Sleep and Dreaming

Second, revised edition

Jacob Empson

HARVESTER
WHEATSHEAF

New York   London   Toronto   Sydney   Tokyo   Singapore

First published 1993 by
Harvester Wheatsheaf
Campus 400, Maylands Avenue
Hemel Hempstead
Hertfordshire, HP2 7EZ
A division of
Simon & Schuster International Group

Typeset in 10/12pt Times
by Hands Fotoset, Leicester

Printed and bound in Great Britain by
Bookcraft, Midsomer Norton.

British Library Cataloguing in Publication Data

A catalogue record for this book is available from
The British Library

ISBN 0-7450-1402-X (pbk)

1 2 3 4 5   97 96 95 94 93

Sleep and Dreaming

The division of one day from the next must be one of the most profound peculiarities of life on this planet. It is, on the whole, a merciful arrangement. We are not condemned to sustained flights of being, but are constantly refreshed by little holidays from ourselves. We are intermittent creatures, always falling to little ends and rising to little beginnings. Our soon-tired consciousness is meted out in chapters, and that the world will look quite different tomorrow is, both for our comfort and our discomfort, usually true. How marvellously too night matches sleep, sweet image of it, so neatly apportioned to our need. Angels must wonder at these beings who fall so regularly out of awareness into a fantasm-infested dark. How our frail identities survive these chasms no philosopher has ever been able to explain.

Iris Murdoch, *The Black Prince*

Contents

Preface to Second Edition

The second edition has the same structure as the first, with one exception: there is a major new chapter, in Part I, on the physiology of sleep. Inevitably, some of the discussion of physiology becomes rather technical, but I have tried, as in the other chapters, to avoid the unnecessary use of jargon and to define new terms as they arise, and to maintain the balance between being readable while remaining authoritative.

Part IV, with the chapters on sleep disorders in both adults and children, no longer offers direct advice on how to deal with sleep problems. Rather, the text, particularly with respect to children's problems, has been made more academic. Other changes have been made, in almost every chapter, to improve clarity or to accommodate new evidence which has come to light in the past few years.

One reviewer was kind enough to say of the first edition, 'Empson has the scope of a textbook without actually writing a textbook, the final aim of the science communicator, while for professionals there are enough references to follow up evidence but not enough to choke the text.' This edition is intended to remain as accessible as the first for the general reader, while being slightly more useful as a source book for the student and professional reader in the treatment of references. I have tried to achieve this by following Nathaniel Kleitman's example, in his monumental *Sleep and Wakefulness*, the second edition of which was published thirty years ago, in using numbered references, and a comprehensive alphabetical list of all the references at the end of the book. The system of numbers allows the reader to choose whether to ignore them, or to follow up any particular assertion to the reference supporting it. The integrated list of 450-odd references at the end of the book also serves as a useful source in itself, particularly to students and professional readers. Alternative conventions, such as the Harvard system of using author's name and date in the text (e.g. Jenkins and Dallenbach, 1924) can make the text unnecessarily cluttered with names and dates if one tries to refer to every paper that one might.

I am very grateful indeed to my assistants in the sleep laboratory who have helped in the preparation of this edition. Caroline Crichton, Linda MacDonald and David Alford did a great deal of work for me in the library, finding the latest papers, and also helped in the redrawing of many of the illustrations, as well as the creation of new ones.

Preface to the First Edition

When people discover that I have been involved in sleep research they often insist on telling me one of their dreams. I tend to reply by telling them one of mine. This sidesteps the issue of providing an instant dream analysis for them. Like other people's children, other people's dreams are also so much less interesting than one's own! The other topic of major interet to many people is that of problems they or their children may be having with sleep. Again, it is not easy to give an on-the-spot diagnosis and suggestion for treatment.

This book is intended to provide answers to many of the questions which people ask about dreaming and sleep. I hope it succeeds in being both an authoritative and readable introduction to what we know about the psychology of sleep, including what can be said about the experience of sleep as well as its psychophysiology. The techniques for recording and scoring sleep stages in the laboratory were established in the late 1960s, using EEG (brainwave) and other psychophysiological measures. This development was crucial in providing a universal frame of reference which has survived for thirty years. It has allowed the accumulation of a body of knowledge about sleep and dreaming which is largely internally consistent and uncontroversial – an achievement of scientific success scarcely matched in other branches of psychology over the same period. Books have of course been written, but some of the best are now somewhat dated, or out of print, and some of the more recent ones have confined themselves to the more recent work. *Sleep and Dreaming* sets out to provide an account of what we know about the subject, regardless of when the research was done.

The book is organized into four parts. Part I describes the context of sleep research, starting with an examination of beliefs about sleep in contemporary Britain, in other cultures and in antiquity. The historical account (in Chapter 2) of the development of electrophysiological measures is intended to provide an understandable introduction to them. Elsewhere, I have avoided using jargon terms wherever possible, and explained technical usages of words wherever they first appear.

Part II is concerned with the experience of sleep, including dreaming. The discovery of REM (rapid eye movement) sleep allowed us to predict mental activity from EEG and other psychophysiological recordings in a way that is virtually impossible in the awake subject. Answers have been provided to questions such as how long dreams last during the state of sleep and whether everybody dreams. Some progress has also been made in establishing the provenance of the content of dreams – such as the events of the previous day, or the dreamer's daytime preoccupations. We are a long way from fully understanding the nature and function of consciousness while we are awake, so, not surprisingly, there are many aspects of sleeping consciousness which remain mysterious. Advances in neurophysiology have, however, provided clues concerning the brain mechanisms governing the generation of dreaming, and recent theories linking the psychological reality of dreaming to these processes are described.

Part III is devoted to the psychophysiology of sleep. The consequences of sleep disturbance, either by reducing sleep, denying it altogether, or selectively depriving subjects of particular sleep stages are considered in Chapter 7. Experimental evidence of perceptual and attentional processing during sleep is assessed in Chapter 8, together with overt behaviours during sleep, such as sleepwalking and sleeptalking. This section of the book includes an account of the sleep of animals, and ends with a chapter on recent theories about the functions of sleep.

Part IV, on problems with sleep, deals separately with sleep disorders in adulthood and the elderly from those of childhood. It provides accounts of the nature of sleep disorders, as assessed in the laboratory.

This book is entended to be accessible to anybody prepared to take an interest in the subject, as well as being useful to students intending to take their interests further. While virtually every assertion is supported by some referenced evidence, which can be followed up by the student, the general reader should have no difficulty in reading straight through the chapters.

I would like to thank John Henry Jones for reading an early draft of Chapter 1. His literate and well-informed suggestions were invaluable. Chris Singleton provided me with much material on childhood sleep disorders, as well as some helpful comments on a draft of Chapter 13. I would also like to thank my colleagues Ray Meddis and Jim Horne for the many opportunities over the years to discuss (and frequently dispute) the functions of sleep. My own initiation into sleep research twenty years ago was at Ian Oswald's laboratory in Edinburgh, and while our paths rarely meet, his untiring work remains an example and an inspiration.

Finally, I would like to thank the staff of the Regents Park Zoo for allowing me to photograph their giraffes sleeping, as well as for the practical help given by the keepers of the Cotton Terrace. These photographs would not have been possible without Kelvin Murray's photographic expertise and help from James Blofeld.

PART I

CHAPTER 1

The Obvious: Beliefs About Sleep and Dreaming

Sleep folklore

For all the time that we spend doing it – about one third of our lives – we have very little natural insight into the sleeping process. Even the simple act of observing a sleeper normally requires forgoing sleep oneself. Typically the object of scrutiny is either a child in bed or our spouse asleep in front of the television. And what is there to see? They may twitch, move around to an apparently more comfortable position, but their eyes remain closed and they remain unresponsive. They offer no clues about whatever mental activity is going on, apart from occasional mumblings. Rarely, they might talk more coherently, but what is said is seldom sensible.

Our memory of our own sleep is usually confined to one or two confusing and ill-recalled dreams, and some individuals claim never even to dream. The quality of sleep is normally judged by the degree of oblivion achieved, in the same way that digestion is counted as most satisfactory when we are least aware of it. Sleep still has no obvious rationale, except that we do it when we feel sleepy or 'tired', and after doing it we're 'rested' – and don't feel sleepy any more.

If you ask a roomful of people whether anybody has not had any sleep in the previous 24 hours, it is very rare indeed to find a serious candidate. In the 15 years that I have been giving lectures on 'Sleep and Dreaming' to many groups of sixthformers as well as undergraduate students I have in fact only once had a single positive response to this question. We all sleep, and as a rule we do it at night in one long session of up to 9 or 10 hours, and during the day we stay awake.

About one-third to half the usable space in any private house is taken up by special rooms devoted to sleeping. It is most unusual for anybody to do it in the kitchen, the hall, the bathroom or the dining room, although naps may be taken in the living room. But doing the whole thing – removing daytime clothes, putting on special sleeping garments, emptying the bladder, cleaning the teeth and finally getting into the purpose-built sleeping furniture is something that is only done in the bedrooms specially built for the purpose. In many households it is conventional for everybody to retire at the same time, and to re-emerge simultaneously in the morning, with scant toleration being shown to individuals who do not conform. A sleepless alien might legitimately conclude that earthlings' central preoccupation was this peculiar sort of inactivity.

What are the obvious truths about sleep? What do most people believe it is for, what their dreams and other experiences during sleep signify, and what may happen to them if sleep is disturbed or prevented? A survey I conducted among Hull University students and staff about their beliefs about sleep and dreaming is fully reported in the appendix. They were asked to indicate whether various assertions (such as 'An hour's sleep before midnight is worth two afterwards') were true, possibly true or untrue. Some of the questions concerned frequency, so answers ranging from 'Never' to 'Always' were available to assertions such as 'Dreams can foretell the future'. The results will be referred to as being from the 'Hull survey' as they become relevant.

The analogy between resting after physical exertion, and the relief from sleepiness offered by sleep, is very compelling, and many people would agree with it. The survey of students and graduates at Hull showed that over two-thirds of them agreed with the statement that 'Exercise improves the quality of sleep'. It logically follows from this that a fit person should need less sleep than an unfit one, or a man than a woman, or a grown-up than a child.

There are plenty of folk remedies for improving sleep, and maxims, adages and proverbs concerning sleep, and they give some insight into received views. My Afrikaaner grandfather was fond of repeating that 'A man needs six hours, a woman seven, and a bloody fool eight' hours sleep – a sentiment which nicely incorporated both his simple male chauvinism and a Calvinist abomination of indulgence. The common English proverb – 'Early to bed and early to rise,' makes a man healthy, wealthy and wise' is less concerned with self-denial than with a prescription for regular habits. Similarly, the Welsh 'Go to bed with the lamb and rise with the lark' allows a generous amount of time asleep, and is more concerned with its timing.

The idea that sleep is especially important in growing children, that it may somehow be essential to growth and development, has always been prevalent. The notion that 'One hour's sleep before midnight is worth two afterwards' has perennially been invoked to put children to bed early (although only 10 per cent of the survey sample believed it to be true). Young ladies proverbially make sure they have 'their beauty sleep' – the statement 'A good night's sleep improves ones appearance' was endorsed by almost two-thirds of the sample. Similarly, the course of improvement from infectious illnesses accompanied by fever has been commonly held to be intimately connected with sleeping, so that a fever typically 'breaks' during the night, while the temperature reaches a maximal high, and then as it reverts to near-normal the patient falls into a deep restorative sleep. The commonsense view of sleep is that it is good for you, providing an opportunity for recovery from fatigue, is essential for growth, and is crucial in recovery from illness.

Co-existing with this view of sleep as a benign restorative has been a certain apprehensiveness about it. We are obviously vulnerable during sleep. This is primarily a physical vulnerability to enemies, both animal and human, because of our obliviousness of our surroundings, and the confused, inert state we can be in when we first wake up. The vampire legend, for example, gains much of its power from the helplessness of the sleeping victim. A collective resolution of this sort of worry at one time was to employ somebody to patrol the streets all night, calling out 'Three o'clock and all's well!' or whatever, at regular intervals, providing reassurance to the sleeping citizens in their beds and even more so to any insomniacs.

Second, our apprehension is aroused by the fact that during sleep we seem to lose control of our minds. Consciousness during wakefulness in a sane person is pretty well ordered and familiar. The happy impression (perhaps totally illusory) that we have when we are awake of being somehow in control of our mental processes deserts us when we are dreaming. On the contrary, while asleep our consciousness seems to happen to us, rather than being under our control. This is particularly disturbing for people who subscribe to the Christian view that sinful thoughts are as wicked as the corresponding deeds, since we cannot help ourselves sometimes dreaming of performing venial if not mortal sins.

In order to understand what is 'obvious' about sleep and dreaming it is necessary to examine some of the conventional ideological baggage which most Westerners carry about with them, and its historical origins. In addition, it will be useful to examine the idea that pre-literate societies, either those in antiquity or those existing in the contemporary world, have more (or more far-fetched) mystical ideas about dreaming than our own.

Dreaming in antiquity

Pre-scientific thinking about sleep and dreaming is often said to have revolved around the two notions of the soul leaving the body during sleep, or of the body being visited by spirits – gods and demons offering revelations and glimpses into the future, or wandering nightmares.

In classical times in Europe and the Middle East dreams were often taken as portents or as guides for action. The Assyrian poem *The Epic of Gilgamesh* (374) is regularly punctuated by dreams, both the hero's and his great friend Enkidu's. They foretell events, providing a sort of rationale for the extraordinary exploits, the failures and the tragedy of Gilgamesh. The poem dates from the third millenium BC and is a eulogistic account of the life of King Gilgamesh of Uruk in Mesopotamia. It clearly ranks as the first written literature of any consequence. It is also remarkable for its universality and its enduring appeal after five millenia. (The tablets on which it was recorded were discovered in the mid-nineteenth century, and their decipherment was only largely completed by the end of that century.) It starts:

> O Gilgamesh, Lord of Kullab, great is thy praise. This was the man to whom all things were known; this was the king who knew the countries of the world. He was wise, he saw mysteries and knew secret things, he brought us a tale of the days before the flood. He went on a long journey, was weary, worn-out with labour, and returning engraved on a stone the whole story.

N. K. Sanders's summary of the plot of the epic sets the scene:

> When the story begins he is in mature manhood, and superior to all other men in beauty and strength and the unsatisfied cravings of his half-divine nature, for which he can find no worthy match in love or in war; while his daemonic energy is wearing his subjects out. They are forced to call in the help of the gods, and the first episode describes how they provide a companion and foil. This was Enkidu, the 'natural man', reared with wild animals, and as swift as the gazelle. In time Enkidu was seduced by a harlot from the city, and with loss of innocence an irrevocable step was taken towards taming the wild man. The animals now rejected him, and he was led on by stages; learning to wear clothes, eat human food, herd sheep, and make war on the wolf and lion, until at length he reached the great civilized city of Uruk.

Enkidu's arrival at Gilgamesh's court was announced to Gilgamesh by two dreams. In the first, Enkidu was symbolized by a meteor falling from heaven, whose attraction to Gilgamesh was mysteriously 'like the love of a woman', and which, when shown to his mother she pronounced to be his brother. In his second dream he found an axe on the streets of his city. Again, he was deeply drawn to it, he loved it like a woman and wore it at his side. His mother Ninsun, a minor goddess, interpreted both these dreams for him, identifying the meteor and the axe as the new friend he was about to make.

Gilgamesh and Enkidu became inseparable companions. When Gilgamesh later dreamt that Enlil, the father of the gods, had decreed his destiny, it was Enkidu who interpreted for him, explaining that it indicated his certain mortality as well as the gifts of unexampled supremacy over the people and victory in battle. When the two embarked on a mission against the giant Humbaba they both had dreams highly significant to their project. These were apparently induced, or incubated, by Gilgamesh, who dug a well, went up to the mountain and poured out a fine meal on the ground before saying 'O mountain, dwelling of the gods, bring me a favourable dream.' Encouraged by their interpretations of each other's dreams they set off against Humbaba to cut down his cedar forests.

As well as killing Humbaba they also slaughtered a semi-divine bull, the Bull of Heaven, which belonged to Ishtar the Queen of Heaven and patroness of Uruk. Enkidu now dreamed that they had offended the gods so deeply that one of them must die, and he promptly declined into a fatal illness. During his illness he dreamed of the afterlife, where kings, rulers and princes were reduced from their high station to fetching and carrying as servants, and only the high priests, gods and one or two favoured dead kings were allowed to preserve their earthly privileges.

After Enkidu's death Gilgamesh wandered far and wide in his grief encountering amongst others the proverbial survivor of the great flood, Utnapishtim, who told him how he had been warned in a dream by a god of the imminent deluge, and instructed to build a great boat into which he was to take the seed of all living creatures. Because of his obedience he had been granted the gift of eternal life. Gilgamesh went on to search for the secret of immortality and according to the legend he almost succeeded.

Gilgamesh is not reported as having any significant dreams after Enkidu's death, and despite his continuing efforts to penetrate the mysteries it becomes increasingly apparent that his powers have waned and the gods have turned against him. As a test of his strength Utnapishtim challenged him to stay awake for six days and seven nights:

> But while Gilgamesh sat there resting on his haunches, a mist of sleep like soft wool teased from the fleece drifted over him, and Utnapishtim said to his wife, 'Look at him now, the strong man who would have everlasting life, even now the mists of sleep are drifting over him.'

Despite his human limitations he managed to retrieve the underwater thorn which would give immortality, although it was stolen from him on his journey back to Uruk by a serpant. The epic ends with his death in his own city, which he was largely responsible for building:

> This too was the work of Gilgamesh, the king, who knew the countries of the world. He was wise, he saw mysteries and knew secret things, he brought us a tale of the days before the flood. He went on a long journey, was weary, worn out with labour, and returning engraved on a stone the whole story.

It is impossible to do justice to the beauty of the poem in such a brief account. As Sanders says, it is a mixture of pure adventure, morality and tragedy, with Gilgamesh the first tragic hero of whom anything is known. It is clear that even five thousand years ago in Mesopotamia people had achieved a degree of subtlety of belief that defies analysis into one or two dogmas. The recognition and acceptance of the mysteries of mortality, earthly hubris, privilege and their futility were carried through two thousand years, as this epic was copied and repeated in different versions. The role of dreaming in all this was to provide a channel of communication for the gods to inform and warn those few mortals sufficiently significant to attract their attention, at critical moments in their lives. Presumably most people's dreams were not interpreted as being messages from the deities, as even Gilgamesh was only favoured with two or three of these in his lifetime.

In some societies the practical importance of dreams as portents of the future and as phenomena with mysterious healing properties was not only recognized but institutions were set up to exploit the fact. In order to achieve both a suitable dream and an explanation of its meaning it would have been necessary to travel to an oracle. There, one would have slept on a special bed (from the sound of it, usually particularly uncomfortable), and any dreams reported would have been interpreted. This process of inducing dreaming is called incubation. It was practised in ancient Egypt and in Greece, and for ordinary people these special dreams were relied on for their curative powers more than their predictive value.

J. G. Frazer (140) in his monumental work on folklore in the Old Testament maintained that the:

> belief that the gods revealed themselves and declared their will to mankind in dreams was widespread in antiquity; and accordingly people resorted to temples and other sacred spots for the purpose of sleeping there and holding converse with the higher powers in visions of the night, for they naturally supposed that the deities or the deified spirits of the dead would be most likely to manifest themselves in places specially dedicated to their worship.

Frazer describes the process of consulting the oracle at the sanctuary dedicated to the soothsayer Ampiaraus, at Oropus, Attica. Patients paid some money, and brought a sacrificial animal (the skin and shoulder of which would be subsequently kept by the priests), and slept in male or female dormitories, on the hides of their freshly killed sacrificial rams. If a cure was achieved then patients were permitted to drop gold or silver coins into the sacred spring. Similarly, at the Aesculapian sanctuary near Epidaurus, dormitories were provided for pilgrims seeking cures. Those who were cured after their night at the sanctuary were permitted to record their dreams and commemorate their recoveries on votive tablets, some of which have survived to this day.

Interpretations were not offered by these priests – rather, the dreams themselves were thought to be curative. Is there much difference between this sort of arrangement and that prevailing at Lourdes today? Priests have always been regarded as healers of the mind, and their modern equivalents in the psycho-analytic movement are similarly preoccupied with the dreams of their patients.

J. G. Frazer further suggests that the story of Jacob's dream (which was deemed so extremely significant that the spot on which it took place was thenceforth sanctified in the Jewish religion) 'was probably told to explain the immemorial sanctity of Bethel, which may well have been revered by the aboriginal inhabitants of Canaan long before the Hebrews invaded and conquered the land'. In this case the dream is used as a political device – not consistent with the idea of credulous primitives believing in the literal truth of supernatural explanations. At least the politicians who told the story can hardly have believed it, and it seems unlikely that people in antiquity swallowed whole everything that they were told by their masters, any more than they do now.

The Assassins, a Muslim sect founded in the eleventh century, were reputed to reward their devotees with visions of heaven by the use of hashish (from which they were widely assumed to derive their name). According to Marco Polo's account, the sect's leader (the 'Old Man of the Mountain'):

> used a special 'Paradise' constructed in a secluded valley. Into this Garden of Earthly Delights the selected trainee Assassins were carried while unconscious with drugs ('assassin' is derived from *hashashin* – 'hashish-eaters'). When they came round in the valley, they were entertained with every delightful variant of wine, women and song promised in the holy scriptures to those who would go to Paradise. Drugged again, they regained consciousness outside the valley in anguish that it had all been a dream. No, they were told, all this will be yours again on completion of your mission. (213)

The point of all this was of course to reinforce the belief that the afterlife was a paradise, even if only achievable with certainty through death in battle, and thus to improve the combativeness of the assassins. This well-known story from Marco Polo's account dates from two hundred years after the sect had been crushed.

Islamic scholars writing in English have come to regard the story as being apocryphal. Even the derivation of the name 'assassin' from 'hashish' is in doubt, according to Bernard Lewis' authoritative historical account of the sect (266). The term *hashshash* does refer to users of cannabis in Arabic, but *hashish* and *hashishi* referred generically to herbage, and only later specifically meant cannabis. In addition Lewis argues that since the name *hashishi* is local to Syria, as a term of popular abuse, it was 'in all probability the name that gave rise to the story, rather than the reverse'. Cannabis was widely used in the Middle East during this period, and it seems unlikely that the practice in itself would seem remarkable enough to cause any comment amongst Arabs.

However, the sect did use assassination as a highly effective weapon against other Persian groups. Their reputation for fanaticism was widespread amongst the Crusaders, and:

> in 1195, when King Richard Coer de Lion was at Chinon, no less than fifteen so-called Assassins were apprehended, and confessed that they had been sent by the King of France to kill him. Before long, such charges became frequent . . . [but] there can be little doubt that these charges are baseless. The chiefs of the Assassins, in Persia or in Syria, had no interest in the plots and intrigues of Western Europe; the European needed no help outside in the various arts of murder. (266)

There is no evidence that the Ismaili Assassins ever made contact with the Crusaders in the relatively short history of the sect. (They were subdued by the Mongols, who destroyed their castles in 1256.)

Speculation about whether the Assassin troops believed that their experiences in the Alamut gardens fitted out as Paradise were really a dream, or whether the gardens' compliant slaves were all too real in the flesh is thus academic. This story is apparently an invention of foreigners, and does not appear in the Arab texts. It seems that fanaticism does not need to be fuelled by credulity, at least about dreaming. Indeed the accounts of the feuds between Middle Eastern factions in the eleventh and twelfth centuries read much like the strife between the militias in modern Beirut, and there is no suggestion that these recent protagonists had particularly mystical views about dreaming.

The conventional Western European view was of sleep as a pleasurable indulgence, like sex, providing a natural avenue for the temptations of the devil. Nocturnal emissions, or 'wet dreams' were an obvious result of demonic intervention. The Christian requirements for chastity in the clergy, and the prohibition against masturbation paradoxically created the conditions most likely to promote these 'pollutions'. St Ambrose (373) accordingly wrote a prayer to guard against them:

> *Procul recedant somnia*
> *Et noctium phantasmata*
> *Hostemque nostrum comprime,*
> *Ne polluantur corpora.*
> 'Let dreams and nocturnal
> Phantasies depart far away,
> And suppress our enemy
> Lest our bodies be polluted.'

St Augustine similarly asked God to keep him in a 'chaste desire' during sleep, and protect him from dreams which, 'owing to animal images', might lead him 'to pollution'.

Although two of the fathers (Tertullian and St Augustine) granted dispensations for these nocturnal pollutions, as they were called, dreams were still regarded with deep suspicion. Dream interpretation had been widely practised in the ancient world, but since Christian theologians could establish no way of telling the difference between divine and demonic dreams, divination of any sort was pronounced heretical. The clerical domination of Western thought during the Dark and Middle Ages resulted in a relative neglect of this subject until the sixteenth century, when the rather trivializing 'dream-books' of Artemidorus were rediscovered.

Can we construe even Freudian theory as a nineteenth-century articulation of these ideas about possession? The id, according to Freud, is uncontainable throughout the night, and instinctual pressure periodically forces unacceptable and deeply disturbing ideas into consciousness. Instead of prayers to protect us from these sources of guilt, shame and terror Freud suggested that dreams took over, transforming the Gothic horrors into cryptic symbols only interpretable by psycho-analysts, the new priests of nineteenth-century rationalism.

In England until the sixteenth century it was unremarkable to speak of visitations from incubi and succubi – evil spirits (male and female, respectively) which were thought to descend on sleepers, seducing them and perverting them to the ways of the Devil. In particular, witches were presumed to consort with incubi. But was this a belief that encompassed the 'normal' dreams that everybody experiences? Pre-scientific thinking in Europe is relatively well preserved in the writings of its poets. The dream-poems of Chaucer and of the French medieval poets before him make clear that such ideas about dreaming were not invariably invoked. There is no hint that dreaming, in this context, was any more than a poetic device, with no connotation of the supernatural simply with the fact that it was a dream

A consideration of two dreams in Shakespeare's plays takes us to a similar conclusion. These are the Duke of Clarence's nightmare in *Richard III*, anticipating his own death, and Caesar's wife's dream in *Julius Caesar*. Both of them seem to involve precognition, predicting dramatic changes in the destiny of great men. The simplest dramatic use of the dream relies on it being ignored or misinterpreted. The audience is thus given a cue as to what is likely to happen, and dramatic tension is created by the characters knowing as much as they do, but carrying on regardless. At a more subtle level, in both *Richard III* and *Julius Caesar* there is a sense in which disregarding portents is part of a more general characterization – of individuals who have taken their destiny into their own hands, or think they have, in contrast to those who consciously submit to their fate (157). However, the context in which dreaming is used in the plot has to be constructed to suit the play – the ideology of the culture in which it is set must condition the characters' responses. It is here that we can gain some insight into the assumptions that Shakespeare and his audience were making about beliefs in antiquity, compared to more modern medieval beliefs – Richard III reigned a mere century before the play was first performed.

In *Julius Caesar* Calphurnia dreamed she saw Caesar's statue which 'like a fountain with an hundred spouts, did run pure blood; and many lusty Romans came smiling and did bathe their hands in it'. Portents in plenty are also reported – 'a tempest dripping fire' (St Elmo's fire?), a lion walking sulkily through the city, the bird of night hooting and shrieking at noon-day and of course the soothsayer's warning to 'Beware the Ides of March.' In this context the portentious dream is used as another example of the superstition of antiquity, rather than as a statement of current belief.

Incidentally a character called Artemidorus appears in the play. He is described as a teacher of rhetoric, but this was probably not a slightly anachronistic reference to Artemidorus of Daldis, whose dream books were becoming popularly available in print in Europe for the first time in the second half of the sixteenth century in Latin and Greek. The play is taken from Plutarch's *Lives*, in which Artemidorus is described as being born in the Isle of Guidos, and a Doctor of Rhetoric in the Greek tongue. Artemidorus of Daldis was not born at the time. The first English translation of Artemidorus' *Oneirocritica*, by Robert Woods, was published in 1606. It must have been a popular book as it had gone to 5 editions by 1656, and 24 editions by 1744. However, when the play was written (in 1601) Shakespeare may well have been familiar with the Latin or Greek version, but his audience in the main would not.

In *Richard III* Clarence has every reason to fear for his life, since he has been emprisoned in the Tower of London. The reason he offered to Richard for his incarceration was that the King was 'hearkening after prophecies and dreams . . . and suchlike toys as these had moved his highness to commit me now'. Here belief in such portents is presented as being highly suspect, and possibly an excuse for more sordid political ends. Clearly Shakespeare's audience was expected to take a sceptical view of dreams as portents although attributing such beliefs to the ancients.

Clarence's dream is much more closely described than any in Julius Caesar, and is a highly believable nightmare of drowning. Clarence has escaped from the Tower, and is crossing the Channel with his brother Gloucester (later to become Richard III). Walking together on the ship's deck, Gloucester stumbled, and Clarence, in trying to steady him, was knocked overboard. A graphic description of drowning is followed by his translation to the 'kingdom of perpetual night'. The two abrupt changes in plot – from walking on the deck to the water, and from the water to the next world – are typical of the 'scene-shift' phenomenon of dreaming. Even more convincing as an account of a real dream is the idea that Gloucester somehow was responsible for his death – but only accidentally. This is a truly classic example of dreamwork as described by the psycho-analysts. The latent thought is the notion that Gloucester may be plotting to murder him – an idea too horrifying to contemplate. The dreamwork process thus thinly disguises it, making Gloucester kill him all the same, but accidentally. 'Gloucester will kill me by accident, though he doesn't want to' (157).

It is my contention here that neither Shakespeare nor his audience believed that dreams predicted the future, although they were certainly prepared to entertain the idea. The interest and subtlety of the plays rely on a considerable degree of scepticism about the infallibility of dreams as guides for the future.

The Grimm brothers, according to Donald Ward (424), introducing his translation of their legends, described the nightmare as being a traveller in physical form. Some shepherds, who observed it regularly using a boat to cross a river and removed the boat, reduced the nightmare to wailing pitifully and threatening them, demanding the return of the boat:

> At night they like to ride horses, and in the morning one can see that they have done so because the horses are exhausted . . . They like to tangle their victims' hair into elflocks, or as they are also called, tangle locks, or mare's braids. They do this by sucking on the hair and twisting it.

Were we really expected to believe this? This account hovers on the brink of farce, and must surely have been intended as a spine-chiller more analogous to a modern horror film than to a literal description of something which was to be believed in. We are invited to thrill to the idea of travelling nightmares, but the essentially humorous style informs us that it isn't to be taken entirely seriously.

To summarize, the upshot of this foray into the literature on beliefs about dreaming in the past seems to be that they were not so extraordinary after all. There was a great deal of credulity, some scepticism, as well as some wonderfully entertaining stories. Much of this, both in antiquity as well as in Shakespeare's day, seems unremarkable in the modern context – the tenets of some fringe cults, the established churches, or even psycho-analysis can seem equally bizarre. As today, people liked the idea of weird beliefs about dreaming, but tended to impute them to others – either foreigners (such as the Assassins) or the ancients.

Modern beliefs about dreaming

The beginnings of modern thought about sleep and dreaming can be traced to the late eighteenth century, the time of the Enlightenment. Scientific writings were read widely by educated people, unlike today, when we are divided into two cultures by the inaccessibility of science to non-experts. Erasmus Darwin published his *Zoonomia* in 1794 (90), which was partly a medical textbook, partly a treatise in biology. Together with his other writings, its profound influence on the Romantic poets illustrates the depth to which scientific ideas which today might remain obscure could swiftly penetrate literary and artistic thinking (242). His chapters on Sleep and Reverie for instance informed Coleridge's development of ideas about dramatic illusion, and his evolutionist ideas found expression in Wordsworth's Ode 'Intimations of Immortality from Recollections of Early Childhood':

> Though inland far we be,
> Our souls have sight of that immortal sea
> Which brought us hither.

Darwin's analysis of the state of consciousness during dreaming is still well worth reading. It was of course self-evident to him as a rationalist that dreams are a product of the imagination, rather than any mystical intervention. The idea prevalent during the 1960s that lack of dreaming might cause madness is anticipated by two hundred years in his writing. Darwin's view was that dreams prevented delirium by allowing trains of ideas to continue in the absence of sensory input:

> if they were to be suspended in sleep like the voluntary motions, (which are exerted only by intervals during our waking hours) an accumulation of sensorial power would follow; and on our awakening a delirium would supervene, since these ideas caused by sensation would be produced with such energy, that we should mistake the trains of imagination for ideas excited by irritation; as perpetually happens to people debilitated by fevers on their first wakening; for in these fevers with debility the general quantity of irritation being diminished, that of sensation is increased.

This argument differs from the more modern notion, that dreaming is involved in the resolution of conflicts, but similarly ascribes an importance to dreams in preserving sanity.

Central to his description of dreaming is the suspension of volition, 'and in respect to the mind, we never exercise our reason or recollection in dreams; we may sometimes seem distracted between contending passions, but we never compare their objects, or deliberate about the acquisition of these objects'. This observation, that we remain uncritical observers in dreaming, forms an important part of some recent theorizing about dreaming by the psychophysiologist Allan Rechtschaffen, who has described dreams as being 'isolated' and even 'un-imaginative' in the sense that we cannot imagine something else during the action of a dream. (This theory is more fully described in Chapter 6.)

Darwin's work shows how little scientific thinking about dreaming has changed over two centuries, and its popularity and deep influence during his own lifetime ensured that these rationalist ideas became an accepted part of literary as well as scientific ideology. However, what can we say with confidence about the beliefs of ordinary people, either in the nineteenth or even in the late twentieth century?

One approach is to consider the usage of words themselves. A very common modern form of expression is the dream *thing* – for instance a dream kitchen or a dream holiday – implying that dreams are simple wish-fulfilments. This usage is now so prevalent that it hardly conveys anything more than the best that could be imagined. When Emerson wrote 'The search after the great is the dream of youth', in 1847, this was a metaphor with considerable impact. The *Oxford English Dictionary* gives no previous examples of this usage, while twentieth-century examples abound, from 'I dream of Jeanie with the light brown hair', and 'I'm dreaming of a White Christmas', to Martin Luther King's dream of a just and non-racist society, the American Dream itself, and every other advertisement for kitchens and holidays in the sun. We can only speculate on whether this is another example of the pervasive influence of psycho-analytic thinking in our culture.

Over the last thirty years the achievements of physiologists and psychologists in studying dreaming have received a good deal of attention in the media, much of it sensationalist, so one might expect some of this information to have percolated through to become common knowledge. While much remains to be explained about dreaming, a number of findings have been made which are by now uncontentious among scientists. Three of the questions in the Hull survey were designed to assess how well known these ideas have become. The statements with which respondents were invited to entirely agree, agree with qualification, or disagree, were:

12. Dreams only occur in the few moments before you wake up.
14. Dreaming sleep is commonly accompanied by flaccid (relaxed) paralysis.
15. Preventing people from dreaming will drive them mad.

We know from experimental evidence that dreams proceed as it were in 'real time', and are just as long as they seem. The flaccid paralysis of rapid eye movement sleep, usually accompanied by dreaming, is also well established. Depriving people of dreaming (rapid eye movement) sleep has indeed been achieved in sleep laboratories. It does not drive them mad any more than depriving them of any other sort of sleep, although one early report did suggest the reverse, and was highly publicized.

The responses of those surveyed revealed some ignorance concerning the first question. Eighteen subjects agreed firmly with the statement that 'Dreams occur only in the few moments before you wake up', and a further 22 thought this was maybe true, out of 148 responents. The second question, asking whether dreaming is accompanied by flaccid paralysis, was agreed with by a surprising 48 respondents, although these people did not show themselves to be well informed about the other questions. There was no evidence for any general consistency in response to this group of questions which may have indicated that subjects responding correctly did so out of knowledge of the scientific findings. The large proportion (33 out of 148) agreeing with the statement that preventing dreams can cause madness suggests, however, that some of the publicity may have got through, although this whole issue may be confounded with ideas of brainwashing and the effects of total sleep loss.

Modern beliefs, one might think, ought to be in the rationalist mould of the Enlightenment, but little or nothing is taught about the psychology of consciousness in schools, except in terms of religious studies. Religion has had a decisive influence on thinking about dreaming, and it is achieving a revival in many parts of the world. In particular, fundamentalism, both East and West, is becoming increasingly popular. The United Kingdom has been spared so far, but while the majority of the population are religiously inactive in terms of church-going, most of them would call themselves Christians, and their spiritual beliefs have been formed by Christian teaching. The established Church of England shares with other Christian churches in upholding the claims of the New Testament, while keeping quiet about some Old Testament stories.

Religious education in schools is of course compulsory in the United Kingdom, and is taught using children's versions of the Bible, such as Horton's *Stories of the Early Church* (211) or *The Ladybird New Testament* (364). The bowdlerizations in these books make it clear that there is little doubt expressed about the credibility of the revelations of the New Testament, and then only about those which occur to people who are awake. That is, biblical accounts of supernatural visitations during dreams, and dreams foretelling the future, are repeated without comment. However, visitations occurring during wakefulness are altered to become visitations during dreams.

The Hull survey included questions on whether spirits visited the body to cause dreams, whether dreams could foretell the future, whether nightmares could be caused by evil spirits and whether the soul can leave the body during sleep. In addition, they were asked whether the dreams reported in the New Testament could be literally true (Table 1.1). Over half the respondents acknowledged that dreams could foretell the future, and amongst those who believed in the literal truth of the accounts of dreaming in the New Testament this proportion was much higher. Very few people indeed agreed that nightmares could be caused by demons, or that the soul leaves the body during

Table 1.1 Can dreams foretell events?

Are the Bible dreams literally true?	Never	Sometimes	Totals
Certainly not	15	11	26
Possibly true	20	21	41
Certainly true	2	13	15
Total respondents	37	45	

sleep. Only two of the fifteen believers in the Bible accounts agreed that spirits could visit us during dreams, although it is crucial to the sense of these accounts that God did make Himself known to individuals during dreams, and actually visited them in their dreams.

This evidence demonstrates how even well-educated people can hold mutually contradictory beliefs (a proposition which social psychologists would find quite uncontroversial). In this context it becomes obvious that we must be careful not to oversimplify the ideology of distant cultures, either in time or space, simply for our own ease of comprehension.

A recent anthropological study of Zulu people in South Africa (324) reported:

> ancestral spirits are believed to visit their descendants in their sleep and through dreams make their wishes known. Sleep is *ubuthongo*, and an ancestral spirit is *ithongo*. The etymology here could well indicate the contact during sleep between the living and the dead, in which case sleep may be regarded as a miniature death that takes a person away from the conscious life of the day.

In imputing this degree of credulity to people who live far away in foreign cultures are anthropologists liable to be careless in the way they ask their questions? The official religion in the United Kingdom – Christianity – crucially invokes supernatural dreams; and yet the most devout Anglican would be most unlikely to interpret one of their own dreams as being a message from a deity. According to my sample of Hull University students, the dreams of Joseph, the Magi, and so on may have been literally true (according to over half of those questioned), but it seems that it would be naive to conclude that they really believe that communications of this sort are still 'possible' – that is, presumably, they happened in the Bible by some unique divine intervention which will never be repeated. A surprising contrast to what any anthropologist would have to report about the religious beliefs of modern Westerners is Turnbull's authoritative and intimate account (413) of the lives of pygmies in the forests of the Congo – containing no references to dreaming at all, and very little evidence of pygmy mysticism.

Rather than modern Western beliefs being less mystic than those in antiquity, or in underdeveloped communities, they seem equally if not more so than some. It could be argued that the very incomprehensibility of the modern world has made us even more credulous. Many of the quite commonplace products of modern technology might as well be magic, for all that any normal person could be expected to understand how they work.

Interpretations of dreams

Lay Interpretations

'Significant' dreams (for instance, communications from deities) are traditionally associated with the great men of history, and not their subjects. It is well known that many modern despots have not only been assiduous hypochondriacs, but have shared this preoccupation with dreams. A Pharoah or a modern dictator would share the conundrum that though apparently so similar to their subjects, with their same mortal limitations, they somehow have acquired the privilege of uniquely determining their country's future, and deciding on matters of life and death perhaps every day. The fact that soothsayers were employed by rulers from the Pharoahs to Hitler is perhaps unsurprising. The advice given by these advisers would properly have been guided by expediency as much as by any rules of interpretation, and as such cannot be taken to represent a body of thought about dreaming. In modern life astrology seems in any case to have taken over from dream interpretation as the soothsayer's preferred technique.

Fragments of papyri from the second millenium BC seem to be the first writings to deal exclusively with the subject matter of dreams, mainly concerning themselves with incest and bestiality with various animals. The only interpretations were that 'That is bad' or 'That is good', with no further elaboration. Assyrian cuneiform texts have also been found which give interpretations of dream topics, many of which, again, are taboo behaviours – eating the flesh of one's penis, killing brothers or sons, eating faeces. According to Becker (33) many more, however, are more mundane:

> To meet a horse was to obtain a saviour. Monkeys, pigs, foxes, mice, cats, birds, snakes and dogs were favourable, indicating posterity and prosperity. But he-goats and sometimes rams were bad omens. Long commentaries were devoted to dreams of flying, even at this period. All, with a few exceptions, signified danger and often death . . . The problems of physiological life are not forgotten. Importance is given to teeth-grinding, interpreted in a negative way, together with speaking, groaning or snoring while dreaming.

The most important dream book of this sort was the compilation made by Artemidorus in the second century AD, taking material from Middle Eastern, Greek and North African sources. His was not entirely a list of subjects and their meanings, and he preferred to make the interpretation by considering a sequence of dreams, and even the personality and circumstances of the dreamer. Quite often, the dream was interpreted as an allegory for what was about to happen to the dreamer. The complexity of some of the interpretations offered in his books, and the attention paid to the dreamer has invited comparisons between his methods and those of Freud, centuries later. Charles Rycroft (372) reports that Artemidorus required to know at least six facts about a dream before it could be interpreted: 'Whether the events depicted in the dream were plausible or bizarre; whether they were approximately interconnected; whether they were customary for the dreamer; what events prior to the dream could have influenced it; and the dreamer's name and occupation.' His books were not widely circulated, and in one of the last two which were dedicated to his son (and unpublished) was the assertion that it contains instances 'that will make you a better interpreter of dreams than all, or at least inferior to none; but, if published, they will show you know no more than the rest' – a sentiment which T. R. Glover (164) rather pithily describes as suggesting science declining into profession. While interpretations had previously derived their credibility from divine revelations of one sort or another, from this time on, in Europe, dream interpretations drew their authority primarily from their antiquity.

A well-developed systematization of dream interpretation apparently existed in China, but was never taken entirely seriously, or at least, being incorporated into the civil service, lacked the glamour of antiquity or divine revelation. Joseph Needham's (322) only indexed reference to dreaming in ancient China is tantalizingly brief:

> Oneiromancy, or prognostication by dreams, was also practised in China, as in most ancient civilisations, though it can hardly be said to have taken a very important place there. Chou Li says that the interpretation of dreams was in the department of the Grand Augur (Ta Pu), and mentions a special expert of lower grade (Chan Meng) who specialised in it. Here again the chief book was late, the *Meng Chan I Chih* of Chhen Shih-Yuan, published in +1562 (Ming). How far certain aspects of Chinese dream-interpretation might be considered, as Chinese themselves are sometimes inclined to think, anticipations of Freudian psychology, would be a subject worth investigating.

The invention of printing in Europe in the sixteenth century soon brought with it a number of books offering dream interpretations for ordinary people. These books typically claimed to be the distillation of wisdom handed down from Arab sages through the centuries, and they all drew heavily on Artemidorus' work. They took the form of dictionaries, with lists of subject matters and their associated meanings. As Raymond de Becker points out, they could have been used as gospel by the naive, or turned into parlour games by sceptics. The *Palais du Prince du Sommeil*, written by Celestin de Mirbel in 1667 actually advises in his preface that, 'The favours of the strictest ladies will be wholly won for you, at the moment when you become the sympathetic interpreter of their dreams' – certainly a pragmatic reason for buying his dream book.

The modern newspaper horoscope has largely taken over from dream books, although they are still published, and still draw largely on the works of Artimedorus (or claim to). The truth is, few people believe that revelations are going to be made to them in dreams – and even on the rare occasions that an individual really felt a dream was of overwhelming 'significance', the so-called dream-books could only take in the most gullible. Nevertheless, we still tell each other our dreams and look them up in these absurd books, and still read our horoscopes – just for fun.

Psycho-analytic dream interpretation: the lay view

Psycho-analytic thinking has had a deep influence on psychiatry and psychology in the twentieth century, but this has been by no means decisive, and its increasingly fragmented theories have been subjected to continuous criticism. Its influence on Western culture has, however, been pervasive, particularly in literature, theatre and the cinema. Its historical importance in the development of modern ideology has come from its unique claim to explain experience, however eccentrically. That is to say, there was, at least in the first quarter of this century, no well-developed rationalist alternative to theology or to a simplistic materialism to explain mental life. Rejection of official religion drove people to the alternatives of magical or spiritualistic fringe cults and rationalism. While psycho-analysis itself probably had little to do with the decline in accepted religious belief its early popularizers only benefited from it. As Geoffrey Gorer (170) has remarked, their books for a lay public implied that psycho-analytic theory gave them an insight into matters of general concern of a depth and quality simply not available to the uninitiated, to people without qualifications. The authority of medicine finally ousted Artemidorus' invocations of antiquity, and the increasingly muted references to the supernatural by the clergy, in explaining life's ordinary ecstasies and tribulations.

The early splintering of the psycho-analytic movement, and the independent developments by the neo-Freudians such as Alfred Adler, undermined the coherence of Freud's original formulations. To the lay outsider psycho-analysis appears a pretty broad church, at least so far as dream interpretation is concerned. The one idea that can be said to have made a firm impression from the psycho-analytic approach to dreaming is that these experiences come from within the mind, rather than from outside (although in the case of Jung's psychology even this is not clear). Many dreams are so bizarre that they seem inexplicable and it follows that only a medically qualified expert could penetrate the machinations of the subconscious mind which produced them. The second psycho-analytic message that has come through to the public is its preoccupation with sex. The idea that dream objects have sexual symbolism can however degenerate into a sort of post-Artemidorian dream-book formula, where anything elongated is a phallic symbol, anything with a hole a vaginal one. This is the layman's view of psycho-analytic dream-interpretation – how any more subtle understanding is achieved is obscure. This obscurity has not detracted from the approach's popularity, and many widely held notions about psychology have originated in the cinema, in magazines or novels, based on interpretations of psycho-analytic thought.

CHAPTER 2

Studying Sleep in the Laboratory

The study of sleep was revolutionized in the early 1960s by the systematization of the previously *ad hoc* methods for estimating sleep depth and quality, using EEG (brainwave) and other measures. These new methods of recording and scoring sleep stages in human beings were based on the use of a piece of equipment available in most hospitals and many university departments of psychology – the clinical EEG machine, or electroencephalograph, a device for detecting and recording the electrical activity of the brain. The ready availability of recording devices contributed to the explosion of research into sleep and dreaming during the late 1960s.

Much of the evidence discussed in the next few chapters will rely on EEG and other electrophysiological information, and some understanding of the basis of these measures is essential to understanding how we know what we do about sleep. The next few pages contains an explanation of the workings of the EEG, written in a non-technical way. It is easiest to understand the modern methods for measuring electrical activity from the brain by looking at the development of these methods over the past 100 years or so. In doing so, the major electrical manifestations of cortical activity will be described, and some important issues will be clarified at a simple, accessible level of complexity which would otherwise possibly remain impenetrable if dealt with in their modern context.

Story of the electroencephalograph (EEG)

The principles of electromagnetism had been established by the late eighteenth century, but it was not until the mid-nineteenth century that any sort of measurements could be made of the small currents produced by living tissue. However there were one or two early attempts to investigate the relationship between electricity and living organisms during the eighteenth century, long before the technology existed to do so properly. According to Grey Walter in his book *The Living Brain* (422), informal experiments on executed criminals showed that electric shocks caused muscles to contract and twitch, and Louis XV 'caused an electric shock from a battery of Leyden jars to be administered to 700 Carthusian monks joined hand to hand, with prodigious effect'. The Leyden jar was simply a primitive condenser, capable of storing static electricity for short periods of time, and more refined experiments had to await the invention of reliable sources of electric current.

Electrical stimulation could produce dramatic effects, but the proper study of electrophysiology had to wait for some time until it was possible to record small electrical potentials. The gold leaf electroscope, available early in the nineteenth century, was too insensitive to register the tiny changes in potential difference associated with nervous and muscular activity.

The first workable device for recording small potentials was the string galvanometer. Although totally obsolete in today's laboratories, a description of this simple device is useful in making clear what is being recorded, and illustrating some of the problems which still confront modern electroencephalographers. Essentially the string galvanometer consisted of a coil of copper wire, connected at either end to two electrodes, and string hanging down within the coil to which was attached a small magnetized mirror. A difference in electrical potential between the two electrodes would cause a current flow through the coil, creating a magnetic field within. The mirror would then rotate in proportion to the strength of the current. A light, shone on to the mirror and reflected on to a fairly distant surface, would provide an initial doubling in amplification of the movement of the mirror, and the further the light was projected, the greater the subsequent amplification of any change in potential difference. An improvement on this basic design was to use a lightweight but rigid rotating rod on which to mount the magnet and mirror, and attach a coil spring at one end, so that once any change in potential difference had been registered the mirror would swing back to its original position.

One way of obtaining a permanent record, in the nineteenth century, was for one observer to watch the galvanometer mirror through a telescope and work a key with his finger that operated a signal pen on a smoked-drum kymograph. The magnitude of excursion of the mirror was read aloud by a second observer (watching the projected light) to an assistant who wrote on the drum next to the appropriate signal.

An apparently apocryphal account is of two Prussian medical officers, Fritsch and Hitzig, who in 1870 took advantage of the opportunity offered by the Franco-Prussian War to study the exposed brains of soldiers struck down on the battlefield. What is certain is that they discovered that electrical stimulation of some parts of the cortex caused movements in the limbs on the opposite side of the body from that of the part of the brain which had been stimulated. Animal experiments showed that these movements could be repeatedly elicited by stimulation at the same place. It was now possible to map what we now know as the motor cortex (i.e. the part of the brain controlling muscle function) in terms of the musculature each section controlled.

The procedure, incidentally, can and has been performed on patients undergoing brain surgery. The surface of the brain is totally insensitive, and operations on the brain in humans commonly involve only a local anaesthetic. The patient is conscious and can even report to the surgeon any experiences he or she may be having as the operation progresses.

It was now obvious that with sufficiently sensitive recording techniques it should be possible to map the parts of the brain responsible for perception – the sensory cortex – in a similar way. This was the task that Richard Caton, working in Liverpool, set himself, using a Thomson reflecting galvanometer and Du Bois-Reymond's coated, non-polarizable electrodes. Caton repeated some earlier experiments on the electrophysiology of nerve and muscle preparations, and then set about recording from the exposed surface of the brain. In doing so he discovered that there were spontaneously ·generated potentials (the EEG) as well as showing that it was indeed possible to detect electrical brain responses to stimuli. While he located the visual cortex in the occiput, or rear of the head, using this technique, he was unable to find any location specifically responsive to sound stimulation. The observation that there was spontaneous electrical activity at the surface of the cortex seemed relatively insignificant at the time, but it was the discovery of the electroencephalogram.

Mary A. B. Brazier has described the work of Hans Berger as the triumph of a man working with equipment inadequate even by the standards of his day (62). Like Caton, Berger attempted to record electrical responses to sensory stimuli in animals, although it seems that the work he did between 1902 and 1910 was in general unsuccessful. It was not until 1924 that he turned to the measurement of human electrical potentials, and delayed publication until 1929, when the first recorded electroencephalogram (of his young son) appeared in *Archiv forschung Psychiatrie*. (See Figure 2.1.)

Note The lower line is a 10 cycles per second sine wave for use as a time marker, the upper line is the recording from Berger's young son made in 1925.

Figure 2.1 Berger rhythm: the first recorded electroencephalogram of man.

Berger discovered the alpha rhythm, running at 10 cycles per second (hertz, or Hz) and also discovered that it disappeared if the eyes were opened, with mental effort (such as doing mental arithmetic with eyes closed) and with loud noises of painful stimuli. Berger's work was disregarded by physiologists, partly because it was published in psychiatric journals, and also perhaps because of his reputation for eccentricity, seclusiveness and his longstanding belief in psychic phenomena such as telepathy. Only after his work was replicated by Adrian and Matthews in Cambridge did he get the credit he deserved, for having laid the foundations of human electroencephalography. Brazier's history (62) of the EEG cannot be recommended too highly for readers wishing to read a full and authoritative account of the early days.

Modern EEG techniques

The modern electroencephalogram

The modern clinical EEG machine is a far cry from the simple galvanometer devices used by Berger and the other pioneers. Entirely electronic amplifiers are arranged in banks, so that between 8 and 16 channels of EEG are transmitted to a bank of galvanometers. The use of multiple recordings has allowed the development of a series of techniques for localizing sources of electrical activity within the cranium. These have been clinically very useful, for instance in localizing sources of abnormal activity within the head, from tumours or foreign objects. Only one EEG channel is necessary for the scoring of sleep stages, although two or more may sometimes be used. The other channels are used to record other sources of electrical activity, generated by movements of the eyes or from the neck muscles under the chin.

The differential amplifiers used in EEG machines use the difference between the voltages offered by the two inputs, which is normally less than 200 microvolts (millionths of a volt), and amplify this difference up to a voltage sufficient to drive the galvanometer pens – perhaps 0 to 5 volts. In addition, there will be a selection of electronic high frequency filters, and of low frequency filters.

Modern EEGs work on the same principle as the sprung mirror galvanometer – i.e. they are capable of measuring very fast changes in potential difference between the electrodes, but are relatively insensitive to slow changes. That is, after a shift in level of voltage difference between the electrodes has taken place, the output from the amplifier gradually returns to the midline. The rate at which it does this is measured as a 'time constant' – defined as the time it takes for the output to return 63 per cent of the way to baseline, after a shift in input voltage level. The shorter the time constant the more attenuated slow activity will be. To pursue the analogy with the sprung mirror galvanometer, the more powerful the spring, the faster the mirror will swing back to its original position.

Recording montages for sleeping subjects

The definitive work, *A Manual of Standardized Terminology, Techniques and*

Scoring System for Sleep Stages of Human Subjects (360), gives a detailed account of the internationally agreed system of recording of sleep stages. EEG (electroencephalographic, or brainwave), EOG (electrooculographic, or eye movement) and EMG (electromyographic, or muscle activity) recordings are simultaneously taken to give the scorer a composite picture of activity throughout the night. The stages themselves are defined in terms of patterns or syndromes of EEG, EOG and EMG activity.

EEG, according to the *Manual*, should be recorded from between an electrode placed centrally on the scalp and one behind the ear. In practice many laboratories use two electrodes on the scalp, one at the vertex (midway centrally between the bridge of the nose and the inion, or bony bump at the base of the cranium), and one frontally, about two centimetres behind the hairline. The EEG is recorded as the difference between these two electrode placements. (Figure 2.2 shows a subject being wired for sleep recordings.)

Eye movements are recorded from electrodes taped above each eyebrow to electrodes taped over the opposite cheekbone, giving two EOG channels. These do not reflect activity from the eyes individually, but between them the two channels will record an eye movement in any direction. What is being recorded here is not the electrical activity associated with the muscles controlling the movements of the eyes, but the change in electrical field caused by the rotation of the eyeballs in their sockets. This is caused by the corneo-retinal potential – a standing potential across the retina of about one-tenth of a volt. EOG changes themselves are of the same order as EEG changes – up to 150 microvolts, and they are typically recorded using the same time constants and level of amplification as the EEG channel. An important point to remember about EOG recordings made using EEG amplifiers is that they never give direct information about the direction of gaze – only changes in direction – and the rate at which the galvanometer pens return to the midline of the paper chart is determined by the time constant setting. Misunderstandings about the nature of the recordings contributed to some confusion in the early 1960s about whether the eye movements of dreaming sleep did or did not actually follow the action of the dream.

EMG recordings made from under the chin reflect the activity of the muscles in the neck. These muscles are under the control of postural reflexes which ensure a level of tonic (continuing) activity almost all the time (unlike, for instance, the large muscles in the arms and legs). This measure gives a good index of the tonic level of muscular relaxation in light sleep, in identifying periods of movement which may contribute to outside interference in the EEG and EOG channels, and is crucial in determining the presence of REM (rapid eye movement) sleep, when there is little or no EMG activity.

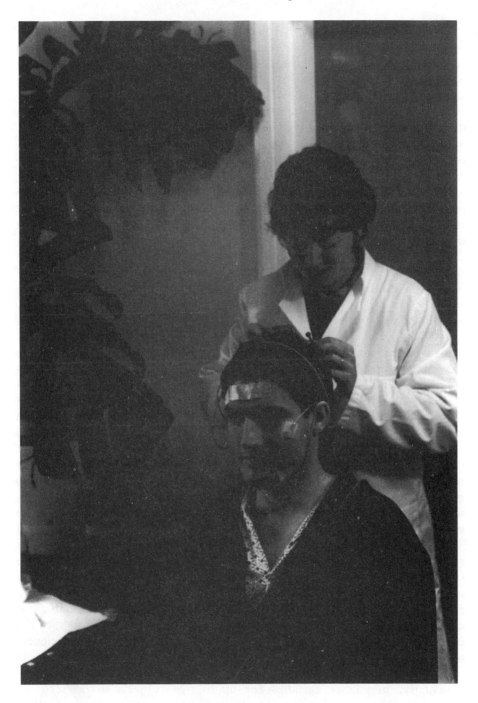

Figure 2.2 Subject wired for sleep recordings.

The EEG during sleep

EEG observations

Early work in the 1930s and 1940s (272) had established that there were systematic changes in brainwaves with sleep, in that large slow waves developed very soon (within fifteen minutes) after a subject fell asleep at night, and during the night the amplitude of these waves waxed and waned. A convention was established of sleep stages, indicated by the numbers 1 to 6, 6 being the 'deepest', with the biggest slow waves. Rather puzzlingly, the EEG would sometimes revert to being low voltage, activated, while the subject was still plainly asleep. These periods of low voltage sleep were called 'emergent stage 1' because subjects were not as easily roused as from 'ordinary' sleep onset stage 1 sleep, and because, being continuous with deeper stages of sleep, these periods of light sleep were obviously not a transition between wakefulness and sleep, in the way that sleep onset stage 1 seemed to be.

In 1953 Eugene Aserinsky and Nathaniel Kleitman (23) reported rapid, saccadic eye movements, similar in appearance to waking eye movements, associated with reports of dreaming. It was not until 1957 that Dement and Kleitman identified 'emergent stage 1' sleep as a completely distinct stage of sleep from other light sleep stages, always accompanied by rapid eye movements, and frequently by reports of dreaming (100). A few years later Ralph Berger discovered the loss of neck muscle tone which accompanies REM sleep (41). These two findings, linking EEG patterns with eye movement and neck and throat muscle activity, have formed the basis of the recording and scoring methods for humans now in use all over the world.

Psychophysiological measures are now used to define sleep states, rather than merely to describe them. Figure 2.3 shows good examples of the psychophysiology associated with relaxed wakefulness and five internationally recognized stages of sleep – four slow wave sleep stages, numbered 1 to 4, and stage REM (rapid eye movement) sleep which is associated with dreaming.

When subjects arrive at the sleep laboratory in the evening for a night's recording they prepare themselves for bed in the normal way. When they are in their pyjamas, or dressing gown if they wear nothing in bed, the electrodes are applied to their faces and heads (see Figure 2.4). It is possible to record from more than one subject at a time on a single EEG machine, so that it is common to have two bedrooms equipped with headboards (into which the electrodes are plugged) as, for example, in the Department of Human Sciences at Loughborough University. Purpose-built accommodation, as for instance in Professor Ian Oswald's laboratory at Edinburgh University's Department of Psychiatry, may have facilities for up to five subjects to be recorded simultaneously, in sound-proofed bedrooms with air conditioning. In Hull we are fortunate in having a newly converted suite, with three single bedrooms,

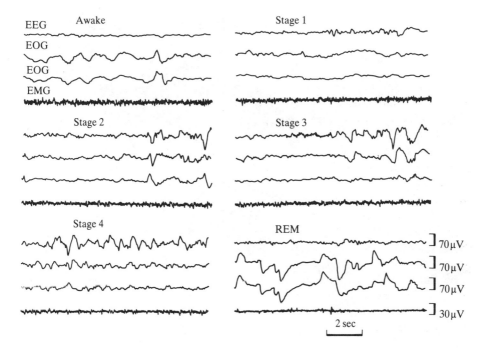

Figure 2.3 Sleep stages.

electromagnetically screened, sound-proofed and environmentally controlled, linked to a control room by hidden cables.

When the experimenter has confirmed that good signals are being recorded from all the subjects involved he or she will say good night and turn out the lights. Most people find the environment of the laboratory unusual, and on their first night they typically take longer to get to sleep than is usual. On the second and subsequent nights in the laboratory a subject will remain indubitably awake, showing alpha rhythm (originally known as the 'Berger rhythm' after Hans Berger, who first reported it) at 10 cycles per second (Hz) in the EEG, and periodic blinks in EOG, for less than ten minutes. Drowsiness is first indicated by a reduction in the frequency of alpha rhythm, from about 10 Hz to 8.5 Hz or so in a young adult, as well as a reduction in its amplitude, and then by its disappearance. It is replaced by a low voltage (i.e. relatively flat) record with slow activity in the range 2–7 Hz. At the same time the blinks typical of wakefulness are replaced by slow rolling movements of the eyes, easily seen in the EOG, as the subject drifts into stage 1 sleep (Figure 2.5).

Stage 1 sleep is defined in terms of the EEG and EOG records as consisting of a low voltage EEG with some slow activity, and occasional vertex sharp waves, and slow rolling eye movements (see example). As they go to sleep, subjects do not usually stay in stage 1 for long – between 1 and 10 minutes.

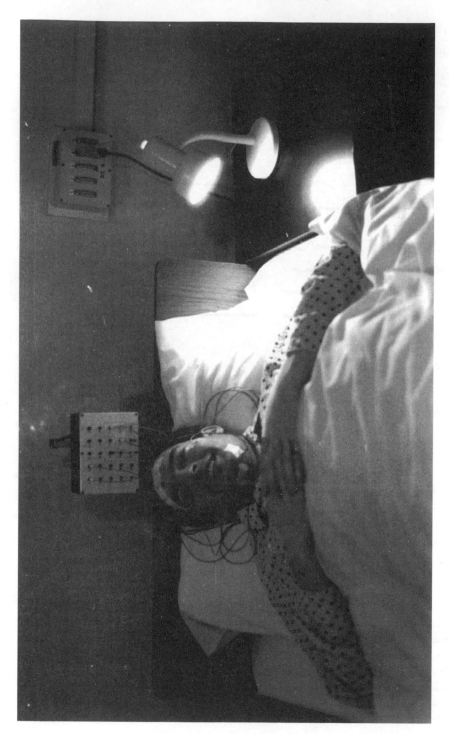

Figure 2.4 Subject ready for sleep in laboratory bedroom.

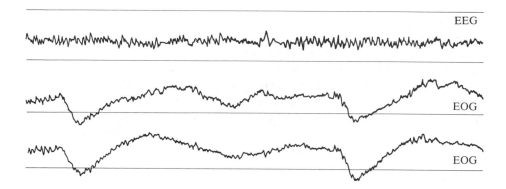

EEG

EOG

EOG

Figure 2.5 EEG/EOG signs of sleep onset.

The less settled subject may alternate for a while between stage 1 sleep and wakefulness, but usually once sleep takes over there is a fairly rapid transition from this stage to deeper sleep stages.

The onset of stage 2 sleep is taken to be the first sleep spindle or K complex. Sleep spindles are bursts of fast (13–15 Hz) EEG activity lasting perhaps 2 seconds which increase in amplitude to about 50 microvolts and then decline, giving them their spindle-shaped envelope. K complexes are phasic events (i.e. isolated occurrences) in which there is a sudden increase in negativity on the scalp, followed by a corresponding positive wave. They last between 0.5 and 2 seconds and while their amplitude may only be in the region of 50 microvolts, they may be as large as 250 microvolts from peak to trough (see Figure 2.6). Stage 2 sleep is defined as comprising a low voltage EEG, with mixed, slow frequencies and periodic sleep spindles and/or K complexes.

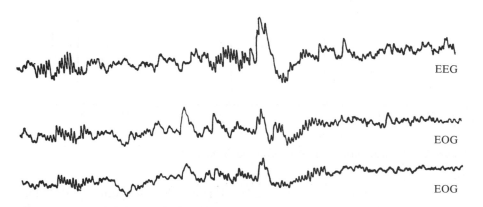

EEG

EOG

EOG

Figure 2.6 Sleep spindle and K complex.

More or less as soon as the subject has settled into stage 2 sleep, at the beginning of the night, larger slow waves begin to appear in the EEG, whose frequency is less than 2Hz. These slow waves increase in amplitude and persistence until when they occupy 20 per cent or more of the record the requirements for the scoring of stage 3 sleep are satisfied. Sleep spindles and complexes may continue during stage 3 sleep. A healthy young adult typically will have reached this stage of sleep within 20 minutes of going to bed, and sleep now continues to deepen, with larger and more persistent slow waves dominating the EEG record. These slow waves pervade the head to the extent that they are also picked up by the EOG electrodes, just as K complexes are. When the slow waves occupy 50 per cent or more of the record the subject is judged to be in stage 4 sleep.

So far as the deep slow wave sleep stages are concerned, therefore, the greater the amplitude and the slower the frequency of the EEG slow waves, the deeper the sleep. Stage 3 is defined as comprising between 20 per cent and 50 per cent slow waves in the EEG, and stage 4 sleep as comprising over 50 per cent of the record dominated by slow waves. It is conventional to regard the NREM stages 1–4 as being on a continuum of increasing depth, and distinct from REM (rapid eye movement) sleep, but to reserve the term 'slow wave sleep' or SWS to indicate stages 3 and 4.

Figure 2.7 shows the typical patterning of sleep through the night, as shown by a healthy adult. On going to sleep, all normal people start with slow wave sleep, and do not have any REM sleep until at least 45 minutes have elapsed. There is then an alternation between slow wave sleep and REM sleep, with REM sleep recurring about every 1½ hours. The first REM sleep period is usually shorter than the subsequent ones – less than fifteen minutes in adults, as against later periods of about half an hour. Deep slow wave sleep (stages 3 and 4) predominates in the first half of the night.

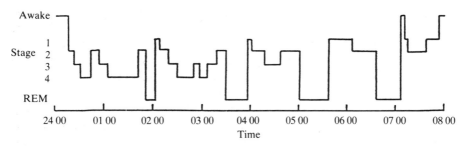

Figure 2.7 Typical patterning of sleep through the night.

The patterning of sleep illustrated in Figure 2.7 is not only typical, but follows conventions which are universal. However much people may vary in their lifestyles during the day, their sleep proceeds in the same regular pattern, obeying the same rules. While it is unremarkable to observe that while some people eat three meals a day, and others miss out breakfast and lunch altogether, taking all their food in the evening, there is no such parallel during sleep – no normal person has been found for example, who takes all their REM sleep in one session of 90 minutes at the beginning of the night, or saves it all up for a session in the early hours of the morning. We are all slaves to the same mechanism, which proceeds every night to control our sleeping brains according to a complex set of rules which are only now becoming apparent.

It has also been very difficult indeed to establish any reliable differences in sleep profiles between different sorts of people – men versus women, the extroverted versus the introverted or the intelligent versus the unintelligent. There are considerable differences between babies, young children, young adults and the aged, which will be dealt with later. The most striking thing about sleep patterns within a broad age group, however, is how remarkably uniform they are.

The first night effect

Looking at the paraphernalia attached to the subject wired up for a night's recording, one might legitimately ask whether anybody could reasonably be expected to feel natural, and get to sleep in their usual way. Might not the electrodes, the constraining wires and the very fact of being observed in a laboratory not only delay sleep but actually alter the quality of sleep from what it might usually be at home?

Experiments assessing the difference between the sleep achieved on successive nights in the laboratory have shown that there is indeed some evidence of difficulty in getting to sleep on the first night (8). The time between lights-out and getting to sleep (the so-called 'sleep-onset time') is increased, and so is the amount of time spent in light sleep at the beginning of the night before deep slow wave sleep (stage 4), and the first REM sleep period. Second and subsequent nights in the laboratory show no progressive changes in young adult volunteer subjects. Most experimental studies of sleep now allow subjects a night of acclimatization to laboratory conditions, so that on their first night they are wired up in the usual way, but whatever recordings made are discarded, and the experiments proper begin on the second night. While most all-night recording experiments are over brief periods (of up to a week), some very extended studies have been done, and there is no evidence that the patterns of sleep we observe over short periods, after the first night, are in any way peculiar to the unfamiliarity of the laboratory environment.

Brainwaves and the experience of being asleep

If we shake somebody and ask them if they were asleep they usually have a definite answer. Everybody is familiar with their own experience of being asleep, and feel they can give a definite answer. As we shall see in Chapter 12 on sleep problems, sometimes the 'insomniac' complaining of never sleeping is in fact, by psychophysiological criteria, achieving normal amounts of sleep, but their experience is that of staying awake. What determines whether people feel they are asleep or awake? A laboratory study (91) using the old (Loomis) classification of sleep stages allowed subjects lying in bed and getting to sleep to indicate when they were 'drifting' or 'floating' by squeezing a bulb. Subjects who characteristically had dominant alpha EEG rhythms when awake were most suitable for this task, as the level of alpha rhythm then acts as a good indicator of alertness. (Some people produce little or no alpha rhythms, even when completely relaxed.) These subjects tended to squeeze their bulbs when alpha rhythm had attenuated – consistent with the idea that these experiences occur when cortical arousal drops.

If the hypnagogic sensation of drifting can be identified with the attenuation of alpha rhythm, should we also define this as sleep onset, or should that be defined behaviourally? That is, should sleep onset be defined as being non-responsiveness to quiet stimuli rather than defined on the basis of EEG? A recent study at the Medical Research Council (MRC) Applied Psychology Research Unit in Cambridge compared a behavioural index (response to a faint auditory stimulus by pressing a button) with subjective and physiological indices of sleep onset (328). While responses became fewer as subjects passed from stages awake (W) to 1 and 2, they only disappeared in stages 3 and 4 and REM sleep. The authors suggest that the behavioural evidence supports a gradual transition between wakefulness and sleep during what they term a 'sleep onset period', despite clearly noticeable psychophysiological changes between stages W, 1 and 2.

The lack of any clear subjective sense of when sleep onset occurs is also shown by comparisons between reports from 'good' sleepers and 'poor' sleepers. When normal good sleepers are woken from stage 1 sleep or stage 2 sleep, and asked whether they were awake or asleep, they tend to report definitely feeling asleep only in stage 2 sleep (193), although this is not necessarily true for poor sleepers, who may deny they were asleep even when the EEG traces show clear signs of stage 2 sleep.

Sleep norms

Individual variations

You don't have to record people's brainwaves in order to know how long people sleep. Surveys have shown that adults sleep an average of 7½ hours, with a standard deviation in the sample of about 1 hour. That is, two-thirds of the population can be expected to sleep between 6½ and 8½ hours per night, about 16 per cent regularly sleep over 8½ hours, and another 16 per cent sleep under 6½ hours.

Healthy individuals regularly sleeping less than 5 hours or even as little as 2 hours in every 24 are rare, but represent a sizeable minority. These people typically have been described as being highly active, personified in individuals such as the successful business man or the former British Prime Minister, Margaret Thatcher. A laboratory study of two short sleepers by Jones and Oswald (225) found that their pattern of sleep was not that of the 'normal' sleeper's first half of the night. Rather, while they showed the same pattern of alternating between slow wave sleep and REM sleep about every 90 minutes, the proportion of light sleep stages (1, 2 and 3) was low. Almost all their time in bed was spent in either stage 4 sleep or REM sleep, giving them a near normal total amount of these two sleep stages, and very low levels of light sleep. Another case study of an elderly lady in poor health who slept very little, by Ray Meddis and associates (297), found that her sleep was light and fitful, and, over a period of a week she only achieved one night's proper sleep. When this occurred her pattern of sleep stages was more similar to a 'normal' sleeper's than a 'short' sleeper's.

There are occasional reports in the medical journals of people not sleeping for extended periods of time when suffering from illnesses interfering with brain function. A recent and very interesting case is that of a 53-year-old man in Italy who suddenly began to sleep less and less (274). His habitual amount of sleep had been 5 to 7 hours per night, with a half-hour siesta in the afternoon. As his sleep problem developed, he could only manage 2 or 3 hours of sleep, frequently disturbed by vivid dreams. Three months after his symptoms had started, he could not sleep at all, and suffered from waking dreams. The last 6 months of his life were spent in hospital, where he rarely slept, if ever, and he suffered from disorientation, inability to concentrate enough to do the simplest task, and was totally unintelligible. He contracted a lung infection which did not respond to treatment. On autopsy it was established that he had suffered from a very rare brain condition in which the thalamus progressively degenerated. Two of his sisters and many of his relatives over three generations had died in the same way, indicating that the condition may be inherited. A follow-up study of 5 more cases from the same family, and a study of 28 affected members of the family from four generations (292), has confirmed that this syndrome is determined genetically. Post-mortems of the five revealed the same pattern of damage to the anterior ventral and mediodorsal nuclei of the thalamus. Age of onset varied between 37 and 61, and death ensued after between 7 and 25 months, during which the same pattern of sleep reduction, then complete insomnia, was accompanied by waking dreams, hallucinations, and finally stupor and coma.

Did lack of sleep alone kill this man and his relatives? We cannot be sure, since the thalamus is a very important structure and damage to it may be lethal for a variety of reasons. In these cases, however, it seemed that the nature of the disease was systematically to destroy those nerve cells essential to the control of sleep, and these unfortunate people probably represent the closest that we can expect to find in the way of a natural experiment on the long-term effects of the denial of sleep in human beings.

Periodically there are press reports of otherwise healthy individuals who need no sleep at all. These people rarely volunteer for investigation in controlled EEG studies. One such case who did submit to continuous observation was reported from Ian Oswald's laboratory in Edinburgh. This was a middle-aged man who had been involved in a road accident after which he suffered from headaches, difficulty in walking and a total lack of sleep. After repeated medical examinations and seven years of litigation he was awarded £12,000 in compensation, and 'aided by continuous benefits, he stayed off work, exhausted through lack of sleep' (334). After an initial two nights in the sleep laboratory in which it was confirmed that he was continuously awake, he returned with his wife for a five-night stay. Over the first three days he was watched increasingly closely, as it appeared that he may have been sleeping during the early evening when no recordings were being made, and during the nights his wife seemed to be doing her best to keep him awake. By the fourth day he had become obviously very sleepy. His speech was slurred, he was making visual misinterpretations, looking very dishevelled, and seeming scarcely able to keep his eyes open. On the fifth night he finally fell asleep when the electrodes were on and recordings were being made, and stayed asleep for 2½ hours until his wife woke him. Oswald reported: 'He appeared disoriented, begged to be allowed to sleep, and said he must have been cured by an injection. The EEG appearances of slow-wave sleep and rapid eye movement (REM) sleep had been normal.' Despite this demonstration of his habitual need for normal sleep, even if only for a few hours a night, this same individual appeared on television a few years later, again claiming never to sleep. Whatever the explanation in this case, it obvious that such claims must be treated with the greatest scepticism. *Nobody* has yet been discovered who maintains any semblance of normal health without sleeping.

Sleep patterns in normal babies

A neonate's (newborn infant's) behavioural repertoire is somewhat limited, and there is of course no question of their reporting on whether they are awake or asleep. A systematic description of neonatal 'states', was first suggested by Wolff (442). Avoiding any 'anthropomorphic' assumptions, observations of the regularity of respiration, open or closed eyes, movements and vocalizations have resulted in the definition of five mutually exclusive syndromes or states which are now widely accepted. Two of these states can be identified with sleep states which show a continuity of development to maturity in the form of REM sleep and deep slow wave sleep. In neonates REM sleep is termed 'active' sleep, and the neonatal equivalent of slow wave sleep is 'quiet' sleep. The greatest changes in sleep in humans take place during the first year of life, with the normal 1-year-old showing essentially the same patterns of sleep as the adult, although in different proportions of stages, and with a recognizably different EEG.

As any parent knows, the neonate does not recognize any distinction between night and day. His or her patterns of sleep and wakefulness are determined by an intrinsic cyclical patterning of alternation of behavioural activity and sleep states, modulated by demands of hunger and thirst, which commonly resolves into a 4-hour 'day' by the end of the first month. While some infants may go uncomplaining through the night without feeding by the age of 2 months they will not have spent the whole time asleep. Observations show that they persist in periodically waking, even if remaining quiet, and the establishment of uninterrupted night-time sleep is uncommon before 3 months of age.

The neonatal infant's EEG during quiet sleep has few slow waves, and no sleep spindles. Slow waves appear in bursts, separated by periods of low voltage activity of about 10 seconds. In the first month after full term these slow wave bursts increase in length until the low voltage periods of quiet sleep are entirely displaced (343). Sleep spindles develop during the first two months of life, varying in frequency between 10 and 14 Hz although showing no systematic tendency to increase in frequency with age (as is the case with the waking alpha rhythm, which progressively becomes faster with age to reach a maximum of 10–11 Hz) (112).

While there has been some disagreement over the incidence of EEG spindling in neonates, the consensus of reports indicates that the development of spindles in the EEG of normal sleeping infants occurs between the end of the second month and end of the fourth, and the appearance of persistent spindling earlier or later than this time window tends to be associated with other clinical abnormalities (307). Normal sleep patterns at this age have, however, been reported in a group with known severe brain abnormalities (441). There are also great individual differences between normal infants which are not always obviously related to maturational age.

Sleep patterns in the first 3 months of life are difficult to categorize and, compared to the remarkable uniformity of adult sleep, show a high degree of idiosyncrasy. Despite this, some consistent patterns have been established. The typical full-term infant can be described as asleep for about 17 hours out of the 24. Active sleep is easily identifiable with adult REM sleep, and the neonate will spend between 60 and 80 per cent of sleeping time in active (REM) sleep – 10 to 13 hours. Unlike adults, infants may show very short delays between sleep onset and active sleep onset, sometimes going straight into active sleep. The time between sleep onset and active sleep onset thus tends to be either very short indeed (less than 10 minutes) or over 50 minutes, as the period of their alternation between active and quiet sleep is of the order of

60 minutes. Active or REM sleep onset will persist for the first 12 months of life in normal infants.

Developmental sleep norms

The definitive work on sleep norms at different ages is by Robert Williams, Ismet Karacan and Carolyn Hursch from the Florida Sleep Laboratory (441) who recorded the normal sleep patterns of over 200 subjects between 3 and 70 years of age and older over a period of 15 years. The descriptions of sleep norms which follow derive largely from their work, with the exception of the norms for infants. While many other studies have been done on the development of sleep their results do not contradict the norms established in Florida, and the principle advantage of the work of the Williams group is that their sample sizes were appreciably large – at least 20 in each of 13 age groups, and a consistent system of recording and scoring was used over all of these subjects.

The considerable differences between infant sleep and childrens' sleep are undeniable, even if there is some lack of unanimity about the precise relative amounts of active and quiet sleep, not to speak of the 'intermediate' stages in very young babies, attributable at least in part to the idiosyncratic nature of neonatal sleep (compared to the remarkably stereotyped nature of adult sleep). The techniques developed for recording and scoring adult sleep are inappropriate for infants, and so a common system of techniques and norms has been developed by Thomas Anders, Robert Emde and Arthur Parmelee, in association with a dozen other leading researchers (13). Uncontroversial normative data on infant sleep is provided, for instance, by Prechtl's (350) recordings of 20 babies. During childhood, adolescence, adulthood and middle age we can be confident of the consistency of evaluation of sleep. In old age there is a different problem from that of infants' sleep, namely that of assessing the amount of deep slow wave sleep (stages 3 and 4). When scoring sleep stages in young and middle-aged adults one encounters individual differences in the amplitude of the slow waves of stage 4 sleep, and there is an understandable tendency to recognize the periods of sleep with the biggest slow waves in any individual as 'their stage 4 sleep'. Typically, the amplitude of slow waves in deep sleep becomes smaller with ageing. When applied to the elderly, this shifting criterion for scoring stages 3 and 4 may tend to inflate the actual amount of deep slow wave sleep actually scored.

Another progressive change with age in sleeping patterns is the number of arousals during the night. The 20-year-old sleeps with fewer interruptions than the 36-year-old (128), and there is evidence that this increasing fitfulness in sleep continues throughout the lifespan, with 66-year-olds sleeping more soundly than 95-year-olds (232). These brief wakenings do not prevent a similar total quantity of sleep for younger men and women, since we tend to stay in bed slightly longer as we get older. There is some evidence that sleep disturbance in normal old men is more frequent than in normal old women. Possibly this increase in the number of wakenings during the night is related to the attenuation with age of the 24-hour (circadian) rhythm of body temperature and other physiological functions.

The pie charts (Figure 2.8) illustrate the major changes in proportions of sleep states taken at different ages. REM sleep can be identified with active sleep in the neonate, who spends about half the time in this state. As the mature version of deep slow wave sleep develops in the first year of life, and daytime sleeping is displaced by wakefulness, the number of hours spent in active (REM) sleep is eroded until by the age of 3 years it has dropped from 12 hours to 3 or 4. After the age of 10 the amount of REM sleep remains constant until old age.

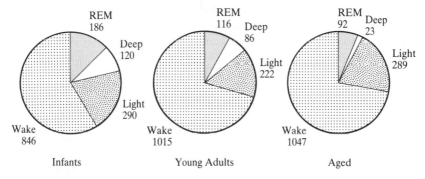

Note The three pie charts show the amount of time (in minutes) spent in wakefulness and sleep by groups of 3- to 5-year-olds, 20- to 29-year-olds and 70- to 79-year-olds, respectively. In these charts 'light' sleep comprises stages 1 and 2, and 'deep' sleep comprises stages 3 and 4.

Figure 2.8 Quantities of sleep at three ages.
Source: (441).

Comparisons between quantities of neonatal quiet sleep and deep slow wave sleep stages (3 and 4) in older children and adults are improper, since quiet sleep develops into the whole range of slow wave sleep stages. However, once well established as in the 3-year-old toddler, stages 3 and 4 slow wave sleep occupy about 3 sleeping hours, reducing with age in the same way as REM sleep. Unlike REM sleep, these sleep stages continue to reduce in middle-aged and elderly groups, so that in the over-70s very little stage 3 or 4 sleep is taken. The typical person over 70 takes half as much REM sleep as the toddler, and about the same amount as a 20-year-old. Their deep slow wave sleep has however reduced to a quarter of the amount taken by the toddler, about half that of a 20-year-old. Even this short period spent in stages 3 and 4 may be an overestimate, as was pointed out above.

CHAPTER 3

The Physiology of Sleep

Biological rhythms of sleep
Circadian rhythms and Zeitgebers

The nineteenth-century 'classical' account of physiology, typified in the work of the great French scientist Claude Bernard, held that physiology functions to maintain a constancy of the internal environment, and the view which would be expressed in modern terms as that physiological control consists of a series of negative feedback systems responding to changes produced either internally, by other systems, or from the external environment. It is certainly true that many biological systems do respond like this. For instance with changes in the environment, pupils dilate in the dark, and perspiration increases in the heat. However, since life began, one of the great certainties on this planet, in all habitable zones, has been that there has been a regular alternation of light and dark, warm and cold, on a 24-hour basis. Despite so much uncertainty in the world confronting organisms, the sun has remained uniquely and totally predictable. It is therefore perhaps unsurprising that physiological systems should have evolved to rely on, and in many cases to anticipate, such a regular routine. That is, rather than simply react to changes when they occur, they can behave proactively, preparing the organism for changes which are known to be about to occur.

It was known over a hundred years ago that body temperature, for example, varied with time of day in a regular way. It was not clear until the middle of this century, however, that variations such as this, and the control of the timing of wakefulness and sleep, were largely under the influence of biological clocks which were relatively independent of external cues. Two facts forced scientists to this conclusion. First, when animals are removed from all external cues as to time of day, they continue to show pronounced rhythmicity in behaviour (alternating wakefulness and sleep) on a 24-hour basis. Second, to bring home the point that this 24-hour rhythmicity was in no way a response to any minimal cues that the experimenters had not been able to exclude from the animals'

40

environment, it was usual for the free-running rhythms to deviate slightly from the exact 24 hours. Figure 3.1, from Jurgen Aschoff's important paper in 1965 (22), showing the activity of a chaffinch in an isolated environment, illustrates the point very well. The horizontal bars denote times of activity. The first four

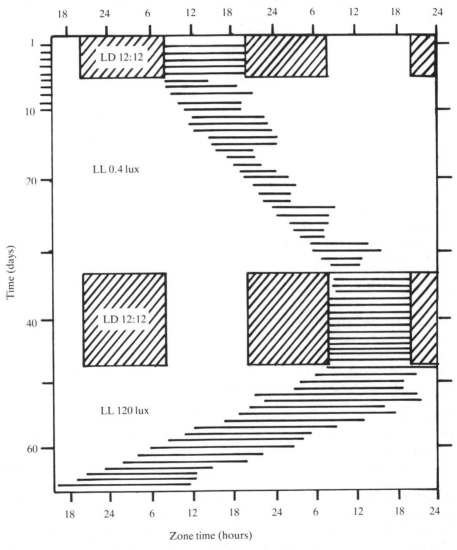

Note Black bars, activity time; shaded area, darkness.

Figure 3.1 Activity ryhthm of a chaffinch (*Fringilla coelebs*) in a light–dark cycle with 12 hours of light and 12 hours of darkness (LD 12:12) and in continuous illumination (LL) with an intensity of 0.4 lux and of 120 lux. Source: (22).

days were under normal illumination (LD 12:12, with lights on for 12 hours, off for 12). The next four weeks were under continuous illumination at a low level (0.4 lux), followed by two weeks of LD 12:12, and then a period of continuous and relatively bright light (120 lux). When under continuous low illumination the animal's pattern of behaviour was governed by a 'day' slightly longer than 24 hours, and while under continuous brighter illumination its day was shorter than 24 hours. Aschoff went on to experiment on human volunteers isolated in an underground bunker for 3 or 4 weeks. Like the chaffinch, these volunteers carried on their lives in a more or less regular routine of wakefulness and sleep, although the human rhythms were almost all longer than 24 hours, whatever the level of illumination. Their rhythms of body temperature and urine excretion followed the same pattern of response to continuous light as the chaffinch, with the period of the spontaneously generated day becoming longer the dimmer the continuous light.

In short, both chaffinches and human beings (and virtually every other animal species) seem to have an independent ('endogenous') biological clock ticking away somewhere inside them, and this clock is instrumental in controlling some of our most important physiological functions, including preparing us for wakefulness and making sleep possible. The study of biological rhythms necessitated the integration of knowledge from a number of disciplines – from mathematics to biology, and has generated a specialized vocabulary of its own. Some useful terms are listed below.

Useful Biological Rhythms Research Vocabulary

General oscillator terms
Amplitude: The peak to trough difference in biological oscillation.
Frequency: The reciprocal of the period of a rhythm: e.g. 10 cycles per second, or once per 24 hours.
Period: The time it takes to complete one complete cycle of a rhythm.
Phase: A particular reference point in the cycle of a rhythm: e.g. sleep-onset times.

Biological rhythm terms
Circadian periodicity: Rhythms of about 24 hours. Franz Halberg (181) first introduced the word 'circadian' to describe such imprecise but highly regular rhythmicity.
Endogenous periodicity: An innate rhythm, apparent in the absence of any time-giving external cues.
Exogenous periodicity: Rhythmic activity derived mainly from external cues: e.g. some flowers opening in response to sunlight (but not the heliotrope, famous since 1729 for opening its flowers on a circadian basis even if kept in the dark).

Entrainment: Coupling of an organism's underlying endogenous rhythm with time-giving external cues (*zeitgebers*).
Ultradian periodicity: Rhythms of less than a 24-hour period: e.g. 90-minute cycles of REM/non-REM sleep.
Zeitgeber: Literally, 'time-giver': a forcing oscillation in the environment.

Biological clocks share many of the properties of mechanical clocks. A surprising property of even the simplest mechanical oscillators at the heart of clocks is that of the tendency towards entrainment. The Dutch scientist Christiaan Huygens, working in the seventeenth century, was one of the first to build reliable pendulum clocks, and he noticed that when they were in close proximity they tended to tick in synchrony, keeping the same time even if they did not do so when restarted in isolation from each other. This tendency, for the frequency of oscillators to adjust in concordance with quite weak rhythmic stimulation, is known as entrainment. In the example of the pendulum clocks, the vibration generated by each activation of the escapement – the tick – was transmitted through the wooden case of one timepiece to the one in contact with it. Similarly, while biological clocks drive physiological functions at a variety of time periods close to 24 hours when in isolation from external cues, all relevant physiological functions settle into an exact 24-hour routine in the presence of natural *zeitgebers*, or time-giving cues such as sunlight.

The suprachiasmatic nucleus, circadian rhythms, sleepiness and bright light

It is obvious from the evidence from isolation studies that biological clocks exist, controlling biological rhythms in almost every important physiological function. Given the phenomena of entrainment, it is logically possible for any organism to have either one biological clock governing all functions, a small number governing important functions or, indeed, a clock in every cell in the body, since they would normally all be entrained upon one another. Experiments like those done by Aschoff, on human beings isolated from time cues, have shown that, given time, different physiological functions commonly become dissociated in phase, even though still exhibiting circadian periodicity. Richard Kronauer and his colleagues at Harvard University report that over extended studies in their isolation facility, every single subject tested developed a dissociation between their temperature rhythm and the sleep–wake cycle by the end of two months isolation (255). On the basis of evidence like this they have constructed a mathematical model involving two major circadian oscillators, one directly governing body temperature, and the other governing rest-activity. According to the model, interactions between these oscillators (and their respective entrainment) normally resolve into a coherent circadian pattern governing all physiological functions.

Neurophysiological evidence is crucial to their argument. Experiments on

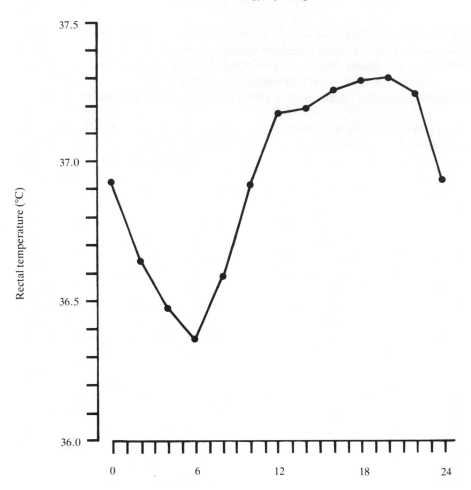

Figure 3.2 Temperature variation in human subjects over 24 hours.
Source: Aschoff, J. 'Circadian rhythms: interference with and dependence on
work–rest schedules'. In L. C. Johnson, D. I. Tepas, W. P. Colquhoun and
M. J. Collingan (eds), *The 24 Hour Workday. A Symposium on Variations in
World-Sleep Schedules*, Washington, DC: National Institute for Occupational
Safety and Health, 1980.

the rat have indicated that in this animal at least, there is only one biological
clock governing circadian activity, and it is located in the *suprachiasmatic
nucleus* (SCN) of the hypothalamus. (In humans, the hypothalamus lies at the
base of the brain, under the thalamus, below and anterior to the third ventricle.
The pituitary gland is attached to the base of the hypothalamus.) Experiments
reported almost simultaneously by two pairs of American scientists, Robert
Moore and Victor Eichler from the University of Chicago (309) and Friedrich
Stephan and Irving Zucker from the University of California at Berkeley (396),

showed that lesions in this area of the brain abolished any noticeable circadian periodicity in activity, hormone secretion, drinking or sleep. The animals continued to eat and sleep in normal amounts, but not at regular times. The question remained whether the clock is really located in this structure, or whether the SCN is simply a vital coordination centre. Subsequent experiments have shown that even when all nerve connections between the SCN and the rest of the brain have been severed, this structure still produced a circadian pattern of discharges, as monitored by microelectrodes (218). (Not surprisingly, the animals showed no circadian patterns in wakefulness and sleep, at this stage.) Finally, there is further evidence that the SCN exerts its control over the rest of the brain largely through the medium of neuromodulators, or local brain 'hormones' (151). If an animal's SCN is destroyed, and then replaced with nuclei obtained from donor animals, circadian rhythms become re-established, even though the grafts have very few neural connections with surrounding nervous tissue (262). These grafts can be effective in re-establishing circadian rhythms in as short a time as a week (92).

To return to the Richard Kronauer group's mathematical model, they argue that the SCN controls the human sleep–wake cycle while the temperature cycle is relatively independent, and governed by a different oscillator. It is obviously impossible to make direct electrophysiological recordings from the human brain to establish whether our SCN is comparable to the rat's. However, anatomical studies show that we do have such a structure (277), and experiments on squirrel monkeys show that their SCN is implicated in control of sleep–wake cycles, but not temperature cycles. Additional evidence for this two-oscillator model comes from studies of jet lag. Fast transmeridian travel (across time zones) results in passengers arriving at destinations whose local time is very different from that of the zone that they left, often on the same day. Body rhythms, including temperature rhythms, subsequently take time to adjust to the new environment. That is, while sleep–wake routines may change within 48 hours to adjust to the new time zone, cycles of body temperature take much longer. According to the Kronauer model, the SCN responds immediately to *zeitgebers* provided by light – particularly bright sunlight – and the sleep–wake oscillator therefore adjusts quickly. It then forces the second oscillator, controlling body temperature amongst other functions, to entrain as well to the new phase of the 24-hour cycle. The Kronauer group studied body-temperature recordings from individuals in their isolation chamber who were exposed to phase shifts in lighting, and in the temporal displacement of regular activities announced by gongs. These subjects were, in one condition (with a 'weaker regime'), given control over reading lamps. In a regime with a 'stronger artificial zeitgeber' the subjects had no control over lighting. They claim a very good match between predictions made by their mathematical model, of the rates of resynchronization of body temperature, for both these regimes. In addition to these laboratory studies, they obtained temperature recordings from four NASA scientists who regularly made international flights involving time-zone changes. Again, good matches were obtained between temperature adjustments predicted by the model and those actually recorded by these scientists (156).

While mathematical models of continuously variable oscillators can naturally be used to predict continuous variables such as body temperature, it becomes less clear how they should predict all-or-none changes such as the transition between wakefulness and sleep. It becomes necessary to postulate a threshold in the circadian oscillation in propensity for sleep, above which one remains awake (or wakes up) and below which one stays asleep (or falls asleep). The Kronauer model is excellent for explaining changes in body temperature, but seems less useful in predicting sleep behaviour itself. Alexander Borbely and his colleagues have developed an alternative model which aims to explain and predict the circadian sleep–wake cycle as well as other circadian variations (59).

Borbely proposes a single 'sleep-regulating variable' which is basically a propensity to sleep, or sleepiness (S). Sleep onset is only possible when this is at a high level, and spontaneous awakening from sleep occurs when it is at a low level. Two factors control the levels of propensity to sleep:

1.   an endogenous circadian, sinusoidal oscillation;
2.   amount of prior wakefulness.

The factor S, or sleepiness, is reduced by deep slow wave sleep, increased by wakefulness. (REM sleep is assumed to be independently controlled, and its occurrence basically determined by the circadian cycle.) A person living a normal regime of regular sleep at night will have a cycle of propensity to sleep as described in Figure 3.3. The endogenous, sinusoidal circadian rhythm (C) summates with the relaxation oscillation described by the 'prior sleep factor' (PSF) to produce a pattern of sleep propensity – S – over the 24 hours. This illustration assumes that the circadian cycle is sinusoidal, peaking in sleepiness at 0600 hours, and that the subject normally goes to sleep at 2300 hours and wakes at 0700 hours. It also assumes that the amplitude in variation in S over every 24 hours is equally influenced by circadian and prior sleep factors – in fact the Borbely team estimate that the amplitude of variation contributed by circadian factors is somewhat less than that contributed by the homeostatic effects of prior wakefulness. All the same, the figure shows how the concatenation of these two simple but different oscillations produces a plausible pattern of sleep propensity. That is, sleepiness does not simply increase progressively with time since the last sleep period – rather, we maintain or increase alertness over the day and into the evening, then rather suddenly begin to feel sleepy as bedtime approaches.

This model has been tested by comparing its predictions for the effects of sleep deprivation (when S, as determined by the homeostatic function would monotonically increase, although modulated by circadian factors) as well as by

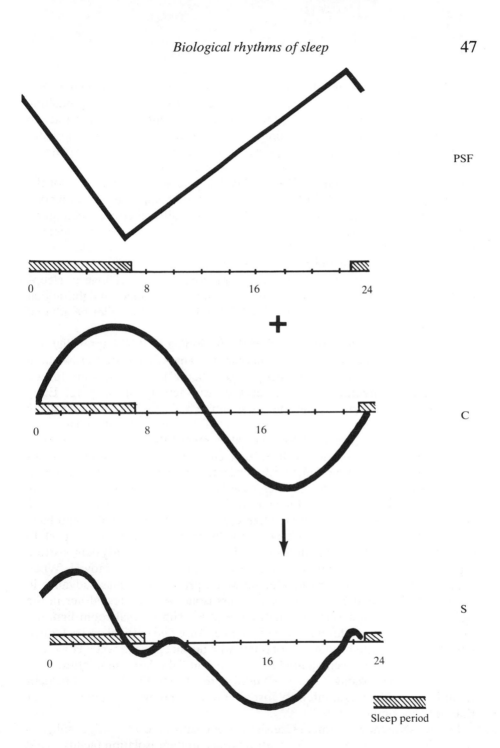

Note Prior sleep factor (PSF) summates with the circadian factor (C) to give propensity for sleep (S) over a typical 24-hour period.

Figure 3.3 Borbely's model (for reference see (59)).

the effects of bed rest, and the effects of shift-working regimes on sleep length. A major virtue of the model is that it addresses the problem of predicting changes in state from underlying factors which are continuously variable. In their terms, 'a model containing only a single circadian pacemaker that gates a noncircadian homeostatic sleep–wake process is sufficient to explain in quantitative detail the major phenomena of human sleep timing.'

Both the Kronauer and the Borbely models give adequate accounts of the nature of circadian rhythms in man, but with different emphases – one on body temperature, the other on sleep–wake cycling. The differences between them, such as the issue of whether there is one major oscillator or two may seem to be of rather academic interest. However, the question of which constitute the most powerful *zeitgebers* in resetting our cycles is undoubtedly of immediate practical importance. After transmeridian flights, is it the change in sleep–wake regimes, the change in mealtimes, or simply the changes in lighting that reset our biological clocks to local time? How should the traveller be advised to ensure speedy adaptation?

As with the chaffinch, illustrated at the beginning of this chapter, lighting schedules are highly effective *zeitgebers* in humans, when tested in isolation facilities. This could be because people go to bed when the lights are turned off, and their rhythms are then reset by the activity of sleeping. Early experiments on human rhythms during isolation had demonstrated that social cues (for instance, receiving a telephone call at the same time every day) were very important *zeitgebers*. It was natural to regard the sleep–wake cycle as being a highly significant synchronizing cue, as it so obviously involves important aspects of brain function. In order to separate out the effects of light from the sleep–wake cycle, Charles Czeisler's group at Harvard University tested a number of elderly subjects in their isolation facility, searching for a subject with a naturally short circadian cycle. Such an individual would have normal sleep–wake cycles, and be normally entrained in every respect to circadian cues in his or her natural environment, but would swiftly demonstrate a phase advance in body temperature when such cues were removed. When they had found such a person, who showed a pronounced phase advance in body temperature after as little as 24 hours isolation, they tested her in the isolation facility on a 12:12 LD lighting routine with normal room lighting. Even under these conditions her body temperature and cortisol cycles tended to drift, advancing to become out of phase with her sleep-wake cycle. However, when exposed every evening for 4 hours to bright light, her temperature cycle was reset on the first day. (The levels used were 7,000 to 12,000 lux, equivalent to ambient outdoor light intensity just after dawn, and over ten times dimmer than midday sunlight) (86).

In a subsequent experiment Czeisler's group subjected 14 younger subjects (aged 18 to 24) to a total of 45 'resetting trials' in their isolation facility. That is, after 3 days of baseline on 'normal' time, the clocks would be put forward or back up to 12 hours, and a variety timings of bright-light exposure were employed. They confirmed that exposure to bright light, particularly in the evenings, speeded adaptation, so that body-temperature, urine-output and plasma-cortisol cycles were all completely adapted after 3 days (88). (Normally, people may take 9 days to adjust completely to a phase advance of 6 hours, such as a winter flight from US Eastern Standard Time – e.g. Boston – to the United Kingdom.) From a practical point of view, this research indicates the importance of going out into the sunshine in the first two or three days after a time-zone shift, particularly in the afternoons and evenings. This advice would also obviously apply to shiftworkers going back on to a daytime shift. The Czeisler group have tested the application of their recommendations on shiftworkers (87). The experimental group were exposed to bright light at night (7,000–12,000 lux) and to complete darkness during the day, while the control group were exposed to normal levels of artificial light during the night, and allowed to sleep at home during the day, with only their own bedroom curtains to keep out the sunlight. Comparisons between the first and sixth days on the regime showed that the experimental group had completely adapted to the new regime, with pronounced phase shifts in plasma cortisol, urine production, body temperature, subjective alertness, and performance on a simple task. As in many previous studies of the circadian rhythms of shiftworkers over this sort of length of time, the control group showed little or no adaptation at all.

Czeisler argues that nightworkers can substantially improve their adaptation to shifts by making use of commonly available heavy curtains, or blackouts, during their sleep periods, and by seeking out, rather than avoiding bright light during the night. As many shift rotation sequences are short enough to allow workers to avoid any adaptation at all, it remains unclear how generally useful this advice is. Some other, and less contentious, applications of the effects of exposure to bright light, are the treatment of early wakenings in the elderly, and in the reinforcement of circadian rhythmicity in people living in the Arctic circle.

Circadian rhythms are all pervasive and highly physiologically significant for sleep-related processes. Other biological oscillators also exist, however, with both long periods and short ones. Those with periods longer than 24 hours are known as infradian rhythms, those with periods shorter than 24 hours, ultradian rhythms.

Ultradian rhythms

Superimposed on the circadian rhythm is the human 90- to 100-minute cycle of REM sleep alternating with slow wave sleep – an important ultradian rhythm. The deep slow wave stages predominate in the first two or three hours, and light slow wave sleep, alternating with relatively long periods of REM sleep are characteristic during the second half of the night.

Is this pattern the result of processes intrinsic to sleep, or do the sleep stages 'belong' to different periods of the 24 hours? Systematic studies in which subjects have been allowed to go to sleep at various times of the day and night have shown that stage 4 sleep can occur at any time, almost always appearing early in a sleep period whenever it starts. In consequence sleep during the day may start well, with some deep slow wave sleep, but then tends to be fitful, as REM sleep fails to sustain itself later in the sleep period (215). It loses out in competition with stage 4 at the beginning of the sleep period (in the morning when it would otherwise be at its most abundant) and then the drive for REM sleep appears to dissipate later in the sleep period, during the early afternoon. The amount of deep slow wave sleep seems to be determined simply by the amount of prior wakefulness, while REM sleep periods are short and relatively unstable at all hours of the day apart from the hours between 2 a.m. and noon (426).

This evidence has been invoked to suggest that the deep slow wave sleep stages are somehow more 'important' than REM sleep, since they seem independent of circadian entrainment, displacing REM sleep even when it 'ought' to appear. A recent study casts doubt on this interpretation. Normally, as we have seen, body temperature and the sleep–wake cycle are in phase, and it is extremely difficult to disentangle the web of cause and effect between sleep processes, arousal, time of day and temperature.

In the isolation bunker at Manchester University, Ken Hume has found that when dissociation between temperature and the sleep–wake cycle occurs, and the onset of sleep coincides with low body temperature, REM sleep can indeed displace the deep slow wave sleep stages in the early part of the sleeping period. When these rhythms are operating normally, and a person goes to sleep in the early hours of the morning when their body temmperature is at a minimum, deep slow wave sleep dominates the first few hours of the sleeping period. Hume's work suggests that while deep slow wave sleep mechanisms normally override considerations of time of day, they do not simply reflect an imperative need more urgent than that of other sleep stages, determined simply by the amount of time elapsed since stage 4 was last enjoyed. Rather, these preliminary results suggest that stage 4 sleep occurs *either* when temperature is high, *or* when cortical (behavioural) arousal is low, but when sleep is achieved with high arousal and low temperature stage 4 is displaced by REM sleep early in the sleep period (214).

Incidentally, body temperature has been shown to affect sleep directly in both crocodiles and human beings. Higher temperatures (induced by sunbathing in the reptiles and hot baths in human subjects) are followed by unusually persistent high amplitude slow waves in the EEG during sleep (see Chapter 9, pp. 140–1). We can only speculate whether crocodiles given hot baths would produce as much slow wave sleep as after sunbathing! More seriously, these results illustrate how although studies of sleep patterns over the day may indicate an apparently simple relationship between pressure for stage 4 sleep and time since it was last taken, the actual drive mechanisms are considerably more complex. Any imputation of functions from drive mechanisms is also hazardous, as we shall see in Chapter 11 (pp. 162–3).

The 90-minute cycle – does it run all day?

The alternation between slow wave sleep and REM sleep during the night was described by Nathaniel Kleitman as the expression of a basic rest–activity cycle (BRAC), which he suggested continued during the day, and on which the sleep–wakefulness cycle was superimposed (247). An alternative explanation is that the cycling is the outcome of a homeostatic interplay between mechanisms controlling REM and non-REM sleep. Ephron and Carrington were among the first to suggest this (120), explaining that the periodic REM sleep phases could be a method of maintaining arousal in an otherwise increasingly unresponsive brain. If this were true we would expect the timing and quantity of REM sleep to be determined principally by the amount and depth of prior slow wave sleep. The evidence for this is equivocal. Gordon Globus has claimed that the timing of REM sleep periods is to some extent 'pre-programmed', so that they occur at the same times of night, regardless of when the subjects went to sleep, or whether they 'missed' an REM period (163). While the entrainment of 90-minute cycles into the 24-hour day has not always been observed in subsequent studies, Globus's work stimulated the study of periodicity during the day, as well as the study of sleeping cycles.

An elegant and ingenious experiment reported from William Dement's laboratory has resolved the question of whether sleep mechanisms for the main sleep states were interdependent in the literal way suggested by Ephron and Carrington (73). Their five subjects lived on a regime of a succession of 90-minute 'days' for almost a week, being allowed sleep for 30-minute periods with waking intervals of 60 minutes. If the Ephron and Carrington model were right, the subjects should never develop any REM sleep, since slow wave sleep could not 'accumulate'. In the event, all the subjects showed all the normal sleep stages, but frequently went straight from waking to stage REM sleep (REM sleep occurred within 10 minutes of sleep onset in 79 out of the 110 sleep periods containing REM sleep). They typically alternated the type of sleep between successive sleep periods, although REM sleep was primarily between 07.30 and 14.00.

Sleep mechanisms are therefore normally entrained to their own internal clock with a period of about 90 minutes, which may itself be entrained to the ubiquitous circadian cycle. It follows from this that the 90-minute clock is also ticking over during the day (and some of Globus's work on the timing of REM sleep periods during afternoon naps supports this idea). If so, does it affect waking behaviour? Two American psychiatrists (150) observed a group of psychiatric patients over periods of six hours, and counted the number and timing of eating, drinking and other oral behaviours. Deeply committed to Freudian theory, they devized a scoring system which gave 10 points, for instance, for a drink of milk (because of its symbolic importance) and only one point for a sandwich. A clear 90-minute cycle in oral behaviour was evident, which they interpreted as being a manifestation of the sublimated outcome of fluctuations in erotic drive level.

This experiment suffers from two major flaws. First, subjects were observed as a group, so that interactions between the patients may have led to them eating and drinking cyclically at the same times. Second, the food and drink available was nutritious, and thus certainly directly affected their level of appetite: the study becomes much less interesting if the results merely reflected the timing of digestive processes. Ian Oswald (336) repeated the experiment using non-nutritive foods and drink, and with the six subjects isolated from one another. A simple count of the timing of feeding and drinking (with no complicated points system) confirmed that there was a 90-minute cycle (see Figure 3.4).

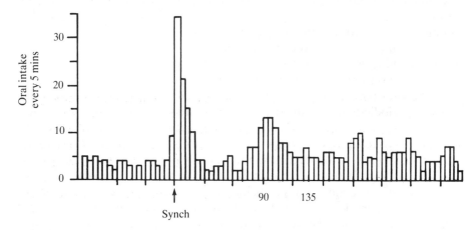

Figure 3.4 Distribution of oral intake scores when peak intakes were synchronized for the period 30 minutes to 2 hours from start. Source: (336).

If the 90-minute cycle (BRAC) persists during the day, how does it affect cognitive processing and performance? There is EEG evidence for relative activation of the right hemisphere during REM sleep with respect to the left, and we know from a variety of sources of evidence that there is some specialization of function between the hemispheres. In most right-handed people, for instance, linguistic skills seem to be a function of the left hemisphere, while skills (for instance the recognition of faces) which demand the analysis of patterns are performed better by the right hemisphere. One could argue that the times of day which would contain REM sleep, were the subject asleep, should also be characterized by right-hemisphere activation, resulting in improved performance on tasks tapping spatial abilities, worse performance on tasks tapping verbal abilities. Tests on 8 subjects over a period of 8 hours, using verbal and spatial tasks, have shown that performance on both gave evidence of periodicity with a peak of 96 minutes. What is more, these cycles in efficiency were 180 degrees out of phase, just as the experimenters had predicted (245). If the two sides of the brain indeed become activated on a 90-minute cycle then this should also be reflected in power in the EEG. Further experiments have confirmed that there is a significant cycling in EEG power over a 72- to 120-minute period during a day of isolation in 8 subjects, although there were no differences between the hemispheres (293).

While these experiments have provided good evidence for 90-minute periodicity in daytime behaviour, and it is reasonable to assume that this is related to the sleeping 90-minute cycle, it remains to be positively demonstrated that day-time fluctuations in performance are determined by the REM/non-REM sleep cycle of the previous night. Readers wishing to follow this up may be referred to recent models of the REM/NREM cycle provided by Achermann and Borbely (1), and by McCarley and Massaquoi (280).

Infradian rhythms

After the alternation of day and night, the next most noticeable cosmological changes we experience are in the seasons. Historically, people got up with the lark and went to bed soon after it got dark. In temperate latitudes this naturally meant that they would sleep longer in the winter than the summer. This pattern still prevails among people living in the Arctic circle, for example in Spitzbergen where it is very difficult indeed to get children to go to bed during the summer in constant, 24-hour sunshine. In the modern world one might assume that city dwellers would be relatively unaffected by the seasons, so far as their sleep was concerned, with the sleep–wake cycle under voluntary control with the help of electric lighting. However, a study at Hokkaido University has shown that the sleep–wake cycle is phase-delayed by 90 minutes in winter compared to summer – a surprisingly big difference, but explicable in terms of photoperiodic time cues (252). More surprisingly, stage 4 sleep duration decreased by 16 minutes in the winter, and REM sleep duration increased by 20 minutes, compared to the summer. The temperature in the recording facility was strictly controlled to be between 20 and 24 degrees C at all times, so ambient temperature cannot be invoked as an explanation, except in so far as the subjects were exposed to seasonal temperatures during the day.

The most pronounced single infradian rhythm is of course the female menstrual cycle. This is not governed by an oscillator, but by the interaction of endocrine systems regulating oestrous. Sleep is not greatly affected by this cycle, except when it ceases with the menopause.

More mysterious, in many ways, than the female's rhythms are those of the male – much less pronounced, and without a well-understood physiology, although there is some evidence of periodic (20-day) changes in urinary 17-ketosteroid excretion, in plasma testosterone, and of a 20-day cycle in pitch perception. A study on body temperature, carried out at Hull University, arose from my work on the 90-minute REM/NREM cycle, using skin temperature as a measure of the penile erections normally accompanying REM sleep (116). (Unlike the EEG and other usual psychophysiological parameters, temperature is easily measured using a simple, portable pen recorder which can be accommodated in one's own bedroom.) Although the recordings did not show stable patterns of REM sleep over 17 weeks in the one subject, analysis of the average temperature values per night did show signs of periodicity at 21 days. Subsequently, 21 more male subjects took part in a study of temperature and mood over periods varying from 49 to 102 days, confirming that there was a weak but reliably detectable periodicity at about 20 days period length, not only in body temperature but in subjective ratings of alertness in the morning. It would be curious indeed if there were a stable intrinsic rhythm of this frequency, since there are no equivalent natural *zeitgebers*. In conversation Simon Folkard has suggested that these findings may reflect the resultant of the interaction between the intrinsic 25-hour circadian rhythm in man and entrained 24-hour *zeitgebers*.

Physiological mechanisms of sleep and waking

Neurophysiology has a specialized vocabulary, as much or more than biological-rhythms research does. This list of words and definitions is a selection of those used in the sections that follow which may need some explanation for some readers. Many of the definitions are taken from Carlson's *Physiology of Behavior* (72).

Useful Neurophysiological Vocabulary

Acetylcholine: A neurotransmitter found in the brain and spinal cord.

Afferent: Toward a structure: all neurons afferent to the central nervous system convey sensory information.

Agonistic drugs: Drugs which facilitate the effects of a particular neurotransmitter.

Axon: A thin, elongated process of a neuron that can transmit action potentials toward its terminal buttons, which synapse upon other neurons, gland cells or muscle cells.

Basic rest–activity cycle (BRAC): A 90-minute cycle (in humans) of waxing and waning alertness, controlled by a biological clock in the caudal brain stem; during sleep it controls cycles of REM sleep and slow wave sleep.

Brain stem: The 'stem' of the brain, from the medulla to the midbrain, excluding the cerebellum.

Caudal: Literally, of the tail. Towards the posterior. (Opposite of rostral.)

Central nervous system (CNS): The brain and spinal cord.

Cerebrospinal fluid (CSF): A clear fluid, similar to blood plasma, that fills the ventricular system of the brain and the subarachnoid space surrounding the brain and spinal cord.

Decerebrate: Describes an animal whose brain stem has been transected.

Diencephalon: That part of the forebrain surrounding the third ventricle.

Dopamine (DA): A neurotransmitter; one of the catecholamines.

Efferent: Away from a structure; efferent axons of the central nervous system control the muscles and glands.

Hindbrain: (In humans) those parts of the brain immediately above the spinal cord; comprising the medulla oblongata, the pons, and the cerebellum.

Hypothalamus: A central region of the brain normally implicated in the control of temperature, hunger and thirst.

Locus coeruleus: A dark-coloured group of nor-adrenergic cell bodies (secreting the neurotransmitter noradrenalin) located in the pons near the rostral end of the floor of the fourth ventricle.

Medulla oblongate (usually medulla): The most caudal portion of the brain, immediately rostral to the spinal cord.

Microelectrode: A very fine electrode, generally used to record activity of individual neurons.

Midbrain: (In humans) that part of the brain directly above the pons and in front of the cerebellum.

Norepinephrine: A neurotransmitter, also referred to as noradrenalin.

Neuromodulator: A naturally secreted substance that acts like a neurotransmitter except that it is not restricted to the synaptic cleft but diffuses through the interstititial fluid. Presumably it activates receptors on neurons that are not located at synapses.

PGO waves: Bursts of phasic electrical activity originating in the pons, followed by activity in the lateral geniculate nucleus (a structure in the thalamus implicated in waking visual processing) and visual cortex; a characteristic of REM sleep.

Pons: The region of the brain rostral to the medulla and caudal to the midbrain.

Projection: The efferent connection between neurons in one specific region of the brain and those in another region.

Raphe: A group of nuclei located in the reticular formation of the medulla, pons, and midbrain, situated along the midline.

Reticular formation: A large network of neural tissue located in the central region of the brain stem, from the medulla to the diencephalon.

Rostral: Nearer the nose and mouth. (Opposite of caudal.)

Serotonin: A neurotransmitter, also known as 5-hydroxytryptamine (5-HT).

Somatosensory cortex: The gyrus caudal to (in front of) the central sulcus, a groove in the surface of the cortex which in humans runs vertically down on either side from the vertex towards the ears. It receives many projection fibres from the somatosensory system.

Synapse: A junction between the terminal button of an axon and the membrane of another neuron.

Humoral systems for controlling sleep and waking

Brain function is easily influenced by drugs, either activating or depressing cortical activity, promoting wakefulness or inducing sleep. It would seem reasonable, therefore, to think of natural sleep normally being induced and maintained by endogenous soporifics, produced perhaps within the brain itself. These would build up during wakefulness, and also be under the influence of the circadian rhythm (rather like Borbely's factor S), inducing sleep when in great enough concentration, only to become dissipated during sleep itself. If this were the case, and such substances could be identified and manufactured, they could become the basis for ideal sleep-inducing drugs, or hypnotics – acting directly on sleep mechanisms without side-effects.

Unfortunately, the evidence is against any *blood-borne* substances having a substantial role in controlling sleep: attaching a second head in a dog did not result in both heads sleeping simultaneously (92). Early this century Pieron had tested the hypothesis that the cerebrospinal fluid (CSF) contained a sleep-inducing factor, by extracting CSF from dogs deprived of sleep and injecting it into the ventricles of animals which were not sleepy (347). While these experiments appeared to be successful in inducing sleep, it now seems that the injection of any fluid into the ventricles is enough to induce apparent sleep. Crucial evidence comes from the dolphin, which sleeps with half its brain at a time. (See Chapter 10 (p. 156) for more details of this animal's sleep.) Such an orderly alternation of sleep by different parts of the brain would be impossible if sleep were controlled by chemicals circulating either in the blood or in the CSF.

The search for such endogenous sleep-promoting substances has been intense – so much so that Borbely and Tobler's review in 1989 cited over 400 papers on the subject (59). While some highly effective soporific substances have been found, it remains unclear whether they normally have an important role in the physiology of sleep. However, as Neil Carlson comments in his text *Physiology of Behavior* (72), it is difficult to imagine a sleep-control system not involving such chemicals, particularly to keep track of sleep debt. Possibly, however, the mysterious chemical accumulates *inside* neurons, rather in the interstitial fluids.

Neural control of arousal

It is clear from the discussion of biological rhythms earlier in this chapter, that the brain does not only become aroused in response to external stimulation: the sleep–wake cycle is controlled by circadian rhythms as much as by alarm clocks. The brain mechanisms governing arousal must therefore be proactive, and capable of causing wakening, or increasing alertness, in the absence of stimuli available to the senses. In 1949 Moruzzi and Magoun discovered that it was an area in the brain stem – the reticular formation – which, when stimulated electrically, increased the level of an animal's alertness (312). Anatomically, ascending afferent neurons carrying signals from the senses (e.g. the surface of the skin) project to the thalamus, and then, in the case of somatosensory neurons, to the somatosensory cortex. There are, however, also collateral axons from these axons which go to the reticular formation. Lindsley, Schreiner, Knowles and Magoun (269) discovered that if the main sensory pathways were disrupted by lesions, animals could still be aroused by touch, presumably by the collateral projections through the reticular formation. On the other hand, if the reticular formation was destroyed, touch stimuli only briefly roused the animals from torpor, even though the main afferent pathways were intact. Microelectrode recordings from the reticular formation have also shown it to be highly active when the animal is alert, less so when it is drowsy. The reticular formation, with its *ascending reticular activation system* has become identified as the major neurological mechanism subserving the functions of arousal and the direction of attention in the brain.

The experiments which drew physiologists to this conclusion about the function of the reticular formation almost all involved immobilized, decerebrate or anaesthetized rats or cats. More recent studies on freely moving cats, using recordings from single units in the brain stem, have thrown considerable doubt on this interpretation. It now appears that the activity of individual neurons in the reticular formation is closely related to specific movements, and not to general levels of arousal. The increases in general activity in the brain stem reported in earlier experiments were interpreted in terms of increases in arousal, or the direction of attention. However, these patterns of activity could equally have been in anticipation of punishment or reward, and related to preparations for movement, or attempts at movement (386, 387).

A specific structure in the hindbrain, the *locus coeruleus*, is now thought to serve many of the functions previously attributed to the reticular formation as a whole. This nucleus, containing predominantly nor-adrenergic neurons has only two inputs, one excitatory and one inhibitory, but its outputs send axons throughout the brain (29). Gary Aston-Jones and his colleagues, recording from unrestrained rats, have found that the rate of activity in this area correlates very well indeed with behavioural arousal (27). Oddly, when the animals were grooming or drinking, activities requiring a relatively high state of arousal, the locus coeruleus was quiet. They have suggested that the function of this nucleus is to increase the animal's sensitivity to environmental stimuli – that is, to modulate its level of *vigilance*, rather than arousal *per se* (27).

Neurophysiology of the sleep states

The control mechanisms for arousal, described in the previous section, have proved to be extremely elusive. Although our understanding seemed almost complete 25 years ago, the more that was discovered about the reticular formation and its functions using single-unit recordings in intact animals in the intervening years, the less certain we became about its precise role. In the same way, our understanding of the mechanisms controlling the initiation of NREM and REM sleep, and their maintenance, is now less confident than it was in the late 1960s.

Slow wave sleep

The neurophysiology of slow wave sleep has proved a very slippery topic for physiologists. A number of brain structures have been identified as being good candidates for control sites, and it now seems that NREM sleep is normally generated through their interaction. Oddly, however, it is also true that NREM sleep may be generated in either half of a brain transected across the axis, implying that multiple generators in brain stem and forebrain are capable of independently maintaining NREM sleep (388). In the following paragraphs a number of structures will be described, with the evidence linking them to NREM sleep.

The *raphe nuclei*, in the hindbrain, are two long columns extending from the medulla to the pons in the midline. It was shown in 1966 by Michel Jouvet's group in Lyons that their destruction led to total insomnia in the cat (229). These nuclei contain the majority of the serotonin-containing neurones in the brain stem. It was also shown that the pharmacological suppression of serotonin production, using *p*-chlorphenylalanine (PCPA), also causes insomnia, which could be reversed by the serotonin precursor 5-HTP (95). The critical site for the action of serotonin in reversing insomnia induced by PCPA has also been shown, by the Jouvet group, to be the anterior hypothalamus (230). These sources of evidence might lead one to think that serotonin, produced in the raphe nuclei, somehow initiated and maintained sleep through the interaction of these nuclei with structures in the hypothalamus. However, it seems that the raphe nuclei are more active during wakefulness than during sleep (283), making any such simple interpretation impossible.

The *nucleus of the solitary tract*, located caudal to the raphe nuclei, has been shown to receive inputs from neurons relaying information about taste, and from the viscera. Electrical stimulation of the nucleus causes EEG signs of sleep (synchronized slow waves) in the cat, which continues after the stimulation is turned off (289). It is well known that feeding promotes sleep (see Chapter 9, pp. 139–40), so it is perhaps unsurprising that the same structure which relays information from the guts is involved with the promotion of sleep. Single-unit recordings have shown that about half the neurons in this nucleus are more active during NREM sleep than wakefulness, but did not show that they became active until after NREM sleep had already become established, ruling this activity out as playing an important part in the initiation of sleep (111).

The *basal forebrain region* is rostral to the hypothalamus, and has also been implicated in the control of slow wave sleep. Lesions in this area cause insomnia in rats and cats. Single neuron recordings (401, 402) have confirmed a correlation between activity changes in this area and sleep. In addition, it has been found that the neurones in this region are thermosensitive, being more active when warmer. In Chapter 9 evidence is discussed linking body warming in humans to increased deep slow wave sleep levels (as well as evidence showing that reptiles may sleep more deeply when warmer). The links between sleep and temperature are at least as strong as between sleep and feeding.

While these findings from neurophysiological studies seem to suggest strongly that the basal forebrain region is an important sleep centre, human clinical evidence points to another structure – the thalamus. Recent post-mortem studies of seven unfortunate members of an Italian family who suffered from a syndrome of fatal familial insomnia showed that they all had a common pathology – an atrophy of the anterior ventral and mediodorsal thalamic nuclei (275). In some patients the basal forebrain region had been completely unaffected.

To summarize, it is clear from the animal studies that the basal forebrain and the nucleus are both important in the control of NREM sleep, and from human clinical evidence that the thalamus is also involved, but the neural circuits by which these structures exert their control have yet to be mapped, and their precise roles have yet to be established.

REM sleep

As described in the previous chapter, REM sleep is characterized by a lowering of muscle tone, low voltage, desynchronized EEG, and bursts of rapid eye movements. Intracranial electrophysiological recordings have shown that there are other typical events – ponto-geniculo-occipital (PGO) waves – which are associated with REM sleep. Michel Jouvet reported thirty years ago that these waves, generated in the pons, propagate through the lateral geniculate nuclei to the visual cortex. These waves typically occur in bursts, starting a little before the other signs of REM sleep in the cat, and then continuing throughout the REM sleep period (e.g. 398). They often seem to precede individual eye movements, and a major theory of the neurophysiology of dreaming (the activation-synthesis theory, described in Chapter 6, pp. 101–5) invokes their activity as being the prime source of dreaming experience.

The total loss of muscle tone in REM sleep, normally kept up to a minimal level by anti-gravity, or postural, reflexes even when we are perfectly relaxed, is general to all mammals, although it is more complete in some than in others. The motoneurons (or 'final common pathway' of the motor system, as Sherrington called it) are hyperpolarized during REM sleep, and incapable of discharge. It is clear the specific inhibition of almost all these post-synaptic neurons comes from the lower brainstem, leaving only respiratory and oculomotor motoneurons unaffected, but, as yet, it has not been ascertained which structures in the lower brainstem are responsible. When a lesion is made caudal of the pons of a cat the muscle atonia (flaccid paralysis) of REM sleep may sometimes be lifted, and the animal apparently acts out its 'dreams'. Michel Jouvet's description of the animal's behaviour: 'There are orienting movements of the head or eyes toward imaginary stimuli, although the animal does not respond to visual or auditory stimuli' (227).

A similar syndrome can occur naturally in human beings, typically as a result of withdrawal from alcohol dependence – giving rise to the apocryphal pink elephants of delerium tremens, and also to waking dreams accompanied by movement. Mark Mahowald and Carlos Schenck of the University of Minnesota have studied over 20 of these cases, using EEG/EOG recordings of their REM sleep to confirm that it was accompanied by high levels of tonic EMG and movement artefacts. These people complain of vigorous and often dangerous behaviour during sleep, accompanied by vivid, striking dreams (290). They are almost invariably older men, often with a history of drug use – either alcohol or other sedatives.

The control of REM sleep is better understood than that of slow wave sleep. In the first place, experiments on cats involving transections have given a good idea of localization of function in REM sleep control, as distinct from control of wakefulness and NREM sleep. Figure 3.5 shows the sites of three different transections of the brain of the cat. When the cuts are made at levels A or B, all the signs of REM sleep are shown caudal to the cut, and these reappear in a regular ultradian cycle (226). The brain left rostral to these two cuts (i.e. in front of them) alternates between periods of synchronized EEG and of desynchronized EEG. During the synchronized EEG periods the cats seem not to be in REM sleep, but in a state more resembling wakefulness, as eye movements are not spontaneous, but occur in response to visual stimuli. Thus, following J. M. Siegel, we can conclude that 'structures rostral to the midbrain are not required for REM sleep and that structures cauldal to the midbrain contain neurons that are sufficient to generate REM sleep' (388). Transection at level C in the figure allows both REM and NREM sleep in the brain rostral to it, showing that spinal cord is not necessary for the development or maintenance of these states.

In a series of systematic experiments such as these, involving transections at a number of levels. J. M. Siegel and others have established that the crucial area of the hindbrain for the generation of REM sleep in the cat is quite small,

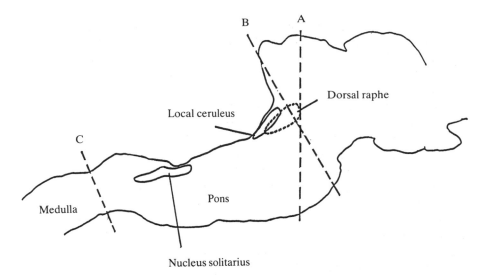

Note The dotted lines (A, B and C) represent the planes of sections whose behavioural consequences are discussed in the text.

Figure 3.5 Sagittal section of cat's brain, displaying five structures important in sleep regulation: the medulla, pons, nucleus solitarius, locus coeruleus and dorsal raphe.
Source: (338).

and is located ventrally to the locus coeruleus (see Figure 3.5). Intracranial, single-unit recordings have confirmed that the activity of cells in this region is uniquely associated with REM sleep. All the evidence points to this area of the hindbrain being essential for the generation and maintenance of REM sleep, including the production of the PGO waves and rapid eye movements. As Siegel points out, it is unlikely that this also means that this small part of the hindbrain is *sufficient* for the complete control of REM sleep, which doubtless requires the interaction of many structures in the brain, some of them quite remote from the hindbrain. Siegel suggests that studies of decerebrate animals may give a misleading impression of an active hindbrain during REM sleep bombarding the relatively passive cortex with PGO waves. The patterns of PGO waves in these preparations appear in regular bursts rather than in the irregular patterns normally seen in the intact animal. The amplitudes of the PGO waves are also very strongly affected. The generation and maintenance of REM sleep is probably the result of a dynamic interaction between cortex and hindbrain. Although the structures in the pons are *necessary* for REM sleep, they are not sufficient in themselves to produce it.

PART II

CHAPTER 4

The Dreams of
Rapid Eye Movement Sleep

In this preliminary chapter on dreaming and REM sleep some of the basic laboratory findings about dreaming sleep will be described. The identification of particular EEG/EOG signs with a sleep state in which people are likely to be dreaming made it feasible to answer a number of questions which had previously only been a matter for speculation, and which are perennially asked by ordinary people. How long do dreams last? Do they really go on for as long as they seem to, or are they, as some people have suggested, fleeting sensations before waking up? Does everybody dream – and what determines whether a dream is remembered? Does everybody really dream in colour? Is dreaming necessary to maintain sanity? If rapid eye movements accompany dreaming, does it mean that our eyes are following the action of the dreams?

Answers to most of these questions were provided in the fifteen years between 1960 and 1975. There are of course still mysteries about dreaming, and for some of them perhaps the technology of the dream laboratory on its own will never provide a solution. As Ian Oswald once remarked, we know very little about the function of everyday, waking consciousness, so perhaps it is overoptimistic to believe that we should achieve a complete understanding of sleeping consciousness merely because we have reliable physiological indices of when dreams are likely to occur.

The natural history of dreaming

How long do dreams last?

The idea that time may be dramatically distorted in dreaming, or even reversed, was given support in 1861 in Maury's book *Sleep and Dreams*. He gave an account of a dream of his own about the French Revolution, and the reign of terror following it. In the dream he became a participant, as a prisoner of a revolutionary tribunal whose judges included Marat and Robespierre.

65

After trial and condemnation to death, Maury was taken to be guillotined in front of a large crowd. He dreamed the actual execution, including his head being separated from his body, and then abruptly woke up to find that his bed headboard had fallen and struck him on the back of the neck in the same place as the guillotine in the dream. The only rational explanation was that the stimulus of being struck must have initiated the whole dream sequence, which although apparently very lengthy, must have proceeded fast enough to be fitted in between the blow on the neck and waking up.

This notion – that dreams are really fleeting impressions formed immediately before waking up, is still fairly prevalent. In the Hull survey one of the statements to which respondents were invited to agree was 'Dreams occur only in the few moments before you wake up'. 18 endorsed this statement, and 22 thought it was maybe true, out of 148. Some of those who thought the statement was true may have had very few experiences of extended dreams, and for them 'dreaming' may literally consist of some recollections of thoughts or images which occurred immediately before waking up. Others may genuinely believe that even lengthy dreams have been compressed into a brief period.

William Dement conducted a number of experiments to establish the extent to which subjects lost track of time during REM sleep, in association with Nathaniel Kleitman (100) and Edward Wolpert (101). In the first of these, reports of dreams were elicited from subjects woken from REM sleep on a total of 126 occasions. As a rough estimate of the amount of dreaming that had been going on, they counted the number of words used by subjects in describing their dream. The longer the preceding REM sleep period before the awakening, the larger the number of words the subjects tended to use. In another experiment, subjects were woken either 5 or 15 minutes after REM sleep had started, and asked to estimate which of the two intervals had been used. They were correct 92 times out of 111, indicating very good awareness of the amount of time elapsed.

A third, and crucially important experiment, involved using external stimuli to influence the content of dreaming itself. Trying a pure tone stimulus, light flashes, and a water spray on an exposed part of the body, Dement and Wolpert found that the water spray was most effective in influencing the content of dreams (although this stimulus also tended to wake the subjects up!) Here is one of their examples:

> The S was sleeping on his back. It was a hot summer night, and he was completely uncovered. An eye-movement period started, and after 5 min. cold water was sprayed on his feet and legs. One minute later he was awakened. The first part of the dream involved being in a room talking to some friends. Then, 'two children came into the room and came over to me asking for water. I had a glass of ice water and I tipped the glass to give it to them. I was sitting, and I spilled the water on myself.

The children wanted the ice and tried to grab it, but it slipped away. I got mad, because they were so greedy, and tried to shove them away from the chair. Then I got out of the chair and was going to change pants. As I left the room I seemed to be in a school and I saw many children in the hall and I seemed to be late for a class. I was starting to climb up some stairs when the bell rang.' (101)

They sprayed the subjects with cold water when they were undoubtedly in REM sleep, and then woke them after varying intervals of a few minutes. Ten of the subjects (like the one above) had unambiguous accounts of cold water in their dreams, and in these subjects their dream-reports showed a very good correlation (in terms of the time that the action in the dream would have taken since the cold water spray) with the actual time elapsed.

Despite Maury's odd experience with the French Revolution, it seems that dreams proceed at a 'normal' temporal pace. Perhaps Maury was not completely woken up by the falling bed to begin with, and dreamt some of his dream with the bedhead lying on him. It seems likely that our dreams are attempts to make sense of experiences which are vivid but inconsequential (as suggested by Perceptual Release Theory, developed by J. L. West to account for the generation of hallucinations and dreams) and this will be dealt with later in the chapter. Maury's dream could be a good example of this sort of attempt at comprehension of a series of striking but unconnected images and sensations, a form of the 'effort after meaning' that the Cambridge psychologist Sir Frederick Bartlett ascribed to normal waking memory processes in the first half of this century.

Does everybody dream?

While most of us can recall dreams at least occasionally, there is a sizeable minority of people who claim never to dream, and who understandably have some difficulty in understanding what everybody else is talking about. Laboratory experiments comparing 'dreamers' with 'non-dreamers' have shown that there is little difference between these groups in their EEG/EOG patterns while asleep (16, 168). In all subjects there was the same orderly sequence of sleep stages, with REM sleep periods recurring at about 90-minute intervals throughout the night. 'Non-dreamers' tend, however, to spend slightly less time in REM sleep than 'dreamers', overall. Is their failure to remember dreams on waking up in the morning because they 'really' don't dream, or is it because they fail to remember them?

Donald Goodenough and his associates (168) canvassed 60 subjects on the frequency with which they remembered dreaming. They then persuaded the 8 highest scorers on their questionnaire, who 'dreamed every night', as well as the 8 lowest scorers, who 'dreamed less than once a month', to submit to laboratory recordings and wakenings during the night. When woken from REM sleep the self-reported dreamers reported dreams on almost every occasion (44 out of 49 wakenings) and also reported dreams on about half the occasions when they were woken from NREM sleep. The 'non-dreamers' reported dreams on less than half the occasions when woken from REM sleep (19 out of 42) and only 7 times in 43 awakenings from NREM sleep. REM sleep is thus even more clearly associated with dreaming in so-called 'non-dreamers' than regular dreamers, who tend to report dreaming whenever they're woken up!

The evidence from these experiments also showed that while waking people up from REM sleep regularly produced reports of dreaming, delaying the awakening until after the end of the REM sleep period produced a dramatic drop in the number of dreams recalled. Even while asleep, we tend to forget our dreams as soon as they are over. People who claimed that they generally did not dream, when woken from REM sleep, did in fact report dreams, but they were particularly prone to forgetting them – if woken after the REM period was over, they recalled even fewer instances of dreaming than those who claimed to regularly recall dreams in the morning (16). In another study generally confirming these findings (168) it was also noticed that 'non-dreamers' tended to report that they were awake and thinking when woken from REM sleep. When their reports of what they were thinking about were examined, it was found that these were frequently bizarre, commonly involved complex stories with visual imagery, and, so far as the experimenters were concerned, were indistinguishable from dream reports. These subjects may therefore have been having the same sorts of experience as 'dreamers', but did not label their REM sleep experiences as 'dreams', but 'thinking'. It seems that while everybody does dream during REM sleep, most dreams are forgotten, and that some people forget more readily than others.

Why are so many dreams forgotten?

The poet Emerson expressed the difficulty in remembering dreams most eloquently:

> Dreams are jealous of being remembered; they dissipate instantly and angrily if you try to hold them. When newly awakened from lively dreams, we are so near them, still agitated by them, still in their sphere – give us one syllable, one feature, one hint, and we should repossess the whole; hours of this strange entertainment would come trooping back to us; but we cannot get our hand on the first link or fibre, and the whole is lost. There is a strange wistfulness in the speed with which it disperses and baffles our grasp. (114)

The experiments discussed in the previous section make it clear that most of the experiences which can be recalled, if people are woken up through the night, are not normally remembered in the morning. Even people who claim to remember dreams every morning only recall their most recent dream, and any dreams they may have had during the two or three REM periods earlier in the night, or even during NREM sleep, are completely lost.

While we are all familiar with (and resigned to) a certain amount of forgetfulness during the day, the equivalent of being unable to remember breakfast or lunch by 3 o'clock in the afternoon would definitely put one in the category of suffering from a severe case of amnesic syndrome. The evidence, however, clearly shows that this sort of wholesale forgetting is normal while we are asleep.

Something about the experience of dreaming makes it peculiarly difficult to remember, even in ideal circumstances. A common method for collecting dream reports is to ask people to keep dream diaries – to write down, as soon as they wake up in the morning, any dreams that they can remember. In one study (79) subjects were required to telephone the local weather information service on awakening, and to record a few details of the weather forecast on the top of their diary sheet before writing down their accounts of their dreams. A control group were instructed to lie quietly in bed for a few moments before writing down what they could recall of their dreams. The experimental subjects, distracted for a moment by having to make a telephone call and record the predicted temperature for the day, recalled very few dreams indeed compared to the control group. Again, while distraction can cause forgetting during the day, this is normally confined to very recent memories which have no obvious meaning (such as unfamiliar telephone numbers that have just been looked up). If briefly distracted from watching a film or television programme we would be very surprised not to be able to remember anything about it afterwards.

Dreams are therefore peculiarly unmemorable – unless remembered! There are two possible sorts of explanation for the difficulties we have in recalling dreams. One is that something about the dream itself (its illogicality perhaps) makes it difficult to remember, and the other that there is something about the physiological state in which we find ourselves when first woken up that makes remembering difficult.

There is a problem about investigating the first of these hypotheses in that the dreams that are remembered are presumably the ones that have more logical structure. The most chaotic experiences are forgotten. However, of the dreams that are reported some are more structured, have more coherent themes and plots, than others. Waking subjects do not have any more difficulty remembering the most chaotic dreams than the most coherent (32). Incoherence *per se* therefore should not make a dream impossible to recall. Another hypothesis is that dreams are forgotten because they are repressed.

That is, their content arouses anxiety causing their recall to become unacceptably upsetting. Freud himself expressed the view that some dreams, but not all, may be forgotten for this reason. (It would of course be inconsistent with his theory if dreams that have already been rendered 'harmless' by the dreamwork during dreaming remained potent sources of anxiety on awakening.) Donald Goodenough, in his scholarly review of the very technical evidence on this issue (167) comparing the recall of dreams by different personality types, comes to the conclusion that while repression may be responsible for the forgetting of some dreams, it is not feasible that it could account for the majority. This is very much in line with the evidence for repression in everyday life – while convincing anecdotal accounts certainly exist, as does some good experimental laboratory evidence for repression, the repression theory remains unconvincing as an explanation for most of what we forget. One obvious counter-example to a repression account of forgetfulness is that of forgetting a telephone number shortly after looking it up; if the directory is closed, and one is distracted for a moment by being asked the time, then merely looking at one's watch and giving the right time is usually enough to prevent a completely accurate recall of an unfamiliar telephone number, but nobody would suggest that repression was at work here.

It seems likely that there is something about the state in which we are in while asleep that prevents memories from being stored in the normal way. The evidence for this proposition will be discussed more fully in Chapter 8 which deals with experiments on sleep-learning, amongst other things. The findings indicate that, as might be suspected from common experience, impressions formed during sleep are not retained. Even if people are woken up and asked to learn something, if they go straight back to sleep they are likely to forget the whole episode. Material presented to people during sleep is not remembered unless they are woken up by it, and remain awake for some time. A minimum period of time filled by waking cortical arousal seems essential for the retention of memories.

Do we dream in colour?

Just as some people claim never to dream, and some say they dream every night, there are those who rarely remember having dreams in colour, and those who always do. A survey of college students showed that 51 per cent of men never dreamed in colour, while only 31 per cent of women never did (304). Calvin Hall's large survey of dream content showed that only about a third of the total number of dreams reported contained references to colour (183). A more systematic study, asking people to match the colours they could recall with colours on a standard colour chart revealed that only about half the dreams contained colour, and many of these were in pastel shades. Fully saturated colours, interestingly, tended to be at the red end of the spectrum for the six subjects involved in this study, and only rarely were saturated blues, purples or blue-greens reported (338).

When subjects are woken from REM sleep and questioned about their dreams Edwin Kahn and his associates found that the incidence of reporting colours increased to 70 per cent (231). Another 13 per cent of the reports were of 'vaguely coloured' dreams. Of the 61 dreams in which colour was reported, it was spontaneously mentioned in only 22 instances, and was elicited by further questioning in the other 39. As the authors point out, colour is not usually the most important aspect of a dream, and similarly might not be mentioned in accounts of events in everyday life. When dreams are recalled during the day, it would therefore be the most salient points that would be recalled, and the colour detail, which would have been available if the dreamer had been questioned about it on awakening, will have been forgotten. Ralph Berger has similarly found that subjects woken from REM sleep report colour in their dreams far more frequently than people do when asked about their dreams during the day – even subjects who claimed never to dream in colour (37).

A simple answer to the question would be that we do generally speaking dream in colour, but that this aspect of the dream tends to be forgotten.

Experimental investigations

Looking at the dreams

Watching the eye movements of subjects during REM sleep, and then obtaining reports from them of intense visual imagery, it seems only natural to assume that one has something to do with the other. That is, the intense visual experiences of dreaming during REM sleep are signalled by eye movements because the eyes are actually scanning the images generated by the dream. It has proved extremely difficult to establish the truth or falsehood of this apparently simple statement.

Some dreams are more visually intense than others, and some REM sleep periods have a great many more eye movements than others. (As explained in the last chapter, REM sleep may be scored as such when hardly any rapid eye movements are occurring, so long as the record of low voltage EEG and reduced EMG continues uninterruptedly.) Ralph Berger and Ian Oswald established that the REM sleep periods characterized by few and small eye movements were accompanied by experiences of what they called 'passive' dreaming, with few events reported that the subject could have been scanning. 'Active' dreams were accompanied by profuse rapid eye movements (39). Even within a period of REM sleep, there are phases of intense eye movement activity separated by intervals of ocular quiescence. Molinari and Foulkes found that subjects woken up following bursts of eye-movement activity reported more vivid dreams than when woken up following intervals of REM sleep in which the eyes had been still (306).

The high correlation of bursts of rapid eye movements with intense dreaming tended to encourage early investigators in their impression that the eye movements were following the actions of 70 to 80 per cent of vivid dreams (365). However when blind matches of EOG records with dream narratives have been made simply on the basis of written evidence and the polygraphic record, matching of reports to records has been no better than chance (312).

Second, while adults who have been blind all their lives report no visual dreams, and have no measurable rapid eye movements using EOG measures, they do have periods of low voltage EEG with reduced muscle tone, consistent with REM sleep (42), and if mechanical sensors are used to assess eye movement, it appears that their eyes do indeed wiggle about during these sleep phases (175). The lack of evidence using standard EOG measures can be attributed to the degeneration of the retina in these subjects. This commonly results in the loss of the corneo-retinal potential, a standing potential difference of the order of one-tenth of a volt across the back of the eyeball which contributes largely to the measurable changes in potential on the face resulting from eye movements in normal, sighted people.

Third, attempts to map the eye movements directly on to the reported dreams (in terms of direction of gaze, and so on), have been dogged by the problem of actually measuring the position of the eyes using standard EEG equipment. (EEG amplifiers record changes in potential, but, because they automatically filter out slow changes, are unable to provide information about the actual position of the eyes. They are not direct coupled (DC) amplifiers.) When recordings were made using DC amplifiers (219) it became apparent that during REM sleep the eyes were almost constantly in motion, making slow, roving movements which would not be picked up by the standard (AC) amplifying equipment. Bursts of fast eye movements were superimposed on these slow movements. In this study it was also confirmed that the fast eye movements were associated with passages of vivid dreaming involving tracking moving images, but the measured direction of movement of the eyes did not correspond very well with reports of direction of movement of objects in the dream.

Waking saccadic (scanning) eye movements are faster when the eye has further to travel, so that while an eye movement over 5 degrees is completed after about 60 milliseconds, so is a movement over 10 degrees. These movements are pre-programmed 'ballistic' responses whose velocities are determined by the anticipated distance of travel, ensuring that the eye arrives at the right place after a fixed period of time. Eugene Aserinsky and his associates (25) have recently discovered that the fast eye movements of REM sleep tend to be consistently slower than waking saccadic movements. In addition, there is no difference in velocity between movements which are long and those which are short. They checked on the possibility that saccadic movements made with the eyes closed, or in the dark, might be slowed, or that the velocity may then be independent of length of saccade, and found that they were not. That is, waking eye movements with eyes closed, or in the dark, are the same as with eyes opened and in the light. The pattern of velocity of eye movements of REM sleep is quite unlike that of waking eye movements, and seems inconsistent with the idea that they reflect scanning responses.

Finally, it can be pointed out that newborn babies have profuse eye movements during REM sleep, although their vision is not good. The weight of the evidence against the scanning hypothesis for REMs is very great. It seems likely that these eye movements are involuntary symptoms of neurophysiological events taking place during REM sleep, with no direct relation to the images generated during dreaming.

'Lose your dreams and you will lose your mind'
Rolling Stones, 'Ruby Tuesday'.

The idea that dreaming is essential for sanity has been prevalent in popular science since the eighteenth century. The modern story of this notion is a good example of the way that the media and the public at large love to incorporate scientific evidence, however slender, to justify what they thought anyway, ignoring any evidence to the contrary.

The discovery that there was a practicable way not only of monitoring dreaming sleep, but possibly of controlling it as well, presented a great challenge. Normal subjects always begin a sleep period with slow wave sleep, and do not start their first REM sleep period for at least 45 minutes, sometimes as long as two hours. They never begin the sleep period with REM sleep. If woken during the night at the beginning of each REM sleep period, and then allowed to return to sleep, would they pick up where they left off, starting REM sleep, or start the night all over again? What would be the psychological effect of preventing the dreams of REM sleep?

William Dement woke 6 subjects in this systematic way over a period of 6 nights, and found that on the first night they did seem to 'start all over again' whenever properly woken, so that by the end of the night they had achieved a good deal of slow wave sleep, and very little REM sleep (96). On subsequent nights it became more difficult to prevent REM sleep, especially in the early hours, and the number of wakenings necessary increased night by night until by the fifth and sixth nights subjects were hardly getting any sleep at all. On recovery nights, when subjects were allowed to sleep undisturbed, they took more REM sleep than usual, as if they were making up to some extent for the amount lost. These findings were consistent with the idea that REM sleep, and perhaps the dreaming associated with it, was especially important, perhaps representing the most important function of sleeping.

In his report of this first experiment Dement also reported that his subjects tended to become paranoid while deprived of REM sleep – ascribing sinister motives to the experimenter, and developing all sorts of unreasonable suspicions, as well as having some bizarre experiences such as hallucinations (seeing or hearing things which were not there). Not only, therefore, did sleep mechanisms rebel against the regime by more and more attempts to initiate REM sleep during the period of deprivation, and 'make up' for the amount lost to some extent when allowed to, but the subjects also showed signs of psychological distress when it was prevented.

Subsequently Dement established that these psychiatric symptoms were not reliably elicited by being deprived of REM sleep (97). Rather, they were probably the consequence of the expectations of the experimenters – the so-called 'experimenter effect'. In this instance these expectations were communicated to the subjects through genuine concern for their wellbeing. Not only were the subjects told of what Dement thought might be the probable results of the regime, but were provided with a psychiatrist on duty all the time to whom they could report any unusual sensations. After the third day of REM sleep deprivation little sleep at all was being achieved, and the symptoms that the subjects showed were a combination of the effects of total sleep deprivation and suggestion.

Despite the fact that Dement performed experiments after this one in which his subjects showed none of the psychiatric symptoms with REM sleep deprivation, and that he himself made clear how his early observations were probably misleading about the effects of REM sleep deprivation, the idea that dreaming preserved sanity had been strongly reinforced. It is not uncommon even now to read in popular science that this notion has firm scientific support. It hasn't.

Many of the American psychiatrists who were doing much of the important pioneering empirical work on dreaming during the 1960s were deeply influenced by psycho-analysis. While a strict Freudian interpretation of the function of dreaming would not necessarily imply that it preserved sanity so much as sleep, the neo-Freudians had developed the notion that during dreams conflicts are resolved, giving dreams a purpose in maintaining psychic equilibrium. Freud himself didn't think that dreaming preserved sanity – on the contrary, as we shall see in the next chapter, the Freudian view was that the function of dreaming was to allow sleep to continue uninterrupted, despite a number of unacceptable ideas being expressed. Dreaming, or the dreamwork, allowed these ideas, which would otherwise be too upsetting to be compatible with sleep, to be dressed up in symbolism, defused of their obviously sexual or aggressive meanings. As it stands, classical Freudian theory should therefore predict that sleep might be disturbed by the prevention of dreaming, but that any untoward effects would be from the prevention of restorative sleep, rather than the prevention of dreaming *per se*.

Dreaming can on the other hand be seen as having a function in resolving emotional conflicts by a process of emotional integration. This neo-Freudian theory has been articulated by Breger (63) and others, and represents the sort of thinking underlying Dement's original hypothesis, that the prevention of dreaming should cause emotional difficulties. The effects of total and of both REM sleep and deep slow wave sleep deprivation on subsequent sleep and performance will be discussed in Chapter 7.

CHAPTER 5

The Quality of Sleeping Experience

The experience of sleep

When I go to bed the experience is oddly similar to getting into a swimming pool. It takes a few moments to adjust – one moment one is dry, wearing dry swimming trunks and walking about, and the next one is progressively getting wetter (including the swimming trunks, which somehow seems particularly inappropriate) – and it's only when half a length or so has been swum that the whole thing seems ordinary again. Similarly, one minute I'm a busy wide-awake person, and the next, when the decision has been made to go to sleep, I'm a wide-awake person lying down in bed. It requires a readjustment before the 'normal' daytime mode of thinking changes to that of drowsiness, and is finally displaced by the onset of sleep.

During this rather curious period when one's thoughts are free to wander we are sometimes aware that the quality of sensations that we are used to when awake has changed. These odd experiences, typical of getting to sleep or of periods of drowsiness during the day, are not uncommon. We accept our experience of waking consciousness as being normal and, for the most part, only professional philosophers spend much time thinking about its significance. For the rest of us, it seems commonplace and obvious that we should be able to think, imagine, perceive and remember in the ways that we do, and we tend to take it for granted that the rest of the world has the same sort of experience of everyday life that we do. Our experiences while asleep, or under the influence of drugs, sometimes seem inexplicable in terms of this rather humdrum awareness, much more personal, and therefore more interesting. Some aspects of drowsiness fit this mould.

Early sleep stages and experience

In the period of drowsiness preceding the oblivion of sleep the quality of

76

thinking changes to become less logical and sometimes bizarre. The incidents that are reported the following day are necessarily the more memorable ones – memorable for their oddity. While much of the thinking during drowsiness may be humdrum, as experiments involving waking people up during this state have shown, there are undoubtedly some unusual characteristics of style of thinking and of dreamlike imagery during drowsiness. The psychologist Clark Hull reported the following sequence of thoughts:

> 'Bill Hambra – Ju (sic) know him?'
> Note: A moment ago while passing in mild lapse of attention, the above came into my mind with great distinctness. It seemed almost as if I were speaking it . . . I have noticed this just as clearly as the above many times while half asleep in bed but never had paper handy and so never wrote it down . . .
> Question: Where in the world could that name have come from? I haven't the slightest recollection of anything like it.
> This human machine is a queer thing! (212)

Apart from thinking of this sort, a large proportion of people report some odd perceptual experiences – not dreams, strictly speaking, but quite different from the ordinariness of waking consciousness. Hypnagogic experiences, as they are called, are characterized by a series of relatively disconnected but vivid images. A survey of Aberdeen University students conducted by Peter McKellar (285) showed that about two-thirds of them had experienced these sensations, which were slightly more often auditory sensations than visual ones.

When asked to describe auditory sensations, McKellar's subjects frequently reported hearing snatches of music which could be recurrent:

> as is illustrated by a subject who recurrently imaged the last movement of Rachmaninov's Second Piano Concerto. This subject added: 'Occasionally I hear the first movement of his Third Concerto, which I do not know well enough to construct in my mind when I am fully consciousness.'

Voices are also very commonly heard in this drowsy state, for instance calling the sleeper's name. These experiences are easily confused with reality, and sometimes result in the sleeper waking up completely and attempting to answer the voices.

Visual hypnagogic sensations may be similarly either isolated images or a series of images. Very commonly, people see static landscapes, moving faces or a sequence of pictures or geometric shapes. McKellar's subjects 'quite frequently likened the images to lantern slides' and furthermore their unrelatedness both to current preoccupations and to each other made them seem like a series of lecturer's slides which had not only 'been mixed up but were really intended for some other lecture'. There have been suggestions that some of these experiences, especially the sequences of geometrical shapes, or flashes, may be the result of discharges from the retina occuring in the absence of any stimulation – the so-called entoptic phenomenon – which can also be observed when the eyes are open in the pitch-dark (377).

Hypnagogic experiences may also reflect after-images of activities protractedly engaged in during the preceding day. When going to sleep after spending a night watching EEG traces of sleeping subjects, for instance, I have had hypnagogic images of the traces (moving backwards) on going to sleep. Incidentally, these images of traces sometimes persisted into my dreams, appearing in the sky above the action of the dream, giving me the impression that I could actually monitor my own sleep stages while dreaming. Donald Hebb, the Canadian psychologist, reported:

> A day in the woods or a day-long car trip after a sedentary winter sometimes has an extraordinarily vivid aftereffect. As I go to bed and shut my eyes – but not till then, though it may be hours since the conclusion of the special visual stimulation – a path through the bush or a winding highway begins to flow past me and continues to do so till sleep intervenes. (195)

One explanation of how random entoptic discharges and after-images are constructed into fully developed perceptions – the Perceptual Release Theory – was first proposed by the neurologist John Hughlings Jackson and later developed by J. L. West as a more general theory to account for both hallucinations and dreams (432). Simply put, during waking consciousness there is a demand by the alert cortex for perceptual information from the senses, and the senses provide an abundance, which is mostly disregarded as only topically relevant information is attended to. In the drowsy state there is very little coming in and yet the cortex is still relatively alert and demanding something to work on, although not alert enough to provide an effective inhibition of nonsense being offered by the senses. Perceptions are constructed or formed from whatever would normally otherwise have been inhibited (such as the low-level random discharges from the retina). According to this theory, half-formed thoughts, memories as well as low-quality visual and auditory inputs now become grist to the perceptual mill, combining to give hypnagogic images.

Estimates of the proportion of people experiencing hypnagogic imagery have varied considerably, depending partly on how exactly they were asked. McKellar (286) argued that while over 70 per cent of people answering a questionnaire reported at least one hypnagogic experience the actual incidence may be even higher, as:

> it can be overlooked for a very long time even by those who subsequently do realize that they have the experience frequently . . . False negatives

seem to occur by a process of ignoring what one is not alerted to notice, as well as from emotional blockage.

McKellar's work has been in the tradition of Francis Galton's inquiries (155) into the considerable variations between individuals in their quality of imagery. One might expect that those who report intense imagery when awake would also report more hypnagogic experiences. The evidence that exists, however, (203) suggests that subjects who are weak imagers in the waking state are just as likely to report hypnagogic images as those who are strong imagers.

Physiological correlates of hypnagogic experiences

When subjects are interrupted on going to sleep and asked to report any mental activity whatsoever they usually have something to say about what was going on in their mind. In Foulkes and Vogel's laboratory study (137) for instance standard EEG/EOG recordings were made and subjects questioned after periods of waking, stage 1 sleep and stage 2 sleep. There was no clear relation between the depth of sleep as indicated by these measures and the incidence of reports. Subjects came up with well-organized fantasy sequences after being roused from some periods with high levels of EEG alpha and saccadic eye movements consistent with relaxed wakefulness. It was difficult to distinguish these reports from those which were more dreamlike, and which were elicited from subjects roused from deeper levels of sleep.

The experimenters categorized the experiences in relation to the sensory modality principally involved and the connectedness of any plot. One example given of a 'dream' in this state of relaxed wakefulness reads more like a fantasy of wish fulfilment rather than a sleeping dream account, although others were remarkably 'dreamlike'. Reports of thinking and imagery were also elicited from subjects woken from light stage 2 sleep.

There were, however, consistent differences in the quality of experience as wakefulness gave way to sleep. Subjects began to feel a loss of control of the course of their thinking. Their level of awareness of being in a laboratory declined, and their awareness that they were under instructions to observe their own sensations similarly became less strong.

Thinking and fantasizing seem to have constituted the majority of Foulkes and Vogel's subjects' reports, but while it is possible to make fine distinctions between levels of sleep depth, using EEG/EOG measures, these did not seem to be very predictive of the quality of experience reported. Most surprising, perhaps, is the number of reports of 'everyday' thinking from subjects who were undoubtedly asleep, by psychophysiological criteria. In addition, there were some reports of dreaming during wakefulness and light slow wave sleep which were bizarre, quite well organized in terms of plot, and involved unusual visual imagery – just like the fully fledged dreams of REM sleep.

Any hope for a unique syndrome of EEG/EOG patterns which might be associated with the odd experiences which McKellar's subjects reported must be abandoned. As we fall asleep our mental state becomes somewhat unpredictable from such gross measures. Sometimes we appear to ourselves to be making sense, sometimes we seem to be obviously deranged, and sometimes our thoughts are driven by the vivid imagery of dreams. The psychophysiologist cannot as yet match the experiences of going to sleep with the measures of brain function that are currently available. While the majority of us, if not all, probably have had hypnagogic experiences of the sort reported by McKellar, they were by no means typical of Foulkes and Vogels's drowsy subjects, and must represent the more memorable events in most people's half-sleeps, rather than the most common.

Are dreams confined to REM sleep?

Aserinsky and Kleitman in 1953 (23) and Dement and Kleitman in 1957 (100) reported 74 and 79 per cent dream reports from REM sleep awakenings respectively, and only 7 per cent reports from non-REM sleep awakenings, indicating a virtually perfect isomorphism between the experience of dreaming and a well-defined psychophysiological pattern. In the first flush of enthusiasm following these unprecedented claims there was a very strong tendency to identify dreaming exclusively with REM sleep, presuming that any lack of identification of dreaming with eye movements could be put down to experimental error. Some researchers, such as Ernest Hartmann, even called it D sleep (for dreaming) to distinguish it from non-dreaming slow wave sleep.

In the context of the reports that subjects make on going to sleep it is clear that much dreamlike activity goes on which is not associated with the syndrome of EEG, EOG and EMG activity defining REM sleep. It was not long before some researchers were also reporting dream recalls following other non-REM sleep awakenings, and a lively controversy began on the question of whether night-time dreaming is confined to REM sleep, or whether it may be continuous through all sleep stages.

A thorough review of the literature on this topic (198) found that reports of dreaming varied in different studies from 74 to 100 per cent from REM sleep wakenings, and from 0 to 75 per cent from NREM sleep wakenings. There were no obvious differences between the studies in the way in which they were conducted which could account for the wide range of rates of dream reporting from NREM sleep. The studies only agreed on a consistently high rate of dream reports from REM sleep. While sleep stages are well defined in terms of psychophysiology, what constitutes a dream is not, and the reviewers suggest that an important determinant of the number of NREM 'dreams' collected is the predisposition of the experimenter. That is, the reports made by subjects woken from NREM sleep are ambiguous, and open to interpretation as being either 'thinking' or 'dreaming', while reports from REM sleep wakenings tend to be indubitably of 'dreams'. What is clear is that mental life does not cease during NREM sleep, and REM sleep is not a necessary condition for dreaming. Primary-process thinking, dream 'logic' and the construction of generally illogical stories all seem to take place throughout the night's sleep. What sets the experience of REM sleep apart is the vividness of the visual imagery and the generally more compelling quality of the dreams associated with it.

Incorporation of stimuli into dreams, and dreamwork

Almost everybody has a story to tell about dream incorporation – for instance dreaming about Arctic exploration only to wake up and find that the covers have slipped off and they're freezing cold, or dreaming of bells ringing only to wake up eventually to find that the alarm clock has been clattering for the last few minutes. Are these dreams really triggered by outside stimuli, or are these reports only the outcome of rather memorable coincidences? Secondly, how frequently are dreams influenced by such stimuli? As we saw in the last chapter, a study in William Dement's laboratory (101) verified that external stimuli could indeed be incorporated into dreams during REM sleep. An example they gave is:

> The S was sleeping on his stomach. His back was uncovered. An eye movement period started and after it had persisted for 10 minutes, cold water was sprayed on his back. Exactly 30 seconds later he was awakened. The first part of the dream involved a rather complex description of acting in a play. Then, 'I was walking behind the leading lady when she suddenly collapsed and water was dripping on her face. I ran over to her and felt water dripping on my back and head. The roof was leaking. I was very puzzled why she fell down and decided some plaster must have fallen on her. I looked up and there was a hole in the roof. I dragged her over to the side of the stage and began pulling the curtains. Just then I woke up.'

Dement reports some further experiments in his book *Some Must Watch While Some Must Sleep* (98). (This book also includes fascinating anecdotes about the background to most of the pioneering experiments of the 1960s: Dement was personally involved in many of them.) Using a variety of sound stimuli, such as bugles, Dement and his students started the tape recordings as soon as a REM period started. They found that the dreams reported by the subjects were noticeably affected by the stimuli on over half of the occasions. The incorporation of stimuli is thus extremely common, if not invariable (given that on many occasions the effects of stimulation on dreaming will be so idiosyncratic that they are not recognized by experimenters).

Ralph Berger assessed the effects of meaningful verbal stimuli on dreaming (37). These stimuli were the names of friends provided by the subject, which, when presented while the subjects were awake, had elicited the largest galvanic skin responses (GSRs). Dream incorporation was judged to have taken place on about half of the occasions. Of the 48 dreams which were judged to have been affected by the stimulus, there were 31 incorporations on the basis of assonance alone – for instance 'Gillian' was represented as 'Chilean', 'Jenny' as 'Jemmy', and 'Mike' as 'like'. Only on 3 occasions did the named individual actually appear in the dream as themselves.

The orthodox psycho-analytic view of the processes underlying dream incorporation is that they maintain sleep. The all-important notion of the dreamwork involves an assumption about the function of dreaming (and possibly of consciousness in general) – i.e. that the dream is controlling the subject's psychological state, and not the other way around. Thus internally generated ideas which would otherwise cause the subject to wake up blushing with shame or racked with guilt are transformed by the dreamwork into a symbolic code. In the same way, external stimuli become incorporated into dreams in order to reduce their arousing effect.

The experimental evidence does not contradict this view, although it doesn't support it very strongly either. While dream incorporations are explained by the psycho-analytic model, it could also be that only stimuli which fail to arouse the brain sufficiently to tip it into wakefulness result in dream incorporation, rather than that the dream incorporation results in continued sleeping. Experimental evidence (61) shows that the incorporation of stimuli into dreaming is indeed associated with continued sleep, rather than wakening. Whether the incorporation actually protected sleep, as the Freudian theory would predict, or whether incorporation is the consequence of delayed arousal remains unclear.

Internally generated stimuli (such as feelings of hunger, thirst or sexual arousal) might also be expected to have an effect on dream content. If dreams are wish fulfilments, thirsty subjects should dream of quenching their thirst, hungry subjects to dream of eating. Primo Levi, who spent a year in Auschwitz, reported widespread dreaming of food amongst the inmates:

> One can hear the sleepers breathing and snoring; some groan and speak. Many lick their lips and move their jaws. They are dreaming of eating; this is also a collective dream. It is a pitiless dream which the creator of the Tantalus myth must have known. You not only see the food, you feel it in your hands, distinct and concrete, you are aware of its rich and striking smell; someone in the dream even holds it up to your lips, but every time a different circumstance intervenes to prevent the consummation of the act. Then the dream dissolves and breaks up into its elements, but it re-forms itself immediately after and begins again, similar, yet changed; and this without pause, for all of us, every night and for the whole of our sleep. (264)

Volunteers in an experiment on the effects of prolonged starvation conducted by Ansel Keys (241) in the 1950s did not report an increase in dreams about food, although their food intake was very low indeed – intended to match the conditions of deprivation suffered by people in places like Auschwitz. Clues for an explanation for this discrepancy may be provided by some laboratory studies.

Dement and Wolpert obtained REM-awakening reports from volunteers who had not had any fluid intake for at least 24 hours. They recorded not one instance of drinking or of thirst in a dream (101). In another study George Bokert increased the degree of thirst in his subjects by not only depriving them of water for 24 hours, but giving them a salty meal before going to bed. Their dream reports included more water-related imagery, such as lakes or snow, as well as some explicitly thirst-satisfying objects, such as Pepsi Cola, than on control nights when they had been allowed fluids ad lib. Subjects reporting gratifying dreams including themes of eating and drinking during the course of the night also drank less in the morning, and rated themselves as less thirsty than those who had not (55).

Thus while drive-related dreams and even simple dreams of wish fulfilment can occur, they are not reliably elicited by the mere existence of an unsatisfied appetite. In this context Primo Levi's account (265) of his recovery from his ordeal in Auschwitz may be relevant: liberated by Soviet troops, he and his fellow inmates spent a year in the Soviet Union. While well intentioned, the Russian authorities in war-time were somewhat unreliable in providing supplies, especially in any variety, and the story of these twelve months is one of continuing preoccupation with food and with foraging. There are, however, no more reports of dreaming about food. Thus, given liberty and the opportunity to cope realistically with the problem of getting enough to eat the dream process was no longer invoked. Ansel Key's subjects knew they were not going to be starved to death, being part of a controlled experiment under constant medical supervision, so in their case the implications of hunger were not life-threatening. The dream process, not perhaps surprisingly, appears to be invoked in response to the meaning of hunger, rather than the level of deprivation in itself. Thirst is a more imperative drive, intruding into dreams even when the subjects know full well that they are merely taking part in an experiment, and that water will be available in the morning.

People who give up cigarettes very commonly report explicit (and guilty) dreams about smoking in the first few weeks, even though there is every reason to believe that sleep actually becomes less disturbed on withdrawal from nicotine. (Withdrawal from other drugs is typically associated with increased REM sleep time, disturbed sleep, and vivid dreaming.) Again, the strength of craving in itself can be sufficient to induce dreams of wish fulfilment, even when the dreamers 'know' that they have no intention of smoking again.

Presleep stimulation and dreaming

It is very well known that dreams often contain elements – visual or ideational – that can be identified as being part of the previous day's experience. Much of our dream content is not so easily traced, but the incorporation of 'day's residues' into dreams is very well established. In a systematic study of his own dream life Freud tried to relate all his dreams to feelings and thoughts experienced the previous day. It was not possible to do this without assuming that dreamwork transformations took place. That is, the 'manifest dream's' apparently irrelevant and unpredictable content was actually deemed to have been systematically arrived at from a 'latent dream', whose implicit content had been the subject of some extensive dreamwork. With sufficient ingenuity, an analyst can therefore trace any reported dream back to certain themes which he or she believes are preoccupying the dreamer. If we could be sure that all dream content is determined in this way then this would not be an unreasonable thing to do.

Experimental studies relating presleep stimulation to dream content are not obviously encouraging in this respect. David Foulkes and Allan Rechtschaffen (136) showed either an amusing or a violent TV western to adult subjects before bedtime, and found that direct incorporation of the content of either film was very rare indeed, although the violent film reliably induced more vivid, emotional dreams. A similar study, using 7- to 11-year-old children as subjects (138) compared dream reports following a violent western compared to a bland film about baseball. Fourteen out of the total of 179 dream reports were judged to contain elements from the films, although there was no difference in the frequency of incorporation of scenes from the two films. The more violent film was not followed by any more intense or hostile dreams than the bland one – perhaps indicating how accustomed these young subjects were to watching violent westerns!

Goodenough's group (169) confirmed that the emotional content of dreams could be affected by presleep stimulation (in this case, a film entitled *Subcision* – explicitly showing a series of operations carried out on the penis as part of a tribal aboriginal initiation rite). They found that the dreams reported following a screening of the stress-inducing film were more anxious than those reported following a neutral film.

A third study of the effects of watching a film on dreaming successfully demonstrates the limitations of this technique and also indicates some important factors in determining what becomes incorporated into a spontaneous dream. Rosalind Cartwright (76) showed a pornographic film to a group of conventional male medical students and to a group of young homosexual men, active members of a national American gay group university chapter. The film included a suggestive 10-minute episode set in an eighteenth-century brothel, in which a male customer chose a female prostitute, helped her undress in a bedroom and finally got into bed with her, and a frankly explicit

10-minute episode of a newly-wed bride and groom set in a hotel bedroom. Both groups of subjects showed signs of sexual arousal during the screening of the film, indicated by penile strain gauges. Their dreams showed marked differences between the groups, perhaps unexpectedly, in that the homosexual men produced a great many explicit sexual dreams, while the medical students tended, when scenes of nudity were included in their dreams, to interpret these in terms of clinical practice, maintaining their professional role. (One might have expected heterosexual young men to be more influenced by what was after all a film of exclusively heterosexual practices.)

Were the gay group's 'control' dreams also more sexually charged than the medical students'? At least were their dreams after seeing the films more sexually explicit than on control nights? Neither the account in Cartwright's book nor the more detailed published experimental reports answers these questions. It is, however, likely that the pornographic film was a potent stimulus for both groups of young men, yet the effect it had on their dreams was only explicable in terms of their ideology – in particular, in terms of how they saw sexuality in relation to their own lives. The homosexual men were deeply preoccupied with their own sexuality, and with proselytizing a liberated view of sexual practices. The medical students, in entering a traditionally conservative profession, were obliged to subscribe to conventionally repressive attitudes. Just as in real life they were assimilating a clinical attitude to human functions many of which are taboo in Western society, so their dreaming interpretations of their own sexuality were also in terms of a medical model.

Both these experiments and the studies on the effects of hunger and thirst on dreaming demonstrate the unpredictability of dreaming, explicable only in terms of semantics. All the evidence points to dreaming being a highly complex cognitive activity. Whatever the limitations of the psycho-analytic approach to dream analysis it does at least attempt to take this into account, and the procedure of showing films, however vivid and disturbing, and then observing spontaneous dream reports, is intrinsically limited by the construction that the individual puts upon the film and the experiment itself.

Two laboratory studies which attempted to assess the effects of real-life stresses on dreams used patients either awaiting major surgery, or undergoing group therapy in which each patient had to prepare themselves for a session devoted entirely to their own problems (64). The major findings of this combination of case study and experimental method in the surgery patients were that:

a) the preoperative dreams of the surgery subjects incorporated stress-related material both directly and symbolically; b) the degree of incorporation was quite marked when the personal meaning of surgery and the individual modes of preparation were taken into account; and c) the content of the dreams was more repetitious and constricted before than after surgery.

Similarly, with the patients anticipating and then undergoing a 'focus session' of the psychotherapeutic group devoted entirely to their own problems, there was evidence that this traumatic event clearly affected dream content. One explanation is that dreaming is an essential part of our adaptation to the demands of the world we face. Not only does it perhaps help in the storage of new memories, but dreaming is actively helping us to solve emotional problems. The dream process is thus not only a way of rehearsing new experiences but of commenting on them and resolving conflicts. A problem with this idea is of course that most dreams are not remembered, so that even if solutions to problems are achieved during dreams they cannot be regarded as adaptive, unless we are to believe that these solutions are somehow incorporated unconsciously. Some more recent theories of dreaming will be discussed in Chapter 6 (pp. 101–6).

Why remember our dreams?

Incubation has of course a long and reputable history in antiquity. In the modern world the reasons for wanting to remember dreams have changed – nobody believes any more that an appropriate dream will cure physical illness, or perhaps predict the future. Rather, the influence of psycho-analysis has encouraged the belief that the analysis of dreams will help cure mental ills. While psycho-analysis itself is very expensive, time consuming, not available on the National Health Service, and therefore practised on only a small number of wealthy neurotics living in larger cities, its influence has been by no means confined to those directly benefiting from treatment. Especially in the United States, a widespread belief exists that people should actively seek ways of developing themselves. Meditation, yoga and psychotherapy have all been taken up by Westerners as ways of helping them cope, and give meaning to their lives. One prevalent notion is that this self-improvement can be achieved through encouraging less rational, more intuitive, styles of thinking, and that dreams represent this ideal.

Modern exponents of this ideal include Anne Faraday and Patricia Garfield, whose books (125, 126, 158) encourage the reader not only to keep dream diaries but to attempt to alter his or her dreams. An experimental study of the ability of subjects to influence their own dreams was conducted at David Foulkes's laboratory (172). Twenty-nine subjects were selected who claimed to have already successfully controlled what they were going to dream, and who were strongly motivated to prove that this was indeed possible. They prepared lists of their own intended dream topics, and kept daily records of their efforts at control and the dreams they recalled. Four judges then tried to match the reported dreams with the topics, identifying between 5 and 9 of the 29 target suggestions, at barely more than a chance rate. This disappointing result indicates that control over one's own dreams is very much more difficult than Garfield and Faraday have suggested.

Some memorable dream themes

While dreaming is inevitably idiosyncratic and personal, a number of scenarios regular recur for many people. Particular sensations, such as of falling or immobility, are occasional but almost universal. Dreams of being chased, or of flying are also more frequent than one might expect, given that neither of these events happen very frequently in real life. The dream topics discussed here are by no means representative of dreams reported from laboratory awakenings, some of them being quite uncommon. In fact one study found that 'typical dreams' (e.g. of loss of teeth, nudity, death, flying, examinations) constituted less than 1 per cent of dreams collected from REM sleep awakenings (389).

Asking people the question 'Have you ever dreamed of . . .' any particular topic (174) gives a different picture. Table 5.1 gives the responses of American and Japanese college students to a variety of dream topics. This survey, conducted in the mid-1950s when differences between American and Japanese culture were even greater than they are now, found a positive correlation of 0.87 between these two samples' dreaming rates for the 34 topics – accounting for over 75 per cent of the variance. (This correlation is somewhat inflated by the number of topics which hardly *anybody* in either group dreamed about – but using only the 15 topics dreamed about by at least half of one of the groups still gives a fairly high correlation of +0.63 between the groups.) There were some differences explicable only in terms of cultural factors which are indicated in the table, but what must be the most remarkable thing about these data is the general unanimity with which these two groups of people thousands of miles apart dreamed.

These commonly reported dreams represent the more interesting and memorable products of our sleeping minds, and it would be churlish not to say anything about them simply because they rarely surface in the laboratory.

Reflective dreams

Some dreams apparently offer a comment on life, and these I have called reflective dreams. The most absurd dreams are probably some of the most difficult to remember, but some are great fun, like this one by the Irish poet Louis MacNeice. He had just returned from a visit in 1937 to the Government fighting front in Spain:

> I had a dream at this time that I was caught by the Nazis. They took me to an enormous wall built of Pelasgian blocks. In this wall was a great wrought-iron gate of eighteenth-century workmanship. They unlocked this gate and thrust me through it, locked it behind me. I found myself in the Alps with a narrow pass before me, began to ascend the rough and

Table 5.1 Dreams reported by Japanese and American students.

Dream	American total (%)	Japanese total (%)	Total	American or Japanese exceed at 0.01 level
Have you ever dreamed of . . .?	(N=250)	(N=223)	(N=473)	
1. Being attacked or pursued	77.2	91.0	83.5	J
2. Falling	82.8	74.4	78.9	
3. Trying again and again to do something	71.2	87.0	78.6	J
4. School, teachers, studying	71.2	86.1	78.2	J
5. Being frozen with fright	58.0	87.0	71.7	J
6. Sexual experiences	66.4	68.2	67.2	J
7. Eating delicious food	61.6	68.2	64.7	
8. Falling, with fear	67.6	59.2	63.6	
9. Arriving too late, e.g. missing train	63.6	48.9	56.7	A
10. Fire	40.8	65.9	52.6	J
11. Swimming	52.0	52.5	52.2	
12. Dead people as though alive	46.0	57.4	51.4	
13. Being locked up	56.4	43.5	50.3	A
14. Loved person to be dead	57.2	42.2	50.1	A
15. Snakes	48.8	49.8	49.3	
16. Being on verge of falling	46.8	45.3	46.1	
17. Finding money	56.0	25.6	41.6	A
18. Failing an examination	38.8	41.3	40.0	
19. Flying or soaring through air	33.6	45.7	39.3	J
20. Being smothered, unable to breathe	44.4	33.2	39.1	
21. Falling, without fear	33.2	39.9	36.4	
22. Wild, violent beasts	30.0	42.2	35.7	J
23. Being inappropriately dressed	46.0	23.3	35.3	A
24. Seeing self as dead	33.2	35.0	34.0	
25. Being nude	42.8	17.5	30.9	A
26. Killing someone	25.6	27.8	26.6	
27. Being tied, unable to move	30.4	20.6	25.8	
28. Having superior knowledge or mental ability	25.6	25.1	25.4	
29. Lunatics or insane people	25.6	13.5	19.9	A
30. Your teeth falling out	20.8	16.1	18.6	
31. Creatures, part animal, part human	14.8	15.7	15.2	
32. Being buried alive	14.8	15.2	15.0	
33. Seeing self in mirror	12.4	11.7	12.1	
34. Being hanged by neck	2.8	4.0	3.4	

Source: (174).

desolate track. Plodding upwards, looking straight ahead of me or hardly looking at all, I was conscious suddenly of something on either side, looked to the right and the left. On the right and the left of my track, padding along in parallel silence were bears. Bears of every size and colour, going inexorably forward, but looking at me sideways. I had the feeling they were 'not quite right', steeled myself to go on, careful not to annoy them. Then ahead of me, higher up the pass, I saw a woman, with a stab of joy in my diaphragm hurried to overtake her. Overtook her; she looked straight out of Bond Street, tall and blonde, the height of elegance. She too had been caught by the Nazis, I walked along beside her and the bears walked on each side of us. But everything was all right now. 'Who are you?' I said at last. 'Oh,' she said suavely, 'I am the Czar's governess.' (287)

What more can one say? It brilliantly combines a legitimate trepidation about the Nazis with a certain ambivalence (perhaps typical of those on the bourgeois Left in Britain at the time) about the Russian bears who may or may not have been rescuing him, resolved in the end by the arrival of the charming governess – 'better keep a hold on Nurse, just in case of something worse'!

A reflective dream of my own occurred when I was in the midst of writing my doctorate on the role of REM sleep in consolidation of memories. One of the hypotheses I was considering was that during REM sleep (and therefore during REM sleep dreams) the entire memory system is accessible – none of the inhibitions present during wakeful life are active, and new memories can be fitted into the appropriate cognitive structures during REM sleep. Habitually a somewhat forgetful person, I had also for a couple of days been trying to remember the name of the director of the film *Such Good Friends*.

In my dream I was alone on an empty road, trying to remember the director's name, when a large open-topped car drove up, full of laughing passengers who seemed to be sharing their jokes in a foreign language. The actor Robert Mitchum was in the back seat, and before they drove off I attracted his attention and said, 'Mr Mitchum, please help me. You starred in a film called *River of No Return* with Marilyn Monroe. Please can you tell me the name of the director, because he also directed *Such Good Friends*, and I haven't been able to remember his name?' Mr Mitchum leaned back, extremely relaxed, and said, 'Very sorry, but I can't remember either.' The car then drove off, but suddenly I set off running after it, shouting, 'Otto Preminger! Otto Preminger!' and woke myself up shouting out loud.

Was my hypothesis correct? Even my dream about it was ambivalent!

Falling

The sensation of falling, typically occurs at the beginning of the night, during stage 1 sleep. It is associated with a muscular spasm of the arms, legs, or whole body which is known as a 'myoclonic jerk', which is common to many mammals. Like yawning and hiccupping, it is involuntary, and yet undeniably under the control of the brain. Ian Oswald has suggested that these jerks may be the outcome of an arousal response, since they can be elicited by sounds heard while dropping off to sleep, and are associated with small K complexes in the EEG (330). These events are not normally associated with any coherent dream sequence, although they may be preceded by a feeling of floating (reminiscent of the 'aura' often experienced by people suffering from epilepsy, giving warning of an imminent convulsive fit). While analogous, in this sense, to an epileptic seizure, there is no evidence that these jerks have anything else in common with epilepsy. It seems likely that the sensation of falling is the outcome of cortical interpretation of the production of this innate response, rather than being intrinsic to its generation.

Falling in dreams is quite common: surveys have found that between 50 and 80 per cent of subject samples report at least one falling dream (376). These dreams tend not to be about sudden drops or stumbles, but of long drops from high buildings or down deep holes, ending in collisions with the ground, or perhaps with miraculously soft landings.

Flying

In *The Interpretation of Dreams* (147) Freud related how a patient regularly dreamed of floating a couple of feet off the ground. His interpretation was that this fulfilled her wish to avoid contamination by other human beings, and to achieve greater stature. (She was a very short lady.) More generally, he attempted to relate the sensation of flying during a dream to sensations from the ventilation of the lungs during sleep, or to childhood memories of being thrown in the air. My 9-year-old son told me of dreaming of swinging violently in the hammock (something he frequently did during the summer) and falling out (again, a frequent occurence), but instead of landing on the ground he floated, and started a floating dream in which he effortlessly travelled around the garden suspended above the ground. Although the hammock episode is explicable in terms of his experience, the subsequent transition to drifting above the ground cannot reasonably be related to his usual fate when falling out of the hammock; these dreams, which are not uncommon, seem uniquely detached from any experience in real life. For Artemidorus, all dreams were classified as being either theorematic or allegorical. The former describe events which are possible if not mundane, while the latter are metaphors. In these terms flying dreams qualify better than most as being allegorical.

Ann Faraday also reports these two types of flying dream, both from personal experience and from reports from her subjects. This sort of dream seems distinct from any recollections of flying in an aeroplane – few people have flown in an aeroplane at roof-top height and in any case the experience would probably be quite different from the drifting and soaring of the typical flying dream. If they are as divorced from experience as they seem, the only explanations for their regular occurrence in a variety of people must be either, following Jung, that these are archetypal dreams with some allegorical significance, or that they represent an attempt to make sense out of experiences really occurring during dreaming sleep – an attempt to make a coherent story out of some pattern of the highly active discharges from the hindbrain which are a feature of REM sleep. This argument will be developed at greater length in Chapter 6 (pp. 101–6). An unusual aspect of these dreams is the cautious attitude that dreamers tend to adopt to flying – a rare example of commentary within a dream, of insight or lucidity. This represents perhaps an indication of the forced nature of the experience – forced by the combination of the sensation of immobility of REM sleep in association with the rich visual experience offered by the over-active hindbrain.

When I conducted a 'phone-in' on sleep and dreaming on a local radio station a few years ago somebody called in to ask what I had to say about flying dreams.

'Do you have them?' I asked.
'Yes.'
'Oh, so do I, aren't they fun?' I said.
'Yes, but how do you get the height?' he replied, 'Most of the time I just float two feet off the ground, and hardly ever get to fly at any decent height.'

This struck me very forcibly, as I too have occasionally had both sorts of flying dreams, and while floating is quite enjoyable, flying at tree-top level is much more satisfactory. I couldn't think of any suitable advice at the time. That night I had a floating flying dream, and, hovering in an upright position two feet or so above the ground I remembered the caller's problem, and immediately found a solution. In my right hand was a small tray, and by tilting it in the breeze I found that I could obtain enough lift to get up to any height I wanted, and was soon soaring into the air and travelling at will. When I woke up it was with the certainty that I solved an extremely important problem, and was eager to try it out at once. It seemed incautious to attempt it indoors, and I was halfway out of bed to get a tray to take out into the garden before I realized the ridiculous nature of the enterprise.

Another solution to the problem of gaining height was told me by one of my respondents, who dreamed of climbing a high flagpole. When at the top he was disappointed to find no flag, but with some cautious experimentation discovered that he did not need to hold on to the pole – he could float. Once confident in his new power he flew at flagpole height with the greatest of ease.

Revelation

A 'feeling of knowing' sometimes accompanies an aspect of the dream which is carried over into wakefulness (for instance the certainty that I could fly when I had my flying dream). This feeling is familiar to heavy drinkers *in vino veritas*, inspiring William James' comment, 'Sobriety diminishes, discriminates and says no; drunkenness expands, unites and says yes' (220). This phenomenon is well known amongst people taking nitrous oxide or mescaline, as well as amongst drunks (285). A revelation which William James experienced when taking nitrous oxide took the form of doggerel, which he genuinely believed to be of enormous significance while he was under the influence of the drug:

Higamous hogamous, women are monogamous,
Hogamous higamous, men are polygamous. (220)

A curious example of the converse situation, in which an accurate perception is achieved, but the subject cannot acknowledge its veracity, is found in patients suffering from Capgras' syndrome. This syndrome consists of the delusion that familiar people have been replaced by imposters. Hadyn Ellis and Andrew Young are two psychologists who have sought neuropsychological explanations for this syndrome, as well as for other disorders of face recognition (113). They suggest that, normally, there is more than one route to the recognition of faces, and that emotional recognition, mediated by different, parallel, neurological pathways, may have to take place at the same time for a normal feeling of knowing. That is, our normal experience of recognition involves the integration of at least two sources of analysis. Patients suffering from Capgras' syndrome have an intact intellectual route for recognition, but a damaged emotional one. Patients suffering from a related condition of being unable to identify faces of people very familiar to them (prosopagnosia) are presumed to have the reverse form of damage. Possibly the same pathways, permanently damaged in these unfortunates, also fail to be coordinated during sleep, and the feeling of knowing becomes all too easily invoked by less than adequate 'intellectual' perceptions.

There are a few instances when genuinely creative thinking has been documented as taking place during dreams. Most popular books on dreaming include Kekule's discovery of the benzene ring and Coleridge's 'Kublai Khan' as examples.

Inspiration without effort is an attractive idea, and in recent history the psychedelic movement of the 1960s promised increased understanding with the use of drugs. The Romantic movement of the early nineteenth century also celebrated personal revelation, inspirational creation, and opium, like cannabis in the 1960s, was a fashionable drug (freely available over the counter in all sorts of remedies). After taking some opium Samuel Taylor Coleridge had been reading Purchas' *His Pilgrimage*:

In Xamdu did Cublai Can build a stately palace, encompassing sixteene miles of plaine ground with a wall, wherein are fertile Meddowes, pleasant Springs, delightful Streames, and all sorts of beasts of chase and game, and in the middest thereof a sumptuous house of pleasure.

Almost twenty years after the incident Coleridge was persuaded by Byron to publish the poem, and he then made the sensational claim that he had been able to remember 200 to 300 lines of perfect poetry when he had awoken from a drug-induced sleep, and was busy writing them down when he was interrupted by somebody from Porlock insisting to see him on business, so that when the visitor had left an hour later he could remember nothing of the rest – hence the uncompleted 54 lines of verse with which we are left. The literary critics such as Elisabeth Schneider and Molly Lefebure (379, 261) have suggested that this account is probably a gross exaggeration – that is, that while Coleridge may have dreamed about Cublai Can, the poetry was not provided in the dream in its complete form, but required years of revision. All the evidence seems to indicate that the account of the dream grew in the interval in accordance with the Romantic ideal of the autonomy of the creative process. William Empson has commented 'I find it a completely achieved poem; probably Coleridge was lying when he told the story of the person from Porlock, nearly twenty years later' (119). Coleridge's other drug-induced efforts are sheer doggerel by comparison and like many drug addicts he was famous for frequently taking great liberties with the exact truth – especially where his drug habit was involved.

The other frequently cited example of creation during a dream is that of F. A. Kekule, a nineteenth-century chemist who knew the composition of benzene – hydrogen and carbon – and its molecular weight, which gave six atoms each of carbon and hydrogen in the molecule. In his attempt to construct a model of the molecule, given the valencies of these two elements there was no obvious way that the twelve atoms could be arranged into a conventional chain, and he had been wrestling with the problem for quite some time. One evening dozing in front of a fire he had a hypnagogic vision:

> this time the smaller groups [of atoms] kept modestly in the background. My mental eye, rendered more acute by repeated visions of this kind, could now distinguish larger structures, of manifold conformation; long rows, sometimes more closely fitted together; all twining and twisting in snakelike motion. But look! What was that? One of the snakes had seized hold of its own tail and the form whirled mockingly before my eyes. As if by a flash of lightning, I awoke as if struck by lightning; this time again I spent the rest of the night working out the consequences.

Arranging the carbon atoms in a ring satisfied the laws of valency, since each of them could share two bonds with one of its neighbour, leaving another one to attach to the hydrogen atoms arranged around the outside. This insight opened up the whole world of aromatic organic chemistry.

A less well-known example is of H. V. Hilprecht, an archaeologist at Pennsylvania University who in 1893 was given drawings of fragments of agate excavated from the Babylonian temple of Bal at Nippur. He thought they might be finger rings, but wasn't sure. In a dream a tall thin priest informed him that the two pieces came from the same votive cylinder and had been cut in two to make earrings for a statue of the god Ninib. Later in the year he visited the museum in Istanbul where the fragments were kept and demonstrated their exact fit.

These two examples of successful problem-solving when dozing or dreaming are typical only in that a feeling of certainty accompanied them – what is unusual is that these were realistic solutions. Just how often is inspiration misguided? Arthur Koestler has commented:

> every original thinker who relies, as he must, on his unconscious hunches, incurs much greater risks to his career and sanity than his more pedestrian colleagues. 'The world little knows', wrote Faraday, 'how many of the thoughts and theories which have passed through the mind of a scientific investigator have been crushed in silence and secrecy; that in the most successful instances not a tenth of the suggestions, the hopes, the wishes, the preliminary conclusions have been realized'. Darwin, Huxley, and Planck, among many others, made similar confessions; Einstein lost 'two years of hard work' owing to a false inspiration. 'The imagination', wrote Beveridge, 'merely enables us to wander into the darkness of the unknown where, by the dim light of the knowledge that we carry, we may glimpse something that seems of interest. But when we bring it out and examine it more closely it usually proves to be only trash whose glitter had caught our attention. Imagination is at once the source of all hope and inspiration but also of frustration. To forget this is to court despair.' (250)

As with all creative activity, the final synthesis of ideas represents the endpoint of a great deal of thinking, of preoccupation with some problem. The nineteenth-century physiologist, physicist and psychologist von Helmholtz, who contributed substantially to every discipline that he engaged himself in, described the process thus:

> It was always necessary, first of all, that I should have turned my problem over on all sides to such an extent that I had all its angles and complexities 'in my head' and could run through them freely without writing . . . To bring the matter to that point is usually impossible without long preliminary labour. (444)

While Helmholtz did not report solving problems in dreams, he did apparently rely to some extent on an autonomous process, so that once he had done the groundwork on a problem he sometimes achieved his insights apparently spontaneously, for instance when out walking. The role of dreaming in this very important process must be regarded as slight. The 'feeling of knowing' offered either when drunk, drugged, drowsy or asleep is no reliable indication of having achieved a real solution to a problem: there are unfortunately no short cuts in that direction!

Exposure – dreams of shame

Freud's comment on dreams of exposure was:

> the dream of nakedness demands our attention only when shame and embarrassment are felt in it, when one wishes to escape or to hide, and when one feels the strange inhibition of being unable to stir from the spot, and of being utterly powerless to alter the painful situation . . . The essential point is that one has a painful feeling of shame, and is anxious to hide one's nakedness, usually by means of locomotion, but is absolutely unable to do so. (146)

Freud's observation that these dreams are fuelled by a sense of shame seems uncontroversial. Interestingly, in the survey referred to earlier (174) twice as many Americans as Japanese reported ever having dreamed of being inappropriately dressed, or being nude. An explanation for this may lie in the way that children are treated in these two cultures: Western conditioning tends to be based on the idea of guilt. Telling a child that he or she is bad when they have behaved wrongly is common in the West, but, as Susan Sontag has observed, it is unheard of in the East, where the child would be told to be ashamed of itself (393). For Westerners the sense of shame and embarrassment has become strongly associated with nakedness and the proprieties of dress and attitudes towards nudity (especially among conventional Protestants). They are also peculiarly prudish and voyeuristic. For the Japanese students the shameful dream may not be confined to these topics – for instance many of their dreams about failing examinations or their schooling in general may have been intrinsically shameful, and they reported both of these more often than the Americans.

Immobility

A sensation of being unable to move is common in many dreams, including some nightmares. Sometimes one can move only excruciatingly slowly, however pressing it seems to move quickly. It is well established that we are in fact in a state of muscular flaccid paralysis during REM sleep, with the exception of the muscles controlling respiration, and the eyes. In some species this inhibition of motor discharge at the level of the pons (a structure at the top of the spinal cord) is more general than others. Dogs in REM sleep sometimes move their legs as if running, and in monkeys the whole face may writhe and twitch.

The sensation of inertia, of being unable to initiate movement during dreams and nightmares, is very common, and it would seem reasonable to interpret this as being a response to an awareness, at some level, of the inability to move. Interestingly, Freud anticipated the discovery of motor paralysis during REM sleep by over 60 years, when in his *Project for a Scientific Psychology* (146) he asserted that there is no motor discharge during dreaming. Later, he addressed the question of why this awareness only arises occasionally in *The Interpretation of Dreams* (147) by saying that it is an expression of conflict about the will. That is, if we do attempt to make a movement during dreaming it is certain to fail, and this provides an opportunity to express the idea that our intentions are being thwarted. One could equally argue that imperative, strenuous movements are rarely dreamed – one tends to be an observer, paying little attention to how one gets about. Only when the dream focuses on the attempt to make a movement is the problem apparent.

Nightmares – dreams of fear

Nightmares can perhaps better be defined in terms of the emotions they evoke, rather than any particular subject matter. These emotions are primarily of fear, guilt and horror, in various proportions, and the dream ends with the subject waking up. While they might be regarded as disorders of sleep, and will be discussed in Chapter 12 and 13, on sleep problems, they are so prevalent, so much a part of normal life, that, like sleepwalking, they deserve a place in any account of normal sleep and dreaming.

Sheer terror in a nightmare can be the result of an unseen, hidden menace – for instance behind a closed door. Unusually for dreaming, the plot is not in this case being driven by the visual imagery, but it is almost as if the feeling of terror is primary, and the process of dreaming is to interpret the somewhat mundane imagery to accommodate the emotion. While some nightmares like this are consummated by the monster actually making an appearance, it is not necessary – the terror may never become actualized.

It is necessary to distinguish 'night terrors' from dreaming nightmares. The former, relatively common amongst children, occur during deep slow wave (stage 4) sleep, and are not accompanied by any visual imagery or a coherent dream (66). Nightmares occurring during REM sleep may be equally frightening, but are accompanied by a story, with vivid visual imagery to sustain it.

The purely guilty nightmare might be illustrated in terms of sexual repression and guilt by Mary Baker Eddy's dream:

> of being assaulted by a strange man while she was with a Christian Science congregation. She managed to disengage herself from this unwanted lover and ran into a house – which unfortunately turned out to be one of ill-repute. The man followed, locked the door, and laughed. Only when Mrs Eddy understood her predicament did the nightmare dissolve. (385)

Nightmares of pure horror are expressed in dreams of cannabalism, gory deaths and graveyard ghouls. The author Gustave Flaubert once dreamed of:

> lying in a curtained bed. He was aware of footsteps on the stairs and, at the same time, a breath of foul-smelling air wafted into his room. Then seven or eight black-bearded fellows entered with daggers held between their teeth. They approached the bed; their teeth made gnashing sounds. Each finger left a tell-tale bloodstain on the white bed curtains. For a long while seven or eight pairs of lidless eyes gazed down at Flaubert. The typical prisoner of nightmare, he could neither shout nor move. When at last they drew back, he saw that one side of their faces was skinless and bleeding. They lifted all his clothes, leaving blood on every item, and sat down to eat. As they broke bread it spurted and dripped blood, and their mirth was the rattle in a dying man's throat. The apparitions vanished to leave the whole room smeared with blood. Flaubert knew a choking sensation and felt as if he had swallowed flesh. Then he heard a long cry . . . (385)

As in a Hammer horror film, the anticipation of something dreadful provides the engine to this dream – the seven bearded men's appalling appearance was not for instance immediately apparent, and even though they removed his clothes and started to eat, there was no explicit imagery of being eaten. In the somewhat incoherent climax Flaubert was himself implicated in the cannabal-istic orgy, tasting flesh – presumably his own. Again, it seems that the emotion of horror came first, and the dream was constructed to accommodate it. How else would the dreamer *know* at the beginning of the dream (as he or she always does) that something horrific was going to happen? There are no screen credits at the beginnings of dreams to tell you what sort of film you are going to see, but they might as well have been in these nightmares, because the terror, horror or guilt is excruciatingly present before the first scenes have even been played.

CHAPTER 6

What is a Dream?

A description of dreaming

While a great deal has been discovered about the physiology of sleep, and psychologists have developed reliable techniques for establishing when people are likely to be dreaming, there has not been an equivalent amount of progress in understanding the nature of dreams. A starting point for any analysis of this nature must be to clearly establish how dreaming differs from waking consciousness.

Dreams happen to us, rather than being a product of conscious control, as fantasies are. When dreaming we are the spectators of an unfolding drama, and only rarely does one have the impression of being in control. 'Lucid' dreaming, when the dreamer 'knows' that he or she is dreaming, and makes decisions about how the dream plot should develop, is unusual. More typically, things happen and we observe. While there may be a coherent plot, events do not unfold in any steady progression – rather, there are sudden changes in scenario, or scene shifts, which are sometimes baffling. Ordinary logic is suspended. One can fly. People can turn into animals. We encounter people who have been dead for years, or we improbably have conversations with film stars or royalty.

The dreams that subjects report in the laboratory tend to be mundane, and lack the bizarre quality of dreams reported in the morning. This is probably because only the strangest experiences are remembered by people waking normally after a night's sleep, and the more everyday the dream content, the less memorable it is. Ann Faraday has also offered some evidence that the last dreams of the night tend to be more vivid than those earlier in the night (125). The oddness of dreaming experience is, however, undeniable. One feature of this oddness which has perhaps been overlooked was pointed out by Allan Rechtschaffen (355), which is what he called the single-mindedness of dreams. When awake, we normally reflect on the stream of consciousness as it goes on. In addition, we can be aware that we are in one place, for instance seated at

98

a desk, and at the same time imagine something else. Rechtschaffen claims that during dreaming this is not possible. He says, 'I cannot remember a dream report which took the form, "Well, I was dreaming of such and such, but as I was dreaming this I was imagining a different scene which was completely unrelated"'. The imagery of the dream totally dominates consciousness. Paradoxically, while dreaming we are without imagination, and we are not aware that we are dreaming. Instances of 'lucid' dreaming, when the dreamer is aware that he or she is dreaming, are rare, even amongst those who claim to frequently experience it. This is totally different from the state of affairs when we are awake, and have taken an hallucinatory drug, when however compelling the hallucination we are well aware that the experience is drug-induced, and not 'real'.

Our conscious control of attention between the reflective, evaluative stream of thought and the thinking essential to the task in hand is vital to our normal processes of registering memories. We form intentions to remember and categorize and order what we are going to remember in terms of our past experience. During dreams there is typically no such facility in our control of consciousness, which is essential to the normal formation of permanent memories. Dreams, by their very nature, impose a strait-jacket of a single stream of thought, driven by visual images, which prevents the formation of any spontaneous intentions, evaluations, the recollection of memories or indeed their storage. As Erasmus Darwin commented in 1794, 'we never exercise our reason or recollection in dreams' (see Chapter 1). Rechtschaffen's is a lucid, insightful account of the phenomenology of dreaming, which, despite the many advances that have been made in understanding the natural history of sleep and dreaming, remains unusual in attempting to deal directly with the experience of dreaming. Of course, the phenomenological approach has been with us for a long time, and has been the primary source of evidence in the psycho-analytic tradition.

The psycho-analytic approach

Freud's analysis of dreaming remains the most influential single account that we have. He and later psycho-analysts have relied on dreams recollected during therapy sessions, or those they could recall themselves. The goal of psycho-analysis was the development of a new set of techniques for use in psychiatry, and in this context dreams tended to be treated as neurotic symptoms rather than as a normal aspect of experience. Dreams seemed to provide a royal road to the understanding of the patients' subconscious. For Freud, 'dreams are the fulfilment of wishes' (148). He asserted that there are two distinct forms of thinking – primary-process thinking, as exemplified in dreaming, and secondary-process thinking, as exemplified in logical reasoning. Primary-process thinking is driven by what he called the pleasure principle, whereby the instant gratification of infantile desires is immediately achieved by making use of a number of irrational but personally satisfying mental tricks (mechanisms he called condensation, displacement, substitution and symbolization). During waking life primary-process thinking is displaced during the child's development by secondary-process thinking, and, in the adult it remains as a neurotic symptom, most clearly during dreaming, but also operating at a subconscious level to influence waking behaviour.

Most dreams are not obviously simple wish fulfilments – dreams of personal glory, gratifying sexual encounters ending in orgasm, or the confounding of enemies. In order to accommodate this fact Freud did not abandon the idea that all dreams were wish fulfilments, but hypothesized a mechanism, the dreamwork, whereby dreams were censored. The manifest dream that is available for recall is thus a compromise, whereby the wish fulfilments have been disguised. The latent dream, only accessible through extensive analysis of the manifest dream, is the 'true' dream – the expression in wish fulfilment of strongly felt desires. Sleep is physiologically necessary, and while asleep there are periodic surges of instinctual energy giving rise to these unacceptable, anxiety-provoking thoughts. Manifest dreams are the outcome of a process which allows the expression of these thoughts, preserving sleep by preventing them from being overtly explicit.

Freudian dream analysis proceeded by the patient lying down on the couch, and in as relaxed a frame of mind as possible recounting their dream, and then considering the dream images in turn, providing free associations to the object represented. This technique of free association, in which the patient is encouraged to say the first thing that comes to mind, reveals connotations of the dream image which might otherwise not have been obvious. In practice, the analyst will direct the patient towards those connotations which seem most pertinent – namely, in Freud's case, sexual connotations. An analysis may go on for years, so the free associations, and the dreams recalled themselves, will be conditioned by the analytic process itself, the patient's contribution increasingly representing the assumptions of the analyst.

Modern psycho-analysts still make extensive use of dream analysis, but are not necessarily interested in uncovering the 'latent dream' – the simple wish fulfilments of erotic urges. Rather, they use patients' dreams to explore their current preoccupations. Charles Rycroft (372), an eminent contemporary British psycho-analyst, has gone so far as to entirely reject the Freudian theory of the origin and function of dreaming. He argues that dreams cannot be regarded as a neurotic symptom if everybody dreams – unless everybody is neurotic. Describing everybody as neurotic makes any distinction between normality and neurosis impossible. In addition, the idea that infants are born with a totally maladaptive nervous system – capable only of primary-process thinking – seems biological and evolutionary nonsense. As he says, quoting from Freud's *Introductory Lectures on Psycho-analysis*,

If we started life as 'a chaos, a cauldron full of seething excitations', with 'no organization' and given to satisfying our wishes by hallucination, it is hard to imagine how we could begin to experience the external world in such a way as to learn adaptation from it. This difficulty does not arise if one assumes that both processes co-exist from the beginning of life, that they both have adaptive functions, and they are not necessarily in conflict with one another – even though they may on occasion be. (148)

Imagination and artistic creation are also, according to a strict interpretation of Freudian theory, neurotic symptoms. Rycroft argues against relegating so much of our mental life to the status of pathology, preferring to liken dreams to waking imaginative activity, such as creative writing. Metaphor and symbolism are intrinsic to both, and it seems only reasonable to attempt to treat dreaming as normal and creative unless good evidence emerges that it is indeed pathological.

Freud was a pioneer in taking dreaming seriously, and in recognizing that the quality of logic in dreams, while sometimes bizarre, may follow certain rules. His psychological theorizing developed throughout his life, but many of the assumptions he made can be traced to an early work, the *Project for a Scientific Psychology* (146). This essay is, incidentally, unusually accessible for the lay reader as it does not rely on any familiarity with the technical terminology that he developed later. In addition to addressing psychiatric issues it also deals, very insightfully in most instances, with topics of general psychology such as primary memory and forgetting. As a trained neurologist, Freud's psychological theory was essentially based in the neurophysiological thinking of his time. Robert McCarley and Allan Hobson (281), in an analysis of Freud's psychological theory, have pointed out how deeply his psychology was informed by these neurological assumptions, which subsequent science has frequently shown to be wrong.

So far as dreaming is concerned, Freud's theory has similarly been overtaken by the evidence. REM sleep – during which our most vivid dreams almost always occur – is universal amongst mammals, which makes it unlikely that its primary role is to be the vehicle for a neurotic defence mechanism, unless gorillas, dogs, cats and skunks are all credited with repressive super egos! Neurophysiological studies have shown that REM sleep is an essential part of brain function – not an optional extra invoked to deal with unacceptable thoughts emerging during sleep.

Some recent ideas

Rather than devoting any more space to criticizing a theory based on nineteenth-century science, it would seem more profitable to follow Freud's example in going to our current knowledge of the biological basis of sleep in building a psychological model of what dreaming really is. Hobson and McCarley (200) followed up their paper on the dated neurophysiological underpinning for Freudian theory in general with an analysis of current knowledge of the neurophysiology of sleep, as applied to dreaming. Following Freud in the spirit of a belief in the isomorphism of mind and body they set out to do what he did, but in the light of modern findings about the physiology of sleep mechanisms. Rather than dreaming primarily being psychologically necessary – a response dealing with occasional neurotic erotic impulses during sleep – they argued that it is in fact the outcome of automatic, pre-programmed neural processes. Like most good theories, theirs integrates a great accumulation of evidence, which, once presented in a single context, makes the theory seem almost self-evident. Relying largely on neurophysiological evidence, the argument for the theory is inevitably rather technical. During REM sleep there is every indication that the cortex is highly active, although little external sensory stimulation is received by it. In addition, although the motor cortex is highly active, generating activity which would normally result in movement, these commands do not reach the muscles controlling the limbs, but are 'switched off' at a relay station at the top of the spinal column, so that we are effectively paralysed during REM sleep. This explains the loss of tone in the neck muscles under the chin, used as one of the defining characteristics of REM sleep.

Not only is the cortex isolated by being unable to control the musculature, but there is also an inhibition of incoming signals generated by sensory systems. That is, perceptions of the 'real' world are selectively attenuated. The hindbrain and midbrain structures normally associated with relaying sensory information to the cortex spontaneously generate signals which are responsible for the cortical activation, and are also indistinguishable from signals which would normally have been relayed from the eyes and ears. This activity is under the control of a periodic triggering mechanism in a structure at the top of the spinal column at the base of the brain known as the pontine brain stem. Activity in giant cells in the pontine brain stem have been shown to precede eye movements in REM sleep in animals (or paradoxical sleep, as it is called in rodents and cats) while there is no evidence that cortical activity can influence these cells' discharges. During REM sleep, they argued, the cortex is largely under the control of these random discharges from the hindbrain. The interaction between stimulation from hindbrain structures normally associated with the transmission of sensory information, and cortical structures normally devoted to integrating sensory input of this sort, gives rise to dreaming. They called this the *activation-synthesis* hypothesis of the dream process, and suggested that dreaming sleep may have a functional role in some aspect of the learning process.

This theory has been elaborated by Francis Crick and Graeme Mitchison (83). REM, or paradoxical sleep is universal amongst mammals. In men, cats and rats, the prevention of REM sleep by selective awakenings results in increased amounts of this sleep stage on recovery, as if what had been 'missed' was then being 'made up', suggesting that not only does this sleep stage have its own drive mechanism, but it may have an important function. Since most dreams are not remembered, this function must either have nothing whatever to do with dreaming, or, if dreaming is essential to the process, the forgetting must be a necessary part of it. According to them the random pontine activity stimulating the cortex during REM sleep therefore has the function of erasing memories, which, in their terms, have become 'parasitic' – interpretations which, whatever their origin, have no place in our latest view of the world, and are redundant but persistent. This accumulation of nonsense is expressed in dreams which are created only in order to be forgotten. Those which are remembered are later repeated, so that frightening dreams which wake people up, and are remembered, tend to become recurrent. The theory is supported by a mathematical model ('the Hopfield net') of the effects of random stimulation on very complex interactive systems – neural nets – accounting for both bizarre and repetitive dreams.

In a subsequent paper (84) Crick and Mitchison have defended their theory from some criticisms, and developed it further, with new evidence. As they point out, selective forgetting of parasitic traces will have the opposite effect, on the memory system as a whole, of simply losing memories. 'The process of reverse learning is designed to make the storage in an associative net more efficient.' In a system as complex as human memory the result of erasing what they call parasitic connections will thus have the effect of sharpening and making more accessible those cognitive structures which represent our worlds. As such this theory may, in practical terms, have no quarrels with Hobson and McCarley's hypothesis that REM or dreaming sleep has a positive function in the learning process.

When a neural net becomes overloaded, memories or concepts which share some simple feature are liable to become conflated – linked together by 'parasitic associations'. Crick and Mitchison argue that the phenomenon of condensation in dreaming, first described by Freud, is specifically predicted by their theory. While most of what Freud had to say about the 'latent content' of dreams is at best arguable, the phenomenon of condensation as part of the 'manifest content' is well established, even in children's dreams (134), and of course, as a neural-net theory would predict, 'in condensation the objects or events brought together always turn out to have some feature in common'.

Additional evidence that Crick and Mitchison produce in support of their theory comes from what they call 'nature's experiments' – in this case the few species of mammals which have no REM sleep. They had already noted that the echidna, an Australian monotreme, lacked REM sleep. It also has, in relation to its size, a very large neocortex, and Crick and Mitchison had attributed the large size of the cortex to the lack of any system for 'reverse learning'. They subsequently learned of Dr Mukhametov's work on the sleep of cetaceans (described in Chapter 10), showing that two species of bottle-nosed dolphin and porpoise show non-REM sleep, but no REM sleep. As is well known, cetaceans have very large neocortices in relation to their size, and this has, in the past, been taken as an indication of great potential intelligence. Crick and Mitchison argue, rather, that these animals are not particularly intelligent, but that REM sleep did not need to develop in them because there was no evolutionary pressure for them to have small heads (being constantly supported by water). Seals, on the other hand, while also sea mammals, do have to support their heads out of water, and they have in fact been shown to have normal REM sleep. Thus, the 'function of REM sleep is to make advanced brains more efficient and, in particular, to allow these brains to have a smaller size than they would otherwise have' (84).

Hobson and McCarley's thesis has also been developed in a recent essay by Martin Seligman and Amy Yellen (380), whose title – 'What is a dream?' – has been borrowed for this chapter. Seligman and Yellen take the theory further, in mapping the psychological reality of dreaming on to contemporary neurophysiological evidence of brain functioning during sleep, accounting for the emotional quality of dreaming as well as its visual content. They invoke three sources of evidence, closely following Hobson and McCarley's arguments to start with. First, the neurophysiological evidence suggests that the hindbrain is in control of the generation and maintenance of REM sleep, and cortical activity is dictated by spontaneous hindbrain activity. Assuming mind–brain isomorphism, it follows that the experience of REM sleep dreaming should therefore be an outcome of this interaction between the cortex and the hindbrain.

Second, rapid eye movements are not continuous during REM, but come in periodic bursts, typically lasting between 2 and 10 seconds, and are separated by periods of sleep lasting up to 3 minutes with low voltage, mixed frequency EEG and muscle atonia. Subjects woken during a REM burst have been shown by Molinari and Foulkes to report highly vivid visual experiences much more frequently than when woken from periods of REM 'quiescence' (306). Categorizing these reports as being either 'primary visual experiences' (PVEs) or 'secondary cognitive elaborations' (SCEs) they found that 82 per cent of reports of mental activity when woken from REM bursts were PVEs, and 12 per cent SCEs. Eighty per cent of reports after awakenings from REM quiescence were SCEs, while only 20 per cent were PVEs. Subsequent work by David Foulkes and others (135, 60) showed that the very striking differences between experience during REM bursts and REM quiescence was not as great when subjects were questioned at any length, rather than being allowed to make spontaneous reports of what had been going on in their minds. It is, however, undeniable that there is a great difference in the quality of experience during REM bursts and REM quiescence, with visual and auditory hallucinatory sensations characterizing the REM bursts, even if the difference is not quite as striking as was first thought.

Given the two sources of evidence outlined above, it would not seem unreasonable to conclude that the discharges from the pontine brain stem are causing the dreams. How is it that what seem like random discharges from a part of the brain that we share with the humblest reptiles can end up as the elaborate, coherent cognitive activity we know as dreaming? Seligman and Yellen invoke evidence showing how adept is the cortex in constructing sense out of chaos. Like John Hughlings Jackson, with his Perceptual Release Theory (see earlier, p. 78) discussed in the context of hypnagogic hallucinations, they argue that dreaming is the outcome of the cortical integration of sensory inputs over which it has no control. In a survey of dreams reported by university students, they found that dream images which were highly vivid also tended to be 'surprising', and at the centre of the visual field. They concluded:

> These results suggest the existence of two different kinds of visual events during dreaming as we predicted. One kind is vivid, detailed, colorful, large, and in the center of the visual field. The other kind is less vivid, less detailed, less colorful, smaller, and in the periphery of the visual field. The detailed are more constrained and continuous with the plot. We suggest that this is so because the vivid events are hallucinatory bursts whose content is unconstrained by the previous visual events, the ongoing emotion, or the ongoing integration; whereas the less vivid events are visual material generated by the cognitive integration, and as such, are constrained in content (380).

In a second study Seligman and Yellen compared the coherence of subjects' dream reports with their ability, while awake, to construct dream plots when shown a series of unconnected slides. They predicted that those who integrated random visual events well in the waking state would also be those whose dream images were very constrained by the dream plot. Those who integrated random visual events inadequately when awake would be those whose dreams images fitted least well into their dream plots. Strong positive correlations were indeed found between measures of the integration of images into dream plots with the integration of the unrelated slides into dream stories made up while awake, showing that their subjects had a consistent characteristic style of integration while awake and asleep. They concluded:

> We suggest that the same process by which individuals make coherent the externally generated visual episodes of daily life is at work during dreaming; when an individual encounters the internally generated visual episodes in REM sleep, he deploys this ability (in whatever measure he possesses it) to make this encounter coherent.

This approach to the nature of dreaming is highly compelling. Because it relies on continuing cognitive synthesis as a mechanism for the construction of dreams, it explains the apparently dreamlike quality of many experiences reported during NREM sleep, including hypnagogic imagery. This description could be described in terms of Freud's dreamwork as a sort of cortical rearguard action in the face of incoherent but highly active discharges from the hindbrain. In Chapter 5 dreams of exposure were described as dreams of shame, nightmares as dreams of fear, guilt or horror. Is it similarly possible that these emotions are not a consequence of the dream but of the apparently haphazard interaction between midbrain and hindbrain activity during REM sleep? That is, just as cognitive synthesis is required to make sense of the input from the visual cortex, so it is needed to comprehend the intense emotions being offered to the cortex by overstimulated midbrain limbic structures.

One problem that remains is to explain the recurring dream – if the stimulation from the hindbrain pontine structures is truly random, how is it that people can have the same dreams repeatedly? If there is such continuity between waking skills in integrating visual material and in the coherence of dream reports, why is it that 'dream logic' follows rules of its own, characteristic of Bleuler's 'A-thinking' or Freud's primary-process thinking? Would waking subjects really respond to dream images in the same way as when asleep? These questions must remain unanswered, but this strategy for understanding the nature of dreaming represents the most promising yet suggested. Our knowledge of the neurophysiology of sleep is highly advanced, while our psychological understanding of dreaming is very limited. If we accept an isomorphism between brain states and mental functioning, taking some account of neurophysiological evidence must represent the most promising approach to understanding dreaming, at this stage in the state of the art.

PART III

PART III

CHAPTER 7

Sleep Disturbance

The effects of sleep deprivation

The experience of sleep loss: heroic experiments

Oliver Goldsmith, writing in 1811, described the effects of sleep loss thus:

> But man is more feeble; he requires its due return; and if it fails to pay the accustomed visit, his whole frame is in a short time thrown into disorder; his appetite ceases; his spirits are dejected; his pulse becomes quicker and harder; and his mind, abridged of its slumbering visions, begins to adopt waking dreams. A thousand strange phantoms arise, which come and go without his will: these, which are transient in the beginning, at last take firm possession of the mind, which yields to their dominion, and, after a long struggle, runs into continued madness. In that horrid state, the mind may be considered as a city without walls, open to every insult, and paying homage to every invader; every idea that then starts with any force, becomes a reality; and the reason, over fatigued with its former importunities, makes no head against the tyrannical invasion, but submits to it from mere imbecility. (165)

Characteristically, he does not cite any source for this assertion. This quotation does, however, sum up what many people might expect of the consequences of going without sleep for any length of time. Floridly psychotic episodes in people's lives, when they experience hallucinations of the sort Goldsmith describes, are often preceded by periods of sleeplessness, or at least of gross sleep disturbance, and this is perhaps why the association between sleep loss and madness has been made. It does not necessarily follow that sleep loss would cause these symptoms in otherwise normal individuals.

Relatively few controlled observations of the effects of sleep loss have continued for longer than 48 hours. When they have, disorders of perception including hallucinations have sometimes been reported, but by no means invariably. A not untypical pattern of distortion of sensation was reported from the first documented vigil of this sort and published in 1896:

> The first subject, J.A.G., is a young man of 28 years, assistant professor in the University. He is unmarried, of perfect health, of nervous temperament, of very great vitality and activity. He is accustomed to about 8 hours of sound sleep from 10 p.m. to 6 a.m. He awoke at his usual time Wednesday morning, November 27, and remained awake until 12 o'clock Saturday night. The second night he did not feel well and suffered severely from sleepiness. The third night he suffered less. The fourth day and the evening following he felt well and was able to pass his time in his usual occupations. During the last 50 hours, however, he had to be watched closely, and could not be allowed to sit down unoccupied, as he showed a tendency to fall asleep immediately, his own will to keep awake being of no avail. The daily rhythm was well marked. During the afternoon and evening the subject was less troubled with sleepiness. The sleepy period was from midnight until noon, of which the worst part was about dawn.
>
> The most marked effect of the abstinence from sleep with this subject was the presence of hallucinations of sight. These were persistent after the second night. The subject complained that the floor was covered with a greasy-looking, molecular layer of rapidly moving or oscillating particles. Often this layer was a foot above the floor and parallel with it and this caused the subject trouble walking, as he would try to step up on it. Later the air was full of these dancing particles which developed into swarms of little bodies like gnats, but colored red, purple or black. The subject would climb upon a chair to brush them from about the gas jet or stealthily try to touch an imaginary fly on the table with his finger. These phenomena did not move with movements of the eye and appeared to be true hallucinations, centrally caused, but due no doubt to the long and unusual strain put upon the eyes. Meanwhile the subject's sharpness of vision was not impaired. At no other time has he had hallucinations of sight and they entirely disappeared after sleeping (345).

Two more subjects then repeated the 90-hour vigil, and similarly became extremely sleepy, especially during the hours between midnight and noon, reviving somewhat during the afternoons. They did not experience any of the hallucinations experienced by J.A.G. In a later experiment conducted at the UCLA Neuropsychiatric Institute, four volunteers underwent 205 hours (8 days) of sleeplessness (344). They became increasingly sleepy for the first 4 days until it became almost impossible for the experimenters to keep them awake. Making them responsible for keeping each other awake at this stage restored a sense of group cohesion and of common purpose, although from this point on some serious changes in behaviour seem to have occurred, marked by emotional outbursts, grossly impolite eating habits and what the authors of the report describe as an 'infantilization of personal habits . . . including toilet and bathing activities'. At one point one of the subjects went berserk during a psychomotor tracking task, screaming in terror and pulling off his electrodes, falling to floor and sobbing and muttering incoherently about a gorilla. Oddly enough, at the end of the 205 hours the subjects claimed that they could go on longer, that after the fifth day things had got easier, and indeed offered to stay awake for another day if paid at the ninth day's rate.

In the 40-odd experimental studies that have been reported to date on periods of sleep loss longer than two days, hallucinations have, however, been uncommon, tending to affect individuals in solitary vigils, rather than those in groups. Similarly, other frankly psychiatric symptoms, such as of paranoia, have affected lone volunteers more than those selected to be in groups.

A study in which the majority of the subjects suffered from mental aberrations of one sort or another required them to perform tasks continuously, and in isolation, for 42 hours (317). Three of these ten subjects experienced actual hallucinations, and seven of them suffered perceptual distortions or illusions. Two other groups of ten subjects were allowed either six 1-hour naps or one 6-hour nap during the experiment, and they both managed to maintain a high level of performance on the tasks. Even in these groups, however, a minority had hallucinations. It is well known that isolation in itself, with no sleep loss, can induce hallucinatory experiences, and it seems that in this experiment the effects of sleep loss potentiated the relatively mild levels of isolation imposed on the subjects.

In these experiments subjects have invariably found it most difficult to remain awake during the hours between midnight and noon, with a revival every afternoon. In addition, it typically becomes very difficult indeed to keep people continually awake without keeping them moving, and this naturally confounds the effects of physical fatigue with those of sleep deprivation *per se* (although purposely increasing exercise levels during a vigil does not seem to increase or decrease the impairments attributable to sleep loss (15)).

After about 72 hours of sleep loss, 'it is impossible to prevent subjects from obtaining brief "microsleeps"' (438) which (when EEG measures are made) have been shown to be indistinguishable from brief periods of natural sleep. Using Dement's analogy, rather than taking their sleep in one meal, subjects may achieve enough to keep going by snatching 'snacks' (99). Such heroic experiments therefore show a diminishing return in giving insight into the effects of loss of sleep, although they have demonstrated that it is an intensely stressful experience, taxing the psychological resources of individuals to their utmost.

Effects on performance and psychophysiology

The sleep-deprived person may feel terrible and look pretty ragged but is typically capable of achieving the same levels of performance on psychological tests as when rested. Many common tests of perceptual functioning, memory or skilled performance seem insensitive to the effects of sleep loss. Despite a good number of studies having been undertaken in the first half of the century it was not until the late 1950s that the particular decrements in performance of sleepy subjects were established. Researchers at the Walter Reed Army Institute of Research in the United States (438) and at the Medical Research Council Unit for Applied Psychology in Cambridge (433) simultaneously identified the tasks sensitive to the effects of even one night's loss of sleep as those which were not self-timed, which went on for at least 10 minutes and which were not intrinsically motivating. While a sleep-deprived subject at the Walter Reed Institute was able to respond as quickly in a simple reaction time task as when rested, his pattern of responses over an extended series of trials, with the experimenter determining when stimuli were to be presented, would include an increasing number of very slow responses.

The Cambridge subjects were faced with the 5-choice serial reaction task, where a subject responds to one of 5 lights coming on by pressing one of 5 buttons on a continuous basis (every time a response is made the relevant light goes out, but another one immediately comes on). Average response speed tended to increase over a period of 20 minutes in sleep-deprived subjects, unlike in rested controls. Their best (i.e. fastest) responses were, however, just as fast as when rested, although the number of slow responses (or gaps in responding) increased dramatically after the first 5 minutes. The effects of sleep deprivation were therefore not simple. For instance, one could not say that the nervous system had simply slowed down, as on occasion the subjects could produce responses as quickly as they could when rested.

The theory developed to account for these findings, Lapse Theory, proposed that the special effect of sleep loss was to increase the number of lapses in attention, possibly through 'microsleeps'. This attentional failure may be caused by a lowering of arousal level, which may be temporarily counteracted by the subject exerting special efforts to remain awake. Evidence supporting the theory has come from experiments on the interaction of sleep loss with other manipulations known to increase arousal level, such as incentives and noise.

Giving the subject an immediate knowledge of the results of a monotonous task provides an intrinsic incentive, which can be sufficient to completely overcome the effects of one night's sleep loss for brief periods (434). This improvement is achieved by the subjects making an extra compensatory effort, measurable in terms of increased muscle tension (EMG). In these subjects the level of EMG has been shown to be well correlated with their level of performance (435). Offering extra payment for good performance, and 'fines' for missed signals in a vigilance task similarly maintained performance after one night's sleep loss at normal levels. This was not maintained after a second night, and after the third night without sleep subjects provided with these incentives could perform no better than those not provided with incentives (207).

Loud noise impairs performance on the 5-choice serial reaction time task in normal, rested, subjects. This has been interpreted as increasing arousal to levels incompatible with that task. Sleep-deprived subjects, however, improve their performance on the 5-choice when subjected to white noise, as if arousal level in their case was being raised sufficiently to allow them to cope with the demands of the task (81).

Lapse Theory can be invoked to explain all the results described above, but it remains unclear whether the lapses in attention induced by lowered arousal are the only important symptoms of sleep loss. For instance, are the fast reaction times of the sleep-deprived subject really as fast as those when they are rested, and is the slightly slower average-reaction time really simply the result of a number of isolated lapses? Analysis of the moment-by-moment changes in performance over a 10-minute period has shown that while the sleep-deprived subject may be performing well at the beginning, *all* responses are slowed towards the end, as well as frank lapses occurring. In a boring, repetitive task these subjects are not only prone to occasional failures to respond, but their 'good' responses are also impaired (270). According to the Swedish psychologist A. Kjellberg, lapses are the most dramatic outcomes of lowered arousal, but as the sleepy subject is performing a work-paced task for any length of time his responses become degraded even before the occurrence of frank lapses in attention (243).

This explanation of sleep-loss effects in terms of lowered arousal is further supported by studies on selective attention. Loud noise (usually delivered as 'white noise' – a wide-band mixture of tones, sounding like a monotonous hiss as from a TV set unconnected to an aerial) as we have seen, is a potent arouser, and in rested subjects it has the effect of focusing attention in a dual component task (201). This involves tracking a moving dot as well as monitoring lights which are either centrally or peripherally placed. When performing this same task for 40 minutes after sleep loss, subjects began by showing faster responses to the centrally placed lights than the peripheral ones, like rested subjects. They gradually demonstrated more and more evidence of defocusing attention as the task went on, consistent with the view that although performance was not disrupted by lapses, habituation was leading to a marked drop in arousal level in these subjects (202). Sleep-deprived subjects similarly have been found to be easily distracted by irrelevant stimuli in a card sorting task, again demonstrating a failure to maintain focused attention on the job in hand (326).

The EEG is probably the best single indicator of cortical arousal at low levels. Recordings of sleep-deprived subjects have shown a reduction in the amplitude of alpha rhythms (53). This is consistent with the view that, even when they are succeeding in remaining awake, these subjects do not manage to maintain levels of cortical arousal which would be normal in a rested person.

In rested subjects alpha rhythm is indicative of low arousal, but sleep deprived subjects commonly only achieve this level of arousal at best. Alpha appears when they are performing the most demanding tasks, and disappears altogether when less is demanded of them and their eyes are closed – almost as if they were drifting into a light sleep. Recordings of EEG while sleep-deprived subjects have been engaged in tasks have disclosed that errors of commission are not associated with EEG patterns different from those during correct performance, while errors of omission (indicating failure to maintain attention) are associated with reduced alpha (53). In addition, slow waves consistent with being asleep may occur during lapses in performance.

This evidence, again, is consistent with the Lapse Theory of sleep loss. Further EEG evidence comes from studies of the contingent negative variation (CNV) – a negative waveform in the EEG which is elicited when a warning stimulus is given, shortly followed by an imperative stimulus which requires the subject to make a response. For instance, a buzzer will sound, followed one second later by a series of flashes of light, which the subject has to turn off by pressing a button. Sleep-deprived subjects have been shown to have lower amplitude CNVs (159, 319), and it could be assumed that this is associated with inattention or poor preparation for making a response. In rested subjects the relationship between response speed and CNV amplitude is not simple (21), but one might assume that if lapses of attention are responsible for the generally lowered CNV with sleep loss, these should be associated with slow responses, when the subject was ill-prepared for the second, imperative stimulus, having failed to notice the warning stimulus. According to a simple application of Lapse Theory, slow responses ought to be preceded by low voltage CNVs, while fast responses (as quick as when rested) should be preceded by high voltage CNVs similar to those recorded from rested subjects.

Studies carried out in Hull (160, 248, 271) did nothing to confirm this prediction. Both fast and slow responses were reduced after sleep loss. Paradoxically, while CNV amplitude was on average lower after sleep deprivation, sleep-deprived subjects produced higher voltage CNVs before the 8 slowest responses out of 60 trials than before the 8 fastest ones. The same subjects when rested had higher voltage CNVs before fast responses than slow ones. These results reinforce Kjellberg's contention that the sleep-deprived person is not, as a strong version of Lapse Theory would suggest, essentially 'normal' but suffering periodic lapses. Rather, the subject's psychophysiological state undergoes a profound change; the resultant of compelling sleepiness inducing inertia and sleep, and a determined effort to stay awake. Neither a simple arousal model nor Lapse Theory is adequate on their own to explain the complex effects of sleep loss.

Effects of sleep loss on subsequent sleep

It is a commonplace observation that if we lose a night's sleep we tend to sleep a bit longer on subsequent nights, as if to make up a 'sleep debt'. Generally speaking, the amount of sleep lost is not made up for entirely on the recovery nights. Recordings of the EEG of recovery sleep have confirmed that the first night's recovery sleep is longer than usual. There is a great increase in percentage terms of stages 3 and 4 sleep, at the expense of the lighter slow wave sleep stages. While more REM sleep is taken than on control nights in absolute terms, this is not because of any increase in REM sleep as a percentage of total sleep. Only during the second and subsequent recovery nights do subjects typically show a relative elevation of REM sleep percentage levels. Thus over the course of two or three nights stages 3, 4 and REM sleep are almost made up, while stage 2 sleep is not (40, 45, 236).

Schedules of sleep

Reduced sleep in the short term

Once the tasks which are particularly sensitive to the effects of even one night's loss of sleep had been identified, it became feasible to attempt to establish how little sleep is enough to prevent any of the effects of sleep loss. Research conducted at the Medical Research Council Applied Psychology Unit in Cambridge has indicated that even short periods of sleep are enough to prevent any measurable worsening of performance (436). In that experiment, 19 enlisted men were repeatedly tested over a period of 6 weeks. Every week their sleep was rationed on two nights to between 0 and 7.5 hours, and they spent the subsequent days being tested in the laboratory on vigilance and adding tasks. These tasks were repetitive, lengthy and lacking in any intrinsic interest. This regime should have been more than adequate to demonstrate any significant short-term effects of reduced sleep. However, performance deficits were only noticeable after 2 hours sleep or less for one night, and after 5 hours or less for two successive nights, showing some evidence of an accumulation of sleep debt potentiating the otherwise rather slight effects of reduced sleep. This finding, that reduced sleep in the short term has little effect on performance, was subsequently confirmed in later work (e.g. 184).

The effect of interrupting sleep after two or three hours is to deny the subject almost all REM sleep, while allowing them much of the deep slow wave sleep that they might be expected to have in a normal night. Only sleep stage deprivation experiments can answer the question whether one stage or another is more restorative, and these are discussed next.

Sleep stage deprivation experiments

Selective deprivation experiments involve highly artificial regimes designed to systematically eliminate one or other of the major sleep stages. They will be discussed again in Chapter 11 in relation to hypothesized functions of sleep, but the effects on subsequent recovery sleep, and the consequences for performance tasks will be outlined here. REM sleep deprivation experiments were also discussed in Chapter 4 in the context of beliefs about dreaming – in particular, the notion that the prevention of dreaming sleep might cause temporary psychosis. Briefly, William Dement's early experimental work which provided some support for this idea (96) was subsequently found, both by himself and others, to be unrepeatable. In retrospect it seems that genuine concern on the part of the experimenters was communicated to the subjects to provide a potent source of suggestion that they should suffer symptoms of paranoia and hallucinations, and a cumulative sleep loss over the six days of the experiment combined to provide a fertile ground for the production of these symptoms. It has also become clear that dreaming is by no means confined to REM sleep (see Chapter 5 pp. 80–1), so even if the theory was correct, the regime of REM sleep deprivation would not have been an adequate test of it.

Well-established aspects of the early results relate to the behaviour of sleep mechanisms when REM sleep is prevented by repeated wakenings. While it may be virtually abolished on the first night by as few as four or five wakenings, on subsequent nights REM 'pressure' increases, and successively more wakenings are required, as the number of times REM sleep is initiated is increased. In addition, on recovery nights the amount of time spent in REM sleep increases. This REM sleep 'rebound' may be of the order of 50 per cent over baseline levels, although the total amount of REM sleep 'lost' during the period of selective deprivation is rarely made up entirely.

It is also possible to prevent subjects from having any (or very little) stage 4 sleep by disturbing their sleep with loud noises, rather than waking them up fully (7). The effects of this regime on subsequent recovery sleep are similar to the effects of REM sleep deprivation, in that a rebound of about 50 per cent occurs on recovery nights.

In two experiments combining total sleep deprivation, stage REM deprivation and stage 4 sleep deprivation, Julie Moses and others at the U.S. Navy Health Research Center in San Diego have compared the effects of a variety of regimes of total and selective sleep deprivation on recovery sleep and performance (274, 223). In their first experiment, subjects were denied all sleep for two nights, and then allowed to sleep under one or other sleep stage deprivation condition. In this way the restorative effects of sleep without stage REM could be compared with those of sleep without stage 4. Whether recovery sleep after two nights' loss of sleep was restricted by excluding stage 4 sleep or most of REM sleep seemed to make no difference – subjects returned to pre-sleep-loss levels of performance regardless of whether recovery sleep was uninterrupted or selectively deprived.

In their second experiment another group of subjects were subjected to REM or stage 4 sleep deprivation for three nights, and then deprived of sleep altogether for one night, again allowing a comparison of the effects of a four-day cumulation of loss of stage 4 sleep with REM sleep. Selective deprivation of neither stage 4 nor REM sleep over three nights had any measurable effects on performance, and after the subsequent night of total sleep deprivation there was no difference between groups in their degree of impairment. In fact their performance was slightly better than a control group of subjects who had one night's sleep deprivation with no prior selective deprivation. These results suggest that *any* sleep is enough to prevent the failures of attention which worsen performance on the tasks which are most sensitive to the effects of sleep loss.

What are the particular psychological effects, if any, of selective deprivation of REM or paradoxical sleep? Research on this question has concentrated on the possible role of REM sleep in facilitating adaptive processes, and in the consolidation of memories. Evidence relating to these issues will be discussed in Chapter 11.

Reduced sleep in the long term

As has been pointed out elsewhere (see Chapter 2), some people seem to require very little sleep, and some take more. Those who sleep less sometimes claim to do so by choice, self-righteously accusing everybody else of being idle who spends more than six hours in bed. How much control do we have over our requirements for sleep, and what are the consequences of an individual taking things into their own hands, and reducing their sleep?

The effects of reducing sleep on sleep patterns have been studied in a number of relatively short experiments, and in one which went on for 2 years. The short-term effects are illustrated by an experiment (74) in which sleep was restricted to 5 hours for 7 days. Sleep onset time was reduced from 33 minutes during baseline recordings to less than 5 minutes by the seventh night, and time spent awake after going to sleep was reduced from about 30 minutes to virtually zero. Sleep efficiency was thus notably improved. While asleep, stages 1, 2 and REM were reduced at the expense of stages 3 and 4, which were maintained at baseline levels. There was a tendency for REM sleep time to recover slightly during the week of restriction, and during recovery sleep an increase in REM sleep time over baseline levels (a REM sleep rebound) indicated an accumulated pressure for REM sleep. These subjects slept like short sleepers in so far as sleep efficiency was improved, and deep slow wave sleep was maintained at baseline levels. Their REM sleep time was, however, reduced.

Longer-term effects were studied in four young couples, three who normally slept about 8 hours every night, and one who slept 6.5 hours a night, who volunteered to attempt to progressively reduce their sleep to 4.5 hours a night over a period of between 6 and 8 months (142). They reduced their time in bed by 30 minutes every 2 weeks until it was down to 6.5 hours, then by 30 minutes every 3 weeks until it was 5 hours, and finally by 30 minutes every 4 weeks. At the final stage, sleeping only 4.5 hours a night, problems arose with subjects complaining of falling asleep during the day, and the reductions in time allowed in bed were discontinued.

Subjective reports on the effects of reduced sleep were that it produced a chronic feeling of sleepiness and, perhaps not surprisingly, increased the feeling of needing more sleep. The estimated time to get to sleep after going to bed was reduced to a quarter of the baseline levels, and reports of difficulty in getting to sleep were reduced to a third of what they had been. More subtle effects on mood are indicated by a quotation from one of the subjects: 'I get discouraged more easily, slightly depressed about overcoming difficulties, very much like when I am sick with a cold' (142).

Despite the reports of sleepiness during the day performance of tasks known to be affected by sleep loss was generally unaffected during this regime (including two tasks developed at the Medical Research Council Applied Psychology Unit, the Wilkinson Auditory Vigilance Task and the Wilkinson Addition Task (142)). Only one test proved sensitive to the effects of gradually reduced sleep – the Rapid Alternation Test – where an increase in the number of long responses, or lapses, was noticed at the lowest sleep levels. Subjects also reported difficulties in maintaining concentration when driving.

After this phase of the experiment was over, subjects were allowed to sleep as much as they wished, but continued to keep sleep diaries for a year. The six who originally slept about 8 hours did not immediately return to their baseline level, and continued to sleep less than they had before, and even a year later they were sleeping 1 to 1.5 hours less than they had been to start with. The two subjects who slept little to start with did not achieve any such permanent reduction in sleep. This experiment is interesting in highlighting how the subjective experience of sleepiness is not necessarily reflected in performance measures, and more importantly in demonstrating some permanent change in the sleep patterns of the group of six 'normal' sleepers. This study included EEG/EOG recordings during sleep, and it is interesting to compare the sort of sleep that these subjects were getting after months of sleep reduction with that of subjects who have reduced sleep for briefer periods of time (316). In particular, did the regime permanently change their patterning of sleep, as well as reducing their sleep requirement by over an hour?

Comparing the 8-hour with the 5.5-hour sleep regimes for the six subjects who had normally taken 8 hours sleep, stages 2 and REM were significantly reduced, while stage 4 sleep actually increased slightly (see Table 7.1). Although REM sleep time was reduced, its proportion of the first 5.5-hours' sleep was increased in the 5.5-hour sleep condition. That is, there was evidence

Table 7.1 Sleep characteristics during gradual sleep reduction.

Sleep phase (hr)	N	Total time (min.)						Stage-onset latencies (min.)				
		W	Stage 1	Stage 2	Stage 3	Stage 4	REM	Stage 1	Stage 2	Stage 3	Stage 4	REM
8.0	6	17	17	228	32	48	116	10	16	28	42	89
7.5	6	14	13	213	37	40	113	7	15	27	39	85
7.0	6	10	14	200	40	43	99	7	14	27	28	86
6.5	6	9	12	163	38	58	101	6	11	21	30	79
6.0	6	12	15	138	37	54	91	6	14	23	40	68
5.5	6	4	9	147	31	56	83	3	9	21	29	78
5.0	4	5	10	111	30	51	80	4	9	26	34	60
4.5	2	3	11	123	27	35	68	2	8	30	41	60
Follow-up	6	13	10	155	35	57	88	11	15	27	32	78
r-ratio (8.0–5.5 hrs)		2.23	1.61	10.77*	0.99	−2.25*	12.96*	3.00*	1.76	1.37	1.16	1.67

Note * Significant at 0.05 level or better, $df = 5$.
Source: (316).

of some compensation, partly due to a shorter time to the onset of REM sleep. On follow-up, when these subjects were sleeping only 6 hours, but not feeling sleepy any more during the day, the proportions of sleep stages were no different from the period in the experiment when they were being restricted to 6 hours sleep (when this restriction did make them feel sleepy).

In a less ambitious sleep reduction study, three pairs of subjects systematically reduced their sleep from 8 to 6 hours over a period of six weeks (209). Recordings of sleep patterns again showed that this was achieved at the expense of REM and stage 2 sleep, leaving stage 4 sleep levels unaffected. As in the longer experiment, the subjects tended to sleep less during a 3-month follow-up, indicating that even relatively short periods of training may be sufficient to reduce sleep requirements by an hour or so, in individuals who wish to do so.

How much sleep do we actually 'need'? The two subjects in the 8-month restriction study who had already limited themselves to 6 hours did not benefit from the regime, and reverted to their own established norms. Many of us who take 7 hours or more may be able to cope with less sleep without feeling sleepy, given training, but only those of us who were sleeping more than we really 'needed' to. On the other hand, there is evidence that, given the opportunity of 'ad lib' sleep, most young adults will sleep longer than usual, the extra sleep being composed of stage 1, 2 and REM sleep (427). Does this imply a chronic sleep debt in these young people? Perhaps not, but while the 7- to 9-hour sleeping habit is certainly based on physiological need, it seems to be a socially defined and somewhat procrustean norm imposed on all of us whatever our individual needs, which are probably genetically determined.

Extended sleep, displaced sleep and the Rip Van Winkle effect

Somewhat surprisingly, the consequences of sleeping longer than usual are similar to sleeping less, so far as performance decrements are concerned. John Taub and others at the University of California School of Medicine required subjects to sleep an hour or more longer than usual, by putting them to bed at either 22.00 or 01.00, but getting them up at the same time – 09.00. They found that the effects on sleep were to increase the total amount of REM sleep and stage 2 sleep. When tested after two hours extra sleep subjects performed worse on a vigilance task, although not significantly worse on a calculation task (405). In another experiment when sleep was extended by a similar amount subjects were tested on a vigilance task, a calculation task and a pinball game. The combined number of omissions and false reports on the vigilance task were 50 per cent greater after extended sleep, and scores on pinball were reduced by 10 per cent. Again, there was no significant decrement on a calculation task (406).

This group of researchers went on to compare the effects of extended sleep with reduced sleep (5 hours), and with displaced sleep, when subjects slept from either 21.00 to 05.00 or 03.00 to 11.00. Both shifting the timing of the sleep period from the habitual 24.00 to 08.00 and either increasing or decreasing the total amount of sleep had similar effects in reducing accuracy and speed of response on a vigilance task (404). They attributed these effects to physiological changes resulting from the disruption of the habitual circadian cycle of sleep and wakefulness, rather than any direct effects of the regimes on sleep itself – correlations between actual amounts of sleep achieved and their performance and mood measures were poor.

The consequences of sleep loss and sleep reduction cannot therefore simply be interpreted in terms of denial of sleep, but must be regarded as the outcome of a combination of sleep loss, causing sleepiness, and the subversion of the normally well-ordered physiological cycles which substantially control our states of arousal. Implications of this conclusion will be further explored in the discussion of shiftwork (pp. 123–4).

Practical implications of sleep disturbance

Apart from any implications for theories of sleep function in physiology, results from experiments on the effects of sleep deprivation have some practical importance. All of us lose sleep at some time in our lives, and many individuals have to lose sleep as part of their jobs, which may be extremely responsible and demanding. Shiftworkers lose sleep progressively while working the night or morning shifts, and may be employed in nursing, in controlling power stations or chemical plants, as well as in manufacturing industries. Airline pilots commonly have difficulty in sleeping properly after long flights, especially when there have been time-zone changes. Young babies inflict substantial disruption on their mother's sleep in their first three months of life, when they are at their most dependent, when the mother's judgement and good temper are most important. Junior hospital doctors may be on call for extended periods and on occasions have to manage with little or no sleep. It is commonplace for soldiers to get very little sleep indeed during a battle. In all these contexts there are high demands on individuals for effective and responsible behaviour, and it becomes crucial to know what precise effects sleep loss has had on normal functioning.

Overwork

When junior hospital doctors have been asked whether their efficiency was impaired by their long hours of duty, over a third replied 'often' and almost half replied 'occasionally' (437). These doctors frequently have the sole responsibility for assessing the needs of patients who are brought to hospitals, for example, to casualty wards in the middle of the night. Tests of efficiency in detecting abnormalities in the electrocardiogram have shown that after a night of reduced sleep doctors were reliably worse (149).

In taking a patient's history the doctor has to listen carefully to what the patient says, which may be incoherent, and extract from this account the elements which are medically relevant. This very important task involves a high memory load, as items mentioned by a patient early in the interview may turn out to be significant later on. Tests of medical house doctors after a night spent on emergency admissions (when they got an average of 1.5 hours sleep) showed them to be significantly worse at a memory task designed to tap these skills than after a night off duty (93). The differences between doctors were very great, not only in their general level of performance, but in the degree to which their level of perform-ance was affected by the lack of sleep. Referring to recent studies indicating that some people are particularly vulnerable to the effects of sleep disruption, the authors of this report suggested that work should be done to identify those doctors who are most at risk, in order to assign them to other duties.

How does sleep loss affect the soldier? A study carried out at the Army Personnel Research Establishment (APRE) in Farnborough simulated war-time conditions for 10 soldiers, who were required to defend a position during a tactical exercise lasting 10 days (190). Military staff ensured that they had no sleep for the first 3 days, after which short periods of sleep (4 hours) were permitted every 24 hours. As well as being kept extremely busy with military duties (digging trenches, receiving signals, countering surprise attacks by 'enemy troops') the men were tested three times a day on logical reasoning, a decoding task, and marksmanship. Scores on tests of logical reasoning and decoding both got worse by the end of 3 days, and recovered significantly, almost to baseline levels, when only 4 hours sleep per night was allowed. Marksmanship was relatively unaffected when the soldiers were allowed to shoot in their own time at a target, but when shooting was combined with a vigilance task (with the target appearing briefly at unpredictable times), the number of hits was dramatically reduced.

In a larger study assessing endurance over 9 days under different levels of sleep loss, the APRE reported that with no sleep at all soldiers could only operate effectively for 4 days, while with 1.5 hours sleep per day 50 per cent of a platoon lasted 9 days in the field, and nearly all of a platoon allowed 3 hours sleep completed the 9-day exercise (189). The same pattern of performance decrements on cognitive and shooting tasks was observed as in the smaller experiment. This combination of good marksmanship with poor reasoning ability can only be described as alarming – in particular when so many military duties may be concerned with public order, as in Northern Ireland, where rules of engagement require the soldier to make decisions on the basis of evidence that is often ambiguous. To quote the Duke of Wellington, 'I don't know what effect these men will have upon the enemy, but, by God, they terrify me.'

Shiftwork

Shiftworkers commonly complain of not being able to get enough sleep, and feeling chronically sleepy. This problem is not confined to night-workers, but also affects those on early shifts (06.00 to 14.00) who may have to allow an hour to get to work (249). Summarizing the results of a number of studies, Andrew Tilley and Bob Wilkinson have described the effects of shiftwork on sleep as being:

(1) A one- to two-hour reduction in the duration of the main sleep period for the nightshift and a reduction of about one hour for a morning or early shift.
(2) An increase in the total amount of sleep per 24 h., as compared with that of non-shiftworkers. This increase, however, can be attributed to long naps taken outside the main sleep period and increased sleep time on rest days. Both effects suggest a compensatory response to shorter main sleep periods.
(3) A change in the quality of sleep (i.e. more time awake, increased stage 1, and sometimes reduced REM) and a disruption of the normal temporal organisation of the sleep stages during daytime sleep. (409)

In their own study which actually involved recording EEG/EOG measures of sleeping shiftworkers in their own homes, using a portable tape recorder, they also found that sleep during the day was generally shorter than night-time sleep, and more frequently interrupted by awakenings. The consequences for the performance of simple tasks was that simple and choice reaction times were worse at night than during the day, and that as days on the night shift went by, simple reaction time tasks became slower. Circadian (24-hour) fluctuations in performance thus seem to combine with the effects of a cumulative sleep loss in a cycle of degradation of efficiency on the night shift.

Some individuals take to shiftworking with no problems, while others find the regime intolerable. Simon Folkard and Tim Monk have suggested that it may be the individuals whose rhythms do adjust to the regime who experience the most difficulty (133). By recording body temperatures throughout the day of groups of well-adjusted shiftworkers, intolerant shiftworkers, and day-workers who had given up shiftwork because they could not tolerate it, Reinberg and others have demonstrated that it is indeed the best-adjusted group whose circadian rhythm was most immutable (361). Intolerant workers tended to show cycles longer or shorter than 24 hours when they were on shifts, although they had normal 24-hour cycles when they had returned to day-work.

As with the effects of sleep reduction, sleep displacement or increased sleep on their own, the effects of shiftworking on performance and mood are a consequence of the interaction of our innate biological rhythms with sleep and arousal mechanisms. The implication of the Reinberg group's work is that rapidly rotating shifts, where no adjustment is made in terms of body rhythms, are preferable to longer cycling systems. Monitoring the body temperatures of shiftworkers might also give early warning of shiftwork intolerance, allowing transfers to day-work before performance has deteriorated.

CHAPTER 8

The Psychology of Sleep

Perception and memory in sleep

We do not in general respond when spoken to, or initiate any coherent actions while asleep. We also have very little to report about our sleep after waking up. Just how oblivious are we when asleep? Our inertia during sleep poses severe practical problems to answering this question, but clues are provided by some common observations. Sleepers can easily be woken up by being spoken to, and yet they can sleep uninterruptedly through loud noise. Anyone who has fallen asleep in a moving car or on a train is surrounded by a very high level of noise, but often relatively quiet sounds – somebody saying that they have arrived, or an announcement on a railway station tannoy system heard in the distance – will wake them up. It follows that since they can choose what will wake them up they must be continuously monitoring what they are hearing while asleep. In psychological terms, it is obvious that attentional and perceptual processes are functioning at some level.

Ian Oswald and his co-workers (337) took advantage of the fact that during stage 2 sleep it is commonplace to elicit very large EEG potentials ('K complexes') of about 150 microvolts from peak to trough which can be elicited with even fairly quiet sounds (although K complexes also occur spontaneously, with no stimulation). They instructed their subjects to listen out for particular names, and then played a variety of names to them when they were asleep, including their own. The K complex responses to the target names were larger and more reliable than responses to control names, and subjects also almost invariably responded to their own name with a large K complex – another example of the so-called 'cocktail party effect', where one unerringly picks out fragments of conversation relating to oneself from a medley of sounds.

An experiment (260) which showed that speed of awakening was faster to a subject's own name played forwards than backwards confirmed this finding. Anecdotal accounts of being able to listen out for babies' cries, or other particular sounds, are of course ubiquitous. Not surprisingly the empirical evidence confirms this universal experience. It could be argued that this behaviour may be supported by attentional mechanisms at a simpler level than the more complex processing that goes on during wakefulness. That is, it is one thing to remain vigilant to one of a small number of predetermined sounds, and another to make qualitative judgements about all the sounds that might be heard in the night. The overwhelmingly large EEG slow waves of stages 3 and 4 make it impracticable to record K complexes, and K complexes are absent during REM sleep, so K complex evidence cannot be used to assess perceptual processing during deep slow wave sleep, or REM sleep.

Two experiments from an American laboratory extended the Oswald group's work. Firstly they confirmed that K complexes were more reliably elicited by a subject's own name in stage 2 sleep, and further showed that this effect was measurable in heart rate (HR) and finger plethysmograph (FP – measuring the blood supply to the skin, which is normally reduced by alerting or alarming stimuli) (281). Using these autonomic measures it was also shown that perceptual discriminations were being made in stage REM sleep, although not in stages 3 and 4.

In the second experiment, subjects were conditioned while awake to associate a highly unpleasant blast of noise (produced by 'two pairs of dual freon boat horns') with either a low-pitch or high-pitch tone of relatively low intensity (40 dB). The conditioned signal elicited FP and HR responses in all stages of slow wave sleep, including stages 3 and 4, and K complexes in stage 2. Interestingly, these conditioned stimuli (undoubtedly well established, since responses were made to them in the other sleep stages) did not produce any response in REM sleep. Since they had established that meaningful stimuli can be processed during REM sleep, the authors argued that these findings support the notion that only cognitively meaningful material is dealt with in this sleep stage. The results could also be interpreted as evidence for the mental activity of REM sleep being peculiarly efficient at coping with stimuli denoting unpleasant consequences. This is, in essence, the Freudian view of what 'dreamwork' does – render potentially upsetting internally generated ideas harmless by transforming them into symbolic codes.

Neither of these studies throws much light on the actual level of perceptual processing going on, however, since only *particular* stimuli, previously defined during wakefulness, were used. Subjects did not have to do more than set up 'templates' to recognize these particular sounds. The experiments have, however, confirmed that some monitoring of the outside world does go on throughout sleep, so that only signals previously defined as being 'important' result in our waking up.

An experiment which goes some way to answering this question (381) was reported by Benny Shanon. Tape-recorded words were played to subjects throughout the night. As in the Oswald experiment, subjects were instructed to listen out for target words (two) and to make a response if they could by pressing a key taped to their right hand. In addition to non-target English words the tape recording contained an equal number of words in French, including translations of the target words. As in other experiments the target words evoked K complexes more frequently than non-target words. Interestingly, K complexes to English words were more frequent than to French words, indicating that some selection of stimuli on the basis of language was taking place, rather than simply the sound of the particular targets chosen for the subject. This work thus suggests that auditory perceptual analysis continues at a high level of semantic complexity even in stage 2 sleep, even though most sounds are then studiously ignored in the interests of staying asleep.

ESP during sleep

Many of us have a story to tell of happenings which seem totally inexplicable unless we resort to a parapsychological explanation. That is, an individual somehow became aware of facts which were inaccessible to their senses (clairvoyance), or had a vision of the future (precognition), or they received a communication from another person with whom there was no physical contact (telepathy). It would be wonderful indeed if we had all these powers, and even the most hardened sceptic is more readily disposed to believe in them than some other equally fatuous proposition, which, if necessary, could be readily disproved.

There is a good case to be made for treating apparently impossible claims with some respect – even if they seem impossible to test empirically. Darwins's theory of natural selection and J. J. Thomson's discovery of electrons are examples of advances which were initially treated with almost universal disbelief by scientists in their own time. The empirical investigation of paranormal phenomena began over 100 years ago, with the foundation of the Society for Psychical Research by Henry Sidgwick and Frederick Myers. Despite a century of effort to establish the validity of these phenomena any unbiased assessment must be that no clear conclusion can yet be reached.

The credulity of many parapsychologists, and their generally sloppy use of scientific control is well documented by David Marks, among others, in a splendid book debunking particular claims about clairvoyance and other psychic powers (141). The most extraordinary story in this context is that of Project Alpha. In 1979 James S. McDonnell, board chairman of the McDonnell-Douglas Aircraft Corporation made a grant of $500,000 for paranormal research at Washington University. The grant-holder announced that he was going to investigating psycho-kinetic metal-bending in children, and advertised for subjects. James Randi, a professional magician, asked two young conjurers he knew to volunteer, and they were the only subjects chosen out of 300 applicants. For three years they were at the McDonnell lab, astounding the parapsychologists with their tricks. All through this period Randi was writing to the grant holder, offering to attend experimental sessions as a consultant, but with no response. The two conjurers were under strict instructions to answer honestly if they were ever directly asked whether they were cheating. They weren't. The account of the simple manoeuvres which were sufficient to delude the team of parapsychologists make hilarious if somewhat chilling reading.

Professor Hansel's book on ESP (185) provides an excellent account of the total failure of scientists and scientific method in the investigation of ESP and other paranormal phenomena, showing (a) how easily otherwise brilliant scientists can be hoodwinked by charlatans, and (b) how difficult it is to deal with outright fraud by investigators themselves. Science crucially depends on honesty and good will and can be subverted all too easily into a spurious scientism, relying on the authority of science more than its methodology. In this century 'racial theory' and genetics have both been exposed to this sort of treatment, with catastrophic political consequences. At least the consequences of people believing psychic flim-flam are of little importance to anyone other than themselves. Fringe science tends not to be good science, and of course bad science is not science at all. Whatever one's own beliefs, it is therefore essential to consider evidence presented as being 'scientific' with a certain degree of scepticism.

Clairvoyance and precognition have both been claimed to take place in dreams. Accounts of prophesies in dreams are common to the scriptures of many religions and may also be invoked in more secular epic legends, particularly to establish the divinity or at least the supernatural authority of great kings. Even as modern a tyrant as Adolf Hitler ascribed such a significance to one of his dreams while a soldier in the trenches in the First World War. This dream (of an explosion and the collapse of the trench) woke him up, and leaving the shelter of the trench for the night air he was saved from an actual direct hit which killed most of his comrades. Soldiers might be expected to frequently dream about explosions, and direct hits on trenches were regular occurrences. It is not reported how often Hitler used to flee his trench during the night, but this may also have been a regular habit. As with many anecdotal accounts of prophetic dreams, the coincidence begins to seem less unlikely the more one considers the matter.

Commoners and humble worshippers are not conventionally expected to presume to prophesy in their dreams. J. W. Dunne's book, *An Experiment with Time*, published in 1927 (107) rekindled the interest of psychical researchers in the topic, as he claimed that in his own dreams he had as much access to future events as to actual memories. Besterman (48) tested this proposition by asking subjects to keep dream diaries, and send him carbon copies every morning, so that a check could be kept on any events which were predicted by the dreams. The results were very disappointing, and even when Dunne himself served as a subject, he only recorded 17 dreams in a 4-month period, and they were inclusively prophetic. Precognition is difficult to deal with in the sleep laboratory because it occurs so rarely (if at all!), and no attempts have been made to collect precognitive dreams from REM awakenings.

Telepathic dreams are, however, more amenable to investigation, and a famous series of experiments conducted by Ullman and his associates and reported in their book *Dream Telepathy* (415) comprise the core of evidence on this subject. The procedure in these experiments was to employ two subjects, one as a 'receiver' who would sleep in the laboratory, and the other chosen by the receiver from members of staff in the laboratory as the 'sender', who would remain awake through the night. The sender would be alerted by the experimenter when the receiver had started a period of REM sleep, and then concentrate on a picture given to him or her by the experimenter. When the REM sleep period was ending, the experimenter awakened the receiver through an intercom obtaining an account of any dreams, and asking questions to clarify the imagery of the dreams. In the morning further questioning took place to establish the precise nature of the images in the dreams that had been interrupted during the night. Tape recordings of the dream reports and interviews were then matched with the stimulus cards used by the senders by an outside judge who had no knowledge of which stimulus related to which REM sleep episode, or by the receivers themselves.

The most spectacular results were obtained with one subject as receiver, Robert Van de Castle, a well-known parapsychologist, whose dreams matched the target stimuli being looked at by the sender on every occasion over eight nights of recording – statistically, a highly significant score. Subsequent attempts to repeat this feat, in which other experimenters well known in sleep and dream research collaborated, failed to achieve results better than chance (34).

Hansel's analysis (185) of the reasons for this failure are that the original experiments were flawed, in that the experimenter knew what stimuli were being telepathically transmitted to the receiver. In their questioning of the receiver they may have even unwittingly provided cues which facilitated the subsequent matching of tape recordings to pictures. When conditions were tightened up, in the subsequent experiments, it was therefore not surprising that the results could not be repeated. In these later studies it was ensured that experimenters remained unaware of which stimuli were being transmitted. The choice of sender was also limited to three candidates previously chosen by the investigators. Adrian Parker in his book *States of Mind* (340) argues that perhaps the less friendly atmosphere in the laboratory when sceptical scientists were present may have put the receiver off his task during his dreams: the more rigorous the methodology, the greater the connotation of suspicion of fraud. This idea, that science may be intrinsically inimical to ESP, is understandably invoked by established charlatans such as Uri Geller, but many investigating parapsychologists also seem to share a certain ambivalence in their attitudes to science as a testing ground for their deeply held beliefs. As with all the other work on parapsychological phenomena, in the case of dream telepathy one has to return a verdict of 'not proven'.

Sleep learning

One of the earliest applications of the EEG in assessing perceptual and memory functioning during sleep was directed at 'sleep learning' – the rather attractive notion that instead of having to work away learning material during the day, it could be painlessly drilled while the student was fast asleep. In order to test this idea Emmons and Simon (115) used EEG recordings to present material only when subjects were indubitably asleep. Subjects showed no recollection next day of this material presented to them during sleep. However, there is evidence that fairly subtle perceptual processing can go on during sleep. Evans (121) made verbal suggestions to sleeping subjects that their left or right leg would become cramped and uncomfortable when they heard a particular word. Subjects moved the appropriate leg as though it was indeed uncomfortable. This 'sleep learning' was retained very well over a week, and one of the subjects tested asleep again after six months still moved their leg when given the word they had learned when asleep six months earlier. No recollection of these cue words could be elicited from the subjects during the day, either by direct questioning or using indirect free associative techniques. This result intriguingly suggests a dissociation between waking and sleeping life, reminding one of the dilemma of Chuang-tzu, the Chinese philosopher who posed the following in the third century BC:

> One night I dreamed that I was a butterfly, fluttering hither and thither, content with my lot. Suddenly, I awoke and I was Chuang-tzu again. Who am I in reality? A butterfly dreaming that I am Chuang-tzu or Chuang-tzu imagining he was a butterfly?

To return to the issue of whether learning can take place during a sleep period, one might ask whether stimuli which woke the subject up would be remembered. Portnoff (349) woke subjects up throughout the night, and presented them with lists of words to remember. They were then either allowed to go back to sleep immediately or kept awake for 5 minutes. Next day the subjects could not recall very many of the words they had seen when they had been allowed to go back to sleep immediately, and recalled many more from the trials after which they had been kept awake for a while, although they had shown just as much evidence of learning in both conditions. Similarly, Koukkou and Lehmann (253) found that sentences read out to sleeping subjects were not recalled next day unless the subjects had both been woken by the presentation and stayed awake (with measurable alpha in EEG) for at least 25 seconds. Awakenings with low frequency alpha rhythm were associated with poorer subsequent recall than those with high frequency alpha rhythm (indicating higher cortical arousal). These experimenters went on to confirm this finding in a later study, also showing that the level of cortical activation during the presentation of the stimulus sentences (which were to be learned) was not so crucial in determining their memorability as the level of activation afterwards (262). Taken together, these experiments suggest that while perceptual processing may go on during sleep, the immediate consolidation of memory in a retrievable form only properly occurs during wakefulness, and is prevented by sleep, or disrupted by going to sleep.

When we are awake a novel stimulus almost always gains our attention, and may elicit a range of physiological responses which are controlled by the autonomic nervous system. Autonomically controlled events such as changes in heart rate, the constriction of peripheral blood vessels and the galvanic skin response all form part of this pattern of responses which are known as the orienting response (OR). The gradual diminution of these responses with repeated stimuli (such as, for instance, the ticking of a clock) is called habituation. Habituation is probably the simplest form of learning in our repertoire, although the Soviet psychologist E. N. Sokolov has established that habituation of the OR can be in response to the meaning of a stimulus, as well as its physical characteristics (390). Conventional methods of assessing whether learning has taken place demand voluntary responses from subjects (for instance in repeating back lists of words or numbers) and these are obviously inappropriate when the subject is asleep. The physiological measures used to measure the orienting response and its habituation make no such demands, and any learning through habituation should be evident in a sleeper as much as in a waking subject. K complex responses during stage 2 sleep and alpha responses (brief bursts of EEG alpha rhythm) during REM sleep are similarly involuntary responses which may be sensitive to the effects of habituation.

The Russian work had established that an OR which had habituated during wakefulness returned with full force (dishabituated) if sleep onset intervened (391). It is, however, a common observation that we can become accustomed to sleeping in a noisy environment, implying that habituation during sleep does occur. During stage 2 sleep auditory stimuli commonly elicit EEG K complexes – the easily recognized excursions of up to 150 microvolts which also occur spontaneously, and form one of the defining characteristics of this sleep stage. Studying the way in which these responses habituate to sounds should cast light on the general issue of how accustomed sounds, whether cocks crowing, traffic noise or nearby church bells, lose their power to disturb our sleep. Unfortunately, despite much experimental work on this subject, no simple answer has emerged.

Evidence for habituation during sleep has been contradictory. A number of studies have shown that K complexes do not habituate. That is, if stimuli are regularly presented during stage 2 sleep they will elicit these arousal responses as much at the end of the night as they did at the beginning, with little evidence of reduction even during particular phases of stage 2 sleep (e.g. 222). On the other hand Hugh Firth has reported habituation during sleep, in that while a novel stimulus almost invariably elicited a K complex, when repeated the rate of responding dropped to about 50 per cent within three presentations (130), and this level of responding then persisted for as long as that particular stimulus is presented. (The level of spontaneous responding, when no stimuli were presented, was about 20 per cent.) If interstimulus intervals are long, and trials are averaged over periods of ten minutes or more (as for instance in Johnson and Lubin's study (223)) no evidence of K complex habituation will be found, while if the intervals between stimuli are short and regular there is clear evidence of habituation. (This very fast habituation to trains of stimuli with short interstimulus intervals has been recently confirmed by some Dutch workers (69).)

This very swift habituation may or may not have any bearing on the issue of how we become accustomed to particular noises over a period of days and weeks. As we have seen, the evidence on learning during sleep is not encouraging in this respect.

Habituation during sleep is therefore swift but incomplete, in so far as the rate of K complex responses in the 'habituated' subject is still over twice as high as when no stimuli are presented. It is also fragile, in that changes in sleep stage for instance may cause dishabituation. In addition, different response systems, indexed by EEG and autonomic measures may habituate independently, and behave differently according to sleep stage and interstimulus interval. In Firth's experiment EEG alpha rhythm responses during REM sleep habituated regardless of the length of the interstimulus interval, and so did skin potential and heart rate responses during stages 2 and 4.

Behaviour during sleep

It might seem a contradiction in terms to talk of behaviour while asleep. We tend to think of sleep as being a sort of oblivious coma, when all interactions with the outside world are suspended, short of being woken up. People move about quite a lot while asleep, and if they didn't they would soon develop bed sores. Time-lapse photography of sleeping subjects shows them in an apparent frenzy of activity during the night, none of which they remember in the morning. Paraplegic patients in hospital who cannot move for themselves need to be turned every two hours. This tossing and turning during the night is obviously adaptive and necessary. Sleepwalking itself is somewhat unusual, although talking, groaning, crying out or laughing is quite common.

Sleeptalking

The idea that we might be speaking in our sleep without remembering it in the morning can be worrying, especially if we have things to hide. In *The*

Adventures of Tom Sawyer Tom and Huckleberry were the secret witnesses to a murder:

> Tom's fearful secret and gnawing conscience disturbed his sleep for as much as a week after this; and at breakfast one morning, Sid said:
> 'You pitch around and talk in your sleep so much that you keep me awake about half the time.'
> Tom blanched and dropped his eyes.
> 'It's a bad sign,' said Aunt Polly gravely. 'What you got on your mind, Tom?'
> 'Nothing. Nothing't I know of.' But the boy's hand shook so that he spilled his coffee.
> 'And you do talk such stuff,' Sid said. 'Last night you said, "It's blood, it's blood, that's what it is!" You said that over and over. And you said, "Don't torment me so – I'll tell." Tell what? What is it you'll tell?'
> . . . after that [Tom] complained of toothache for a week, and tied up his jaws every night. He never knew that Sid lay nightly watching, and frequently slipped the bandage free, and then leaned on his elbow listening a good while at a time, and afterwards slipped the bandage back to its place again. Tom's distress of mind wore off gradually, and the toothache grew irksome and was discarded. If Sid really managed to make anything out of Tom's disjointed mutterings, he kept it to himself. (414)

It is difficult to estimate how many people talk in their sleep, because if they do they are probably unaware of it unless somebody hears them, and tells them about it afterwards. A survey has shown that about two-thirds of college students know that they have talked in their sleep at least once in their lives, and about half the sample were, by their own accounts, persistent sleeptalkers (152). Since these frequencies are probably an underestimate of the actual prevalence of sleeptalking, as many who do may be unaware of it, this aspect of sleeping behaviour must be regarded as commonplace, and essentially normal.

Some people talk more in their sleep than others, varying from the odd word to continuous, understandable monologues. One individual's utterances, tape recorded by friends while he was asleep, have been collected and published as a book (284). Arthur Arkin, an American psychologist who specialized in the study of sleeptalking, quotes this example:

> Attention! Attention! Let me stand on that table, they can't hear me. Attention! Now this is a scavenger hunt. You all got your slips. First one there; a yellow robin's egg! Second one: a wolf's dream! Third: a Welsh shoelace! Fourth: a dirty napkin used by Garbo! Fifth: a tree trunk! Sixth: Valentino's automobile hubcap! Seventh: one of the swans in Swan Lake!

Eighth: a Chattanooga choo-choo! Ninth: a bell from the Bell Song in Lakme! Tenth: Yrma Loy! Eleventh: the Hudson River! Twelfth: a teller from the San Francisco Bank of America! Thirteenth: a witch's tail! Fourteenth: David Susskind's mother! Fifteenth: nobody and his sister: That's it! That's it! Now everybody disperse, disperse. Meet back here – three-quarters of an hour, three-quarters of an hour. Come on, we can win, you know we can. Now first of all – oh, let's see – you get one, three, five, seven, nine and twelve; you get two and four: I'll get the rest! O.K., let's go. O.K., everybody back, three-quarters of an hour are up! IT'S OVER!!!!! Uhhh! Aaaahhhh! Ummmmmmmmhhhhh! (18)

This was the shortest of his published somliloquoys. According to Arkin (who met him) Dion McGregor, a professional writer of lyrics, seemed perfectly sane when awake, even if slightly odd. This individual was simply unusually articulate when asleep, and the somewhat weird ideas expressed may represent the sort of autistic (or A-type, as described by Bleuler) thinking typical of dreaming sleep (discussed in Chapter 6, pp. 98–105).

In a laboratory study of self-confessed chronic sleeptalkers Arkin and co-workers (18) confirmed previous findings that for most people sleep-talking occurred mostly during NREM sleep, although about a quarter of the episodes occurred during REM sleep. He noted large individual differences among his 13 subjects, one of whom was garrulous enough to have contributed almost half the total number of utterances collected, mostly during REM sleep. The distribution of talking across sleep stages for the other 12 subjects was 19 per cent REM sleep, 28 per cent stage 4, 26 per cent stage 3, 28 per cent stage 2 and 1 per cent stage 1. Sleeptalking thus occurred in all sleep stages approximately in proportion to their relative prevalence in the night, with the exception of stage 1 sleep, when subjects remained unusually silent. Arkin points out that while sleeptalking may be said to be *associated with* a particular sleep stage, the EEG, EOG and EMG measures tend to be so contaminated with movement artefacts during utterances that precise definition of sleep stage is not normally possible.

In a further experiment Arkin and his associates (20) woke sleeptalkers up after they had made an utterance to ask them what had been going through their minds. Having recorded what had been said by the sleeping subject, they could compare the waking recollections with the content of the utterances. Evidence of concordance of subject matter between the utterance and the recollections were clearest after REM awakenings, least clear after stage 3 and 4 awakenings, and intermediate after stage 2 awakenings. Thus REM sleeptalking typically provides a commentary on the dream in progress, while no obvious relationship between what is spoken and what is remembered exists for stage 3 and 4 sleeptalking, possibly because of a failure to recall non-REM sleep mentation in any detail rather than because what was said had no bearing whatsoever on what the subject was thinking about.

Arkin (19) also reports experiments in which he attempted to engage sleeptalkers in conversation. Many anecdotal accounts exist of such conversations which can be quite extended, but which are not recalled by the sleeping talker next day. Arkin tried responding to sleeptalkers when they started talking in their sleep, and also initiating conversations himself, trying at all times to get into the spirit of what the sleeping chronic sleeptalker seemed to be saying. He was generally unsuccessful in maintaining any extended dialogues, and attributes this to the lack of intimacy between himself and his subjects – most such dialogues are reported from between husband and wife.

Sleepwalking

Getting up and walking about is not consistent with our definition of sleep, so sleepwalking is an intrinsically paradoxical activity. It is, however, not uncommon – a recent survey in Sweden found that 75 out of 212 children had at least one episode (244) and a similar American survey found an incidence of 15 per cent. It can persist into adulthood, and like other disorders of arousal, as somnambulism, enuresis, bruxism and night terrors have been called, will tend to reoccur during periods of psychological stress. It will be discussed in this context in Chapters 12 and 13, on sleep disorders. However, a behaviour which is experienced by such a large minority of the population can hardly be called abnormal, so it will also be considered here.

After getting out of bed the sleepwalker may get dressed, and then walks about, often repetitively, or may remain standing still. He or she typically returns to bed spontaneously after as much as 30 minutes of activity, and remembers nothing about the incident in the morning, when there may be some puzzlement at finding clothing scattered, removed or put on. Observations of sleepwalkers (366) describe them as being able to avoid obstacles, and even on one occasion to negotiate a dangerous walk along the edge of a roof. They tend to adopt rigid, unnatural postures when not moving about. These can be adjusted by the waking observer, and the sleepwalker will passively adopt whatever position is imposed on them. This cataleptic behaviour (typical of some schizophrenic patients) is also shown by subjects who have been deprived of sleep for an extended period (14). Sleepwalkers will respond to verbal suggestions, but do not engage in coherent conversation.

EEG recordings have shown that sleepwalking episodes always begin during stages 3 or 4 (66). While walking about, the delta waves may attenuate in the adult, to be replaced by faster frequencies, and when returning to bed the subject normally enters stage 2 sleep. EEG recordings of sleepwalkers naturally tend to be confounded by signals produced by actual physical movement, but careful analysis of the EEG in children (66) has shown that the episodes are preceded by an unusual pattern of high voltage delta rhythms which are in synchrony on both sides of the head. These persist during somnambulism. Sleepwalking is therefore unlikely to have anything to do with dreaming. It is rather a condition in which sleep and arousal mechanisms seem to have become locked in an unresolved conflict, with the sleeping victim behaving with the inappropriateness of a malfunctioning automaton.

There is good evidence for a genetic determination for sleepwalking. Monozygotic, or identical, twins show a 47 per cent concordance for this behaviour, while dizygotic, or non-identical, twins only show a 7 per cent concordance (31). There are many anecdotal accounts of families whose members all walk in their sleep. For instance, a student who consulted me about problems caused by sleepwalking in her hall of residence revealed that the whole of her family had once woken up in the early hours of the morning seated around the kitchen table, where they had all congregated in their sleep.

Waking up

The ending of sleep is as much a function of sleep mechanisms as its initiation. What normally determines when we wake up? The answer to this question will depend to a great extent on factors determined by the circadian (24-hour) rhythms which crucially affect sleep, discussed in Chapter 3 (pp. 40–9). Assuming, however, that sleep has not been displaced from its proper time, at night, what is it that wakes us up in the morning?

Arousal thresholds

We are all exposed to some level of noise during the night, whether living in the depths of the country, next to a busy urban thoroughfare, or under an approach flight path to a nearby airport. It is of some practical importance to know what levels of noise disturb sleep.

A number of experiments were done to estimate arousal thresholds through the night before EEG measures of sleep depth were available, beginning in 1862 when a student of the psychophysicist Fechner established that there was an early maximum threshold followed by a progressive reduction through the night (251). Michelson's work (303), published in 1897, is illustrative of the methods used in those early days. He varied the amount of noise by dropping steel balls on to a metal surface from different heights, increasing the length of drop progressively until the subject woke, and did this every half-hour through the night. Figure 8.1 shows a general decrease in threshold towards the early hours, superimposed on what looks like a 90-minute cycle.

The relation between sleep depth and the EEG was first assessed in the 1930s (54), using a constant tone stimulus and then asking subjects whether they were awake. The nineteenth-century findings on the decline in depth of sleep over the course of the night were confirmed. Thresholds for awakening were also

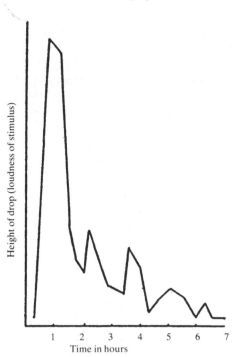

Figure 8.1 Awakening threshold through the night.
Source: (338).

found to be highly correlated with the amplitude and prevalence of delta waves in the EEG. Later work (56) has established that slow wave sleep depth, defined in terms of awakening threshold, is best predicted simply by the number and size of slow waves in the EEG. Estimates of sleep depth during REM sleep have varied somewhat, but it seems roughly similar to that of stage 2 sleep. Absolute magnitudes of stimulus intensity required to wake people up have also varied between different laboratories, from around 40 dB to over 90 dB, for instance, in stage 4 sleep. The rank order of slow wave sleep stages in terms of sleep depth has, however, been consistently confirmed.

The elderly seem particularly sensitive to noise at night, despite their hearing loss. Sounds which cause sleep stage changes in middle-aged and young subjects will wake up people in their seventies. In one study (276) 70-year-olds were shown to be particularly sensitive to sudden loud noises (a sonic boom) compared to 45-year-olds and 8-year-olds, almost invariably waking from REM or stage 2 sleep and about half the time from stage 4, while the younger subjects almost always slept through, whatever their sleep stage. Flyover noise – lower in volume but sustained for longer – woke the elderly up on about one-third of the occasions, compared to about one-tenth of the occasions for the younger subjects.

Waking at a particular time

While most of us would rely on an alarm clock if we had to get up at a particular time there are many individuals who claim to be able to wake up whenever they wish. They may have a ritual such as banging their head on the pillow as many times as the time at which they plan to wake – 'seven times before going to sleep, you'll wake at seven o'clock in the morning'.

How reliably can they estimate time during sleep? People who claim to be able to do it have been shown to be remarkably accurate in their times of awakening (329) and it seemed that they did not achieve their punctuality by, for instance, periodically waking up and looking at the bedside alarm clock. Those who claimed not to be able to wake at a specific time were much worse at achieving a wakening on time than those who claimed to be able to do it. A more recent experimental study (451) using EEG/EOG recordings involved a randomly selected group of 22 subjects, who had made no particular claims about being able to wake up at a particular time. They were required to wake up at a pre-arranged time between 02.00 and 05.00, and were promised extra payment for their services as subjects if they managed to ring a bell within 10 minutes of their allotted time. They were only allowed one response, and had no clocks available to them in the laboratory bedroom, which was windowless, air-conditioned and sound-proofed, so no cues as to time could be picked up from the outside world.

There was no evidence that sleep patterns differed on experimental nights from the two adaptation nights, so far as the proportions of sleep stages were concerned, but there were 33 awakenings with bell responses out of the 44 experimental nights, and 14 of these were within 10 minutes of the target times. While this level of accuracy is not as good as self-described 'reliable wakers' can be at a reasonable time in the morning, it was still strongly statistically significant, indicating that most of us have some ability to assess the passage of time while asleep, and then have some control over waking up. (It may have been instructive to perform the same experiment on subjects while awake, without access to a clock and in a featureless environment for between 2 and 5 hours – I suspect that people would perform little better when awake, and perhaps worse.)

CHAPTER 9

Determinants of Sleep Quality

This chapter is concerned with the effects of various regimes on sleep itself, rather than any behavioural consequences, or with the influence of biological rhythms on sleep patterns. It is normally very difficult to observe spontaneous behaviour in adult human beings without the mere presence of the observer strongly affecting what is observed. When sleep mechanisms take over there is little scope for self-consciousness, and psychophysiological recordings then allow direct measurement of the sleeping brain's free-running rhythms. Its response to experimental manipulation, including for instance changes in the times available for sleep, the deprivation of food, or the effects of exercise, not only inform our knowledge of sleep mechanisms but even provide clues as to the function of sleep itself.

Food, exercise and sleep

Food and sleep

People will frequently ascribe the quality of sleep (or lack of it) to the previous night's food intake. It is undoubtedly true that indigestion will disturb sleep, but does food have any more subtle effects? A test of the efficacy of Horlicks as a night-time drink, intended to induce sleep, at Ian Oswald's laboratory in Edinburgh, used a young adult group (mean age 22 years) and an older group (mean age 55 years) (65). While Horlicks (or in fact another malted milk drink) had little effect on sleep onset time in either group, restlessness during the night was reduced in both, and in the older subjects the advantage conferred by the nourishing bedtime drinks was greatest in the second half of the night, reducing restlessness and increasing total sleep time.

Drastic reductions in food intake are symptomatic of anorexia nervosa, and patients suffering from this condition have been found to sleep little and fitfully (85). When the same people were putting on weight they slept more, and with fewer interruptions. Also, there was a change in the proportion of different stages of sleep during remission, so that there was a massive increase in the amount of deep slow wave sleep at the expense of light slow wave sleep stages. These findings are consistent with the idea that slow wave sleep is concerned with bodily anabolic (growth) processes, which will be discussed more fully in Chapter 11 (pp. 163–7) in the context of sleep function.

Exercise and sleep

As with food, folklore has much to say about exercise and its effects on sleep – to claim a good night's sleep to be the result of strenuous exercise the previous day is entirely uncontroversial. However, the experimental evidence on the subject is by no means unambiguous. A number of studies have found that human sleep was unaffected by high amounts of exercise the previous day (30, 191, 449), although evidence from experiments on rats had shown that prolonged exercise increased the amount of slow wave sleep.

Other experimenters have compared the effects of exercise in trained and untrained subjects, some finding no effect of exercise (420), while others have reported an increase in slow wave (stage 3) sleep only in trained subjects (173). The large number of studies addressing themselves to this issue have varied considerably in the amount of exercise used, the physical fitness of the subjects, length of time over which they were monitored, and the scoring system for slow wave sleep. Jim Horne's work has indicated an increase in stage 3 sleep in the first half of the night following exercise (206) and from a comprehensive review of the evidence Horne has concluded that untrained subjects show little if any sleep EEG effects following daytime exercise, while trained subjects do have increases in stages 3 and 4 in the first recovery night after raised exercise *rate*. That is, the deep slow wave sleep stages are elevated if the rate of energy expenditure during the day is increased, rather than merely the total amount (204).

This suggestion was followed up by an experiment in which subjects' rate of energy expenditure (REE) was elevated to a high level, but not for long enough to significantly affect the total energy expenditure (TEE) for the day. The increase in stages 3 and 4 sleep before the first REM sleep period of the night was of the same order as had been found in other experiments when both REE and TEE had been increased (67). The idea that exercise might increase the need for bodily restitution through its heavy energy demands, and that deep slow wave sleep would then be increased to accommodate this requirement is unsupported by this evidence. Rather, the effects are probably mediated through some other change caused by exercise, such as increased body temperature.

Horne has further shown that athletes who exercised strenuously in their tracksuits, with no cooling, showed elevations in rectal temperature of over

2 degrees Celsius, and elevated levels of stage 4 sleep the following night. When exercised in light, damp clothing, under cooling fans the same athletes showed an increase of rectal temperature of only 1 degree Celsius, and no change in sleep from baseline levels (205). In a further study he demonstrated that passive heating (by lying in a warm bath for 90 minutes) also caused increases in stage 4 sleep (208). Body temperature clearly affects sleep, in reptiles as well as in mammals: a study on crocodiles has shown that warming the animals produced evidence of slow waves in the sleeping EEG which had not hitherto been observed in reptiles. Since the total amount of exercise expended does not determine sleep quality so much as the rate achieved, it is unlikely that this effect is mediated through the effect on metabolic rate over the day. It is unclear as yet whether the changes in human sleep are caused by the effects of warming on the musculature, or whether brain temperature itself can be altered by these procedures, and affect the quality of sleep directly. These findings are interesting in suggesting a common sleep mechanism between reptiles and ourselves, and, again, will be discussed further in Chapter 11, when the functions of sleep will be considered.

Effects of drugs on sleep

The most widely used drugs in our society are nicotine, alcohol, caffeine, and the benzodiazepines, or minor tranquillizers, some of which are marketed as hypnotic, or sleep-inducing, medicines. All these drugs are taken regularly over long periods of time by a large proportion of the population, so their effects on sleep, if any, must be assessed carefully. Prescribed drugs which affect sleep include the anti-depressants, the major tranquillizers, the barbiturates and opiates, and while the numbers of people involved are small (compared for instance to smoking) some of these drugs' effects on sleep are considerable. Other 'recreational' drugs such as cannabis, amphetamine, cocaine and LSD are commonly taken only periodically, except by a few.

Smoking

Comparing 50 smokers with 50 non-smokers, researchers at Pennsylvania State University found that the smokers took longer to get to sleep than the controls, although other sleep parameters were unaffected (394). Of course comparing self-selected groups like this may not tell us so much about the effects of smoking on sleep as about differences between people who take up smoking and those who choose not to. For instance, the smokers generally drank more coffee than the non-smokers (although the two groups did not differ in their regular consumption of alcohol or other drugs). However, within the smoking group those who drank more than three cups of coffee a day did not take any longer to get to sleep than those who drank less than three cups a day, suggesting that coffee consumption was not an important influence on how long these people took to get to sleep.

Crucial evidence on the effects of smoking on sleep came from 8 heavy smokers (consuming an average of two packs a day for over two years) who abruptly stopped smoking. Time spent awake during the sleep period, and sleep-onset latency were immediately reduced, with the time taken getting to sleep dropping from an average of 52 minutes when smoking to 18 minutes on the first two nights after giving it up. This improvement in sleep quality was maintained by the four subjects who continued to abstain for two weeks.

While smokers adapt to some of the effects of nicotine, such as nausea, studies have shown that it persists in elevating heart rate, blood pressure and general psychophysiological arousal in even the most dedicated addicts. These immediate effects of nicotine are probably sufficient to explain the delay of sleep onset by an average of half an hour.

Alcohol

Much interest has been focussed on REM sleep following drinking, as alcohol is essentially a sedative, or cortical-depressant drug like the barbiturates, which are known to suppress REM sleep. The effect of 1 gram per kilogram body weight (equivalent to about a quarter of a bottle of spirits for an average-sized man) taken on one occasion only has been reported to inhibit REM sleep to some extent for the following night (171, 446). When this regime was continued for five days, however, REM sleep time recovered, and in fact exceeded baseline levels. Over a four-day recovery period REM sleep time declined to baseline values. This finding was in general confirmed in another study using a slightly lower dosage (0.9 gm/kg) and appreciably more subjects (371). Some evidence was also found for the reduction in REM sleep to be confined to the first half of the first night after drinking. In those subjects REM sleep levels in the second half of the night were elevated as if in compensation for the REM sleep lost in the first half. On the second and third nights after the same dose there was no reduction in REM sleep time, and no REM 'rebound' was noticeable on recovery nights.

Sleep-onset latency has been found to be reduced with moderately high doses, and while objective measures with lower doses (0.32 and 0.64 gm/kg) did not show statistically significant effects on latency, the subjects involved did reliably report that they felt they had got to sleep sooner (399).

Alcohol is metabolized relatively quickly, so that of a dose of 1 gm/kg taken before bedtime, about 50 per cent will be eliminated in the first four hours. The effects on sleep are consequently not simple even within a night, and over extended periods of regular drinking sleep patterns may also show progressive changes. Evidence from young healthy volunteers suggesting that moderate levels of drinking does any harm to sleep is inconsistent, and a nightcap may actually help them get to sleep. If it were being assessed as a hypnotic drug, alcohol would come out as being moderately effective and relatively harmless (compared for instance to the barbiturates).

A possibly serious side-effect of drinking has however been reported amongst elderly patients suffering from chronic emphysema (a chronic obstructive pulmonary disease) (109). In these patients 1gm/kg alcohol reduced total REM sleep time from about 1 hour to about 25 minutes and also reduced total sleep time by almost an hour. In addition, oxygen levels in arterial blood, estimated from analyses of expired air, were found to be significantly lower than on control nights, and was accompanied by an average elevation in heart rate. The oxygen desaturation was especially marked during REM sleep. Although alcohol did not seem to directly cause any cardiac arrhythmia, as the authors point out, any failure to maintain adequate levels of oxygen in the blood will provide an additional challenge to the cardiovascular system. Some widely advertised palliatives for bronchial conditions (such as Night Nurse in the United Kingdom) contain an appreciable amount of alcohol which, added to a moderate intake earlier in the evening, might be enough to disturb and reduce these patients' sleep, rather than improve it.

Caffeine

The effects of caffeine are not simply to 'keep you awake' – i.e. to increase sleep latency. Rather, it reduces the amount of deep slow wave sleep, increases the number of arousals, and, at high doses (300 mg) will cause early waking after only three hours or so of sleep (154). A cup of strong coffee contains about 100 mg caffeine.

Anxiolytics

The minor tranquillizers, or anxiolytics (anxiety-reducing drugs), first became available in the early 1960s after the discovery and patenting of chlordiazepoxide (Librium) and diazepam (Valium) by chemists at Hoffman-La Roche. While many different benzodiazepines have now been developed, these two remain typical, and are still brand leaders. Their usage consistently increased over 15 years, reaching a peak in the mid-1970s.

Chlordiazepoxide is widely prescribed as an anxiolytic, but, like some other benzodiazepines, is also quite frequently prescribed to patients who present themselves with sleep problems. Ernest Hartmann has reported that it increases the time spent asleep without reducing REM sleep (186). It has also been found to reduce the amount of deep slow wave sleep (stage 4), and over long periods there is evidence that REM sleep may be reduced (187). However, after a month of drugged sleep in that study there was no strong evidence of REM rebound in a recovery month. Diazepam's effects on sleep seem to be similar in most respects (188).

Hypnotics

The barbiturates used to be widely prescribed as hypnotics. Non-barbiturate alternatives, developed from benzodiazepines, have now almost entirely replaced them. The change in prescribing habits in hypnotics took place in the late 1960s, and was not only a response to the epidemic of deaths through overdosing, and the availability of relatively non-toxic alternatives, but because of advances in understanding of the effects of barbiturates on sleep, and of their addictiveness, gained through EEG studies. Studies from Ian Oswald's laboratory, among others (335), showed that barbiturates reduce the amount of REM sleep when first taken, like many other drugs. As tolerance developed over a few days the level of REM sleep returned to normal, but on withdrawal the habitual user experienced vivid dreams and nightmares, with frequent night-time awakenings caused by a massive REM sleep rebound, with double the usual amount of REM sleep, lasting for five or six weeks. These symptoms may often have led patients to return to their doctors to ask for repeat prescriptions of the sedatives, ensuring a drug-dependent way of life in an otherwise healthy person.

The benzodiazepine-derivative hypnotics (such as nitrazepam, or Mogadon) appeared to be innocuous in comparison, and by the mid-1970s they had become the drugs of choice for doctors prescribing for sleep disorders. Since then it has become apparent that some patients, at least, could become very dependent on these drugs, and, in some patients, the effects of withdrawal could be very severe. There has been a consistent reduction in the numbers of prescriptions for benzodiazepines given for anxiety, from about 16 million in 1976 to under 5 million in 1991. The number of prescriptions for the hypnotic benzodiazepines levelled off at about 18 million per year since 1982, although there has been a reduction over the last five years. Figure 12.1 in the chapter on adult sleep disorders (p. 182) shows graphs for prescriptions in England over the 10-year period 1981–91.

There have been a good number of EEG studies of the effects of various hypnotics on sleep, but not all of them have been as extended as they perhaps ought to have been, or have used appropriate subjects. Prescriptions for hypnotics are usually for a fortnight or a month, and may be repeated many times. The time course of drug use and recovery is normally of the order of weeks rather than days. However, most empirical studies of the psycho-physiological effects of these drugs only take recordings for a week or so – typically, two nights' baseline recordings, three nights on medication, and three nights' recovery. This may be sufficient to give an indication of the pharmacological action of the preparation but cannot be taken very seriously as ecologically valid data about the effects of the drug in the real world. An honourable exception to the snapshot approach is the work of Ernest Hartmann, who in a series of experiments published in 1976 (187) studied the effects of a variety of drugs on sleep, taking periods of drug use of three weeks, rather than three days, and following up for up to six weeks after withdrawal. More recent studies of the long-term effects of these drugs, and the effects of their withdrawal, as well as the short-term effects of drugs with short half-lives in the body, will also be discussed in Chapter 11.

Another fault of many laboratory studies of the effects of hypnotics on sleep is that they usually involve healthy volunteers in their early twenties – typically university students. The majority of patients receiving medication for sleep problems are over forty, and many are quite elderly. It is admittedly quite difficult to recruit older people to sleep laboratory experiments – perhaps the development of home recording systems will facilitate this sort of research in the future.

Nitrazepam (marketed as Mogadon in the United Kingdom) is widely prescribed as a hypnotic in this country and in Australasia. Flurazepam, a similar drug, is more often the drug of choice in the United States. They are both benzodiazepine derivatives, like Valium and Librium. Unlike barbiturates, they do not suppress REM sleep when used in normal clinical doses (180, 221). Another popular benzodiazepine, flunitrazepam, tends to suppress the first REM sleep period of the night, increasing REM onset latency, although not depressing the total amount of REM sleep in the night by very much (35). On the first dose stage 4 sleep is increased in the first half of the night, but decreased later. With repeated doses, stage 4 sleep may be abolished altogether. Growth hormone is normally released in the early part of the sleep period at the same time as the first episodes of stage 4 sleep. However, despite abolishing stage 4 sleep, it seems that flunitrazepam does not interfere with the timing of growth hormone release (431). It has also been reported that the amplitude of slow waves is reduced by benzodiazepines, and not the actual number, making the scoring of stage 4 sleep particularly difficult (127, 153). Possibly, therefore, the effect of flunitrazepam may not be as disruptive to slow wave sleep as a reading of the stage changes may suggest: that is, while the drug modifies the EEG signs of deep slow wave sleep, it may not interfere with sleep's essential physiological functions.

Chloral hydrate, like the barbiturates, suppresses REM sleep initially, and causes a massive rebound on withdrawal (188). It is, however, rapidly metabolized, unlike either the benzodiazepines or barbiturates, whose half-lives in the body are between 14 and 30 hours.

Most hypnotics have a long half-life in blood, so that their effects are not confined to the night, if taken in the evening. Experiments have shown that both a benzodiazepine and a barbiturate can depress performance on simple psychomotor tasks on the day following administration (423), not surprisingly perhaps in the case of the barbiturate, but somewhat unexpectedly in the benzodiazepine, which is normally credited with tranquillizing without sedating. Benzodiazepines with short half-lives (3–5 hours) have been developed recently (such as temazepam) but have not received overwhelmingly enthusiastic medical approval, perhaps because they are (by definition) ineffective in maintaining their hypnotic effect over a whole night, while the more commonly prescribed drugs, like nitrazepam, build up over a period of days. None of these drugs are ideal, but the benzodiazepines are perhaps the least harmful, and are the hypnotics most likely to be prescribed by doctors in the United Kingdom. It is perhaps the case that they have become over-prescribed, especially in repeat prescriptions. Like other benzodiazepines they are habit-forming in some people, when taken over extended periods of time. The Committee for the Safety of Medicines in the United Kingdom has recently warned that as many as 40 per cent of patients regularly taking benzodiazepines may have become physiologically dependent on them. That is, they suffer withdrawal symptoms, including anxiety attacks and sleeplessness, when they stop taking them.

Tricyclic anti-depressants

Amitryptyline is regularly prescribed to relieve depression, and also frequently prescribed to elderly patients presenting with sleep problems. It has been shown to slightly increase total sleep time, to reduce REM sleep time with no adaptation over a 30-day period, and to cause a relatively short-lived REM sleep rebound on withdrawal (105). In the United Kingdom the number of prescriptions for these drugs fell from about 3 million in 1975 to less than 1 million in 1986. This does not indicate that there were fewer people complaining of depression, but more probably that doctors increasingly tend to prescribe non-barbiturate hypnotics for patients to whom they might have given tricyclics in the past.

Monoamine oxidase inhibitory anti-depressants

Monoamine oxidase inhibitors (anti-depressants acting directly on brain metabolism) actually abolish REM sleep as they take effect on the patient's mood, and it has even been proposed (105, 418) that it is the deprivation of REM sleep that brings the therapeutic effect. While this is the most marked effect of these drugs on sleep, it is misleading to state that this is their only effect. Phenelzine also reduces the amount of slow wave activity in the EEG in slow wave sleep, virtually abolishing stages 3 and 4 sleep just as it does REM sleep. Another, shorter-acting, monoamine oxidase inhibitory drug, brofaremine, similarly suppresses REM sleep and reduces deep slow wave sleep (397). Surprisingly enough, patients seem to cope without these stages of sleep, even getting less depressed. EEG/EOG measures of sleep processes seem to be so stereotyped in the population as a whole, following such formal rules, and so successful in predicting mental states such as dreaming, that one might identify them as not only indexing normal sleep processes but being an inevitable consequence of them. Evidence such as this may suggest that they are merely the epiphenomena of (or signs normally accompanying) processes which can, in certain circumstances, carry on without them. Otherwise we would have to conclude that the benefits normally conferred by deep slow wave sleep and REM sleep were in fact unnecessary in these patients suffering from depression. If this were true, what would it say about the function these sleep stages have for the rest of us?

Beta blockers

These drugs blockade beta adrenergic receptors, and are normally prescribed to control the cardiovascular system, reducing heart rate and blood pressure. Another of their effects is to reduce muscular tremor, and they have been used by musicians and competitors (such as pool and snooker players, marksmen and markswomen) to control anxiety-related tremor in public performances and competitions.

Patients taking these drugs for control of hypertension, angina or cardiac arrhythmias have often complained to their doctors of vivid dreams and nightmares disrupting sleep. These drugs achieve their desired ends peripherally – with no need to cross the blood–brain barrier into the central nervous system. Some beta blockers (the hydrophilic group including atenolol) do not have any effects on sleep parameters, or produce dream disturbance (49). The hydrophilic drugs do not cross the blood-brain barrier very effectively, unlike the lipipholic drugs (e.g. propanalol and metoprolol) (443), and these lipophilic drugs seem to be the ones responsible for the dream disturbances. In high doses they can also suppress REM sleep, and have even been used in the treatment of narcolepsy (299).

CHAPTER 10

The Sleep of Animals

All animals sleep for at least part of the 24 hours. The majority of species sleep at night, when the temperature drops over most of the earth and it is dark and cool if not cold. Others have evolved to take advantage of prey, or the absence of daytime predators, by being active at night. All nocturnal animals also sleep, either during the day, or during naps at night, or both. In this chapter some general points will be made about sleep in animals, and the sleep habits of a selection of species will be described, using both observational and electrophysiological evidence.

Goal-directed (appetitive) behaviours before settling down to sleep consist at their simplest in finding an appropriate place and adopting a sleeping posture. More complex 'sleep rituals' are displayed by some animals. In his book *Secrets of Sleep* Alexander Borbely (57) describes how the fox begins by digging a shallow hole in the ground, and then walks around it in tight circles until its nose is almost touching the tip of its tail. It finally lies down and lifts it head to look around before burying it under its tail. Dogs will show a similar circling behaviour, although less obsessively. Only a narcoleptic (animal or human) drops down asleep from standing without some preparatory activity.

The postures adopted by sleeping animals are also highly predictable. It may be unclear whether this is the result of instinct or an aspect of synergy – the inevitable outcome of anatomy. An adult giraffe cannot curl up like a kitten, and is obliged by its anatomy to sleep sitting. Bats, on the other hand, could presumably sleep lying down, but always choose to roost hanging upside-down. Sleep habits can be among the most stereotyped behaviours that animals display, and it would not be difficult to justify describing them as instinctive in the same sense that one might describe courtship rituals or nest-building in birds.

Appetitive instinctual activity usually leads to some active consummatory behaviour (such as feeding, copulation, or egglaying following foraging, courtship or nest-building). This appetitive behaviour has been shown in many animals to be composed of a series of highly specific sequences of action,

148

triggered by appropriate cues in the environment, normally offered by other animals. Thus, for instance, courtship behaviour in the male stickleback is triggered ('released') by the sight of a female with a bulging abdomen full of eggs ready to be fertilized. Sleep is much less socially determined. It could perhaps be thought of as a function as inevitable as defecation (which also involves stereotyped behaviour in some animals). The ethologist Niko Tinbergen has nevertheless argued that behaviours which are followed by sleep or rest ought to be described as goal-directed, appetitive activities, and despite the inactive nature of sleep it may still be regarded as a consummatory activity so far as ethology is concerned (410).

Mammals

Electrophysiological studies have shown that the sleep of mammals is strikingly similar to human sleep, in that slow wave sleep alternates with REM sleep (or paradoxical sleep, as it is more usually called in animals.) The only exception is the echidna, or spiny anteater, a burrowing egg-laying Australian monotreme. This animal has been reported as sleeping over eight hours a day without showing any signs of paradoxical (REM) sleep (11). During sleep, the changes in brain state in animals measured by EEG/EOG recordings are just as predictable as in human beings.

Inevitably what we know about animal sleep either comes from detailed laboratory studies (including EEG/EOG recordings), or from less well-controlled observations in the wild of the amount of time that animals spend resting, together with more or less anecdotal accounts of the behaviours animals engage in before they sleep. Estimates of typical amounts of sleep from laboratory studies can, however, be misleading, in both under- and over-estimating sleep duration in the free-living animal. A frightened or distressed animal may not sleep, and one report on the sleep of cattle actually claimed that they do not sleep at all, because the two animals involved did not sleep for a 24-hour period (301). Animals which have become accustomed to the laboratory environment, however, may sleep considerably more than usual. Estimates of the amounts of sleep taken by rabbits and cats, for instance, can vary considerably, depending presumably on how tame the individuals are, and the amount of environmental stimulation to which they are exposed in the laboratory. The amounts of reported sleep per 24 hours range from less than 3 hours in some grazing animals to almost 20 hours in bats and opossums.

Both sleep quantity and quality vary enormously amongst the mammals, but some coherence is apparent when style of life is taken into account. Animals which normally rest underground or in a den are 'secure' sleepers, and sleep longer and more soundly than those which sleep in the open. In addition, animals which spend a good deal of their time actually feeding (such as the grazing ungulates) sleep less than, and differently from animals which have no such demands on their time, such as omnivorous pigs or rats. Predators such as lions with little to fear sleep differently from animals which are regularly preyed upon.

From an analysis of known sleep habits and ecological variables such as safety of sleeping place and severity of predation Truett Allison and Dominic Cicchetti (10) concluded that overall precariousness of lifestyle tended to be associated with reduced levels of paradoxical sleep, while the amount of slow wave sleep was predicted best by overall body size. That is, larger species have less slow wave sleep. The significance of correlations such as these will be discussed more fully in the next chapter. In this descriptive chapter it is only necessary to indicate the importance of lifestyle in determining sleep habits.

The rat

The laboratory rat is one of the most thoroughly studied animals in terms of sleep. It sleeps 'polyphasically' – that is, periods of sleep lasting 10 minutes or so are interspersed with short periods of wakefulness throughout the day (the rat is also nocturnal). About 13 hours in every 24 may be spent asleep. Each sleep period begins with slow wave sleep, as in humans. The rat's EEG changes from a low voltage pattern with theta rhythms (about 7 cycles per second) to large slow waves (58). Muscle tone drops, and then drops further when the animal enters paradoxical (REM) sleep, when the EEG is again low voltage (although not as low as when awake), with rapid regular fast activity. Not only are there rapid eye movements during this sleep stage, but the paws and whiskers twitch and quiver.

When sleeping in the light, the rat keeps its eyes closed, and typically curls up, but light-sensitive camera observations made at the University of Nijmegen (78) have shown that in the dark the animals go into paradoxical sleep stretched out, with their eyes open. (See Figure 10.1.) Periods of slow wave sleep prior to paradoxical sleep onset were found to be very short indeed, and the animals occasionally even went straight into paradoxical sleep with open eyes from wakefulness. Although the animals sleep mainly in the light periods it is likely that wild rats withdraw to dark places in order to do so, when their sleep must follow the rather paradoxical pattern observed by the Nijmegen group. Despite years of study by humans the rat seems to have preserved some of its secrets of sleep!

Figure 10.1 Rats sleeping in the light (left) curl up with their eyes closed, while in the dark (right) they stretch out with eyes open.   Source: (78).

The rabbit

Rabbits differ from rats in sleeping less – about 8 hours – and having less paradoxical (REM) sleep (just under an hour in all). During paradoxical sleep they do not show the suppression of muscle tone typical of REM sleep in humans, and paradoxical sleep in other mammals (348). Rather, the rabbit flattens its ears against its neck during paradoxical sleep, as if there was some relaxation of the muscles controlling the ears. Like rats, rabbits sleep polyphasically. In the wild they are active at dawn and dusk, and rest during the day.

The cat

Cats may lie down to sleep, but sometimes fall asleep crouching. Unlike rats and rabbits, they may sleep continuously for hours on end, and have no clear circadian cycle, taking naps at any time of day or night. Cats in the laboratory will sleep for up to 16 hours a day (95).

Reidun Ursin, of Oslo University, has devised a classificatory system for the scoring of feline EEG which gives two distinct slow wave sleep stages, as well as paradoxical (REM) sleep (416). Most other animals (except primates) have only been credited with a single, undiffcrentiated stage of slow wave sleep, unlike humans, who have four. Ursin found that EEG in the awake alert cat was low voltage, with fast activity (above 16 cycles per second) while in the resting animal there were occasional bursts of 4 to 8 cycles per second waves. During light slow wave sleep the cat's EEG showed signs of spindles of 12 to 14 cycles per second, not unlike the human sleep spindles of stage 2 sleep. There was also some higher voltage activity at 1 to 4 cycles per second. During deep slow wave sleep the EEG was dominated by high voltage slow waves of 1 to 4 cycles per second, together with sleep spindles. In paradoxical sleep there was low voltage, fast activity in the EEG, with frequent eye movements, and a lack of muscle tone in the neck.

As in normal human beings, paradoxical sleep never made its appearance in Ursin's cats at sleep onset, and a period of slow wave sleep invariably preceded the first paradoxical sleep episode. The feline cycle length (between successive periods of paradoxical sleep) appeared to be relatively constant at about 30 minutes. In this study the cats which slept soundest (with the most deep slow wave sleep) also had the most paradoxical sleep, and light slow wave sleep appeared to replace deep slow wave sleep in the lighter sleepers, which slept just as long as the 'deep' sleepers. These differences between individuals may reflect degrees of tameness in these animals, which were recruited from Norwegian farms.

Farm animals

Dr Yves Ruckebusch and his associates at the National Veterinary School in Toulouse have studied a variety of farm animals' sleep patterns – horses, cattle, sheep and pigs (368). Cattle, they found, spend about 12 hours out of every 24 lying down, and about a third of this time is spent asleep, according to EEG criteria. During paradoxical sleep the cow's muzzle, which is otherwise kept cool and moist if not wet, becomes suddenly dry, causing its surface temperature to rise by as much as 4 degrees centigrade. This temperature rise is in spite of a general reduction in blood flow to the snout and the peripheral blood vessels in the cow's head. and is a direct consequence of the lack of regular cooling by evaporation of nasal fluids (411).

The other two-thirds of the time lying down is characterized by a drowsy state, varying in depth, but which seems to be a state intermediate between wakefulness and slow wave sleep in terms of EEG. In humans drowsiness normally very quickly resolves into deeper sleep, or is terminated by an awakening, while in all four of these animal species it seemed a stable, distinct state. Horses spent relatively little time in this state (2 hours) while sheep, pigs and cows drowsed 4, 5 and 7 hours per 24 in the laboratory (see Table 10.1 for a summary of findings). Ruckebusch acknowledges that animals in the field may spend less time asleep than these creatures chosen for their docility did in the lab, but what remains important in this study is the discovery of a stable drowsy state distinct from sleep, and the charting of broad patterns of sleep in these different species.

Table 10.1 Time in hours and minutes in each 24 hours over 2 to 3 days measured on 3 animals for each species.

	Awake	Drowsy	SWS	PS	Standing
	hr. min.	hr. min.	hr. min.	hr. min.	hr. min.
Horse	19 13	1 55	2 05	47	22 01
Cow	12 33	7 29	3 13	45	9 55
Sheep	15 57	4 12	3 17	34	16 50
Pig	11 07	5 04	6 04	1 45	5 10

Note   PS = paradoxical (REM) sleep; SWS = slow wave sleep.
Source: (368).

Drowsiness in the cow is a time of rumination. When Ruckebusch changed the feed of cattle from long hay to pelleted ground grass their need to ruminate was greatly decreased, and consequently the time spent in drowsiness reduced from 30 per cent of the 24 hours to a mere 5 per cent, with increases in slow wave sleep and wakefulness. Observations of free-ranging cattle and horses show that the amount of time spent lying is less variable than the time spent resting and standing (which depends largely on the amount of time spent standing and feeding) (21). The weather, however, does affect the amount of time spent lying, with cattle tending to stand in the shade on hot days (above 24 degrees Centigrade) when humidity is high. On windy cold days cattle tend to lie down when resting, while on milder winter days they stand more than in the summer, perhaps minimizing heat loss (and discomfort) from lying on cold wet ground.

Free-ranging horses similarly vary somewhat in the amount of rest they take lying down, and observations of the wild horses of the Carmargue have shown that stallions spend twice as long lying down as mares (370). The reason for this is obscure.

Ruckebush has also reported on sleep in the foetal and newborn lamb. Of course lambs are born at a much later stage of development than human babies, being able to stand up almost straight away, and run about on their first day of life. Gestation in the sheep is 150 days. By two weeks before parturition the foetus has fully developed sleep patterns, alternating between slow wave sleep, paradoxical sleep and wakefulness, with short periods of drowsiness. The full-term foetus enjoys over twice as much slow wave sleep as the adult, and about 10 times as much paradoxical sleep. During the first day of life the amount of wakefulness increases dramatically, mainly at the expense of paradoxical sleep (which is still 4 to 5 times as much as in the adult). Drowsiness in the lamb does not seem to have the stability it has in the adult sheep, with most episodes lasting less than 10 minutes (369).

Giraffe

This beautiful and improbable animal feeds and ruminates almost constantly, and sleeps very little. It is also an extremely timid creature, which makes systematic observation difficult. Studies at the Frankfurt Zoo (217) and the Buffalo (New York) Zoo (254) indicated that sleep is polyphasic, with 3 to 8 reclining episodes per night, which last between 1 or 2 and 75 minutes. The animals would hold their heads and necks erect most of the time while on the ground, with eyes sometimes open. One or two episodes of paradoxical sleep per night began with the animal lowering its head, either along its back, like a swan, or on to the ground facing its tail, or in front. There is some evidence that younger animals favoured the swan posture.

The photographs (Figure 10.2) were taken by myself and Kelvin Murray at the Regents Park Zoo in London, and are of a 7-month-old giraffe. Taken by time-lapse (every 10 minutes) with infra-red film with a 4-second exposure, they show the typical reclining posture with head and neck erect. The eyes are in fact shut. (The lids are light-coloured, and comparisons with photographs taken during the day show that when the eyes are open they appear dark on this film.) The rather blurred photograph of the same animal with its head on the ground is presumably of it resting during a period of paradoxical sleep. The long exposure would result in blurring with any slight respiratory movement.

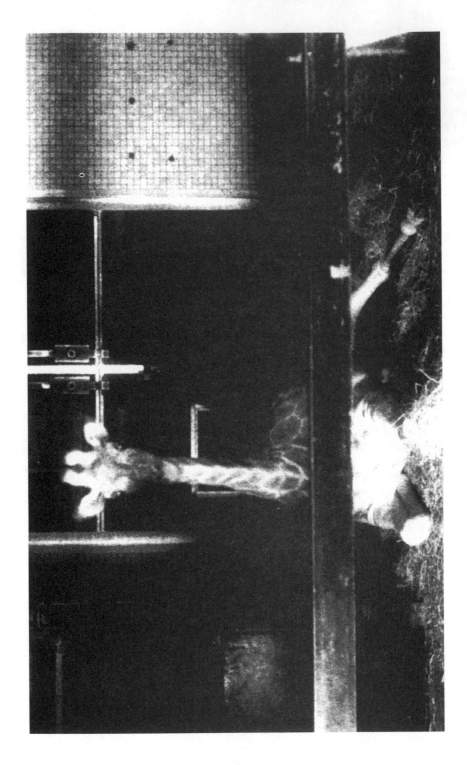

Figure 10.2 Infra-red photographs of sleeping giraffe taken at London Zoo.

It would take a chapter to itself to give an account of the taking of these photographs, which not only presented considerable technical difficulties photographically, but which was made extremely difficult by the timidity of these animals. (Even after a month of regular visits most of the five giraffes – all zoo-bred and handled daily by their keeper – avoided the camera by retiring to the pen next door).

Dolphins and porpoises

These animals, as improbable in their own way as the giraffe, may spend most of their lives in deep water which is rarely calm enough to rest on the surface without continuing to swim. EEG recordings of Black Sea porpoises and dolphins (314, 315) by scientists from the Severtsov Institute in Moscow have shown that they do, however, sleep regularly. The most surprising aspect of their sleep is that it was normally hemispherically independent. That is, one half of the brain showed all the EEG signs of slow wave sleep while the other remained alert, with low voltage, mixed frequency EEG patterns. Over an 8-hour period the two halves of the brain took turns to sleep, showing both light and deep slow wave sleep. Muscle tone was always high, and there were no rapid eye movements indicating paradoxical (REM) sleep. In fact one or other eye was commonly open all the time. In these animals each eye's neural output is entirely connected to the opposite hemisphere. It seems, however, that the opening and closing of the eyes was unrelated to which hemisphere was asleep at the time.

It is possible that the cortical arousal in the 'non-sleeping' hemisphere reflects some sort of paradoxical sleep, or that the functions of paradoxical sleep are served during this state in some way as yet unclear. This odd arrangement has obviously evolved to make it possible for an air-breathing animal to maintain respiration in the water while sleeping, and, interestingly, in this animal there is never any period when it is completely immobile. (Some theories of sleep function argue that the primary purpose of sleep is to conserve energy by maintaining immobility.)

Primates

The sleep of the chimpanzee is very similar to human sleep. Frank Freemon and his associates (145) found that it was even possible to directly apply the criteria for human sleep stages, using the standardized scoring system for human sleep stages (46). The only difference was that EMG (neck muscle tone) was not very helpful in discriminating REM sleep in the chimpanzee. Their two 4-year-olds slept for about 10.5 hours per night. The proportions of the four slow wave sleep stages, and REM sleep, were in the normal range for human subjects, although stage 4 (at 10 per cent) was slightly less than what one might expect in an adolescent. Another study (47) using adult chimpanzees reported essentially similar results, except that the proportion of REM was only 15 per cent compared to the 4-year-olds' 23 per cent, and the total time spent asleep was about an hour shorter. These differences could be entirely explained in terms of the age differences between the animals in the two studies.

Birds and reptiles

Birds

Birds have been found to sleep, in may ways, rather like mammals. That is, EEG recordings show periods of high voltage slow wave sleep alternating with periods of low voltage EEG, associated with rapid eye movements (REMs). As in mammals, paradoxical (REM) sleep always follows a period of slow wave sleep, although in birds the length of time spent in paradoxical sleep is very short, varying between 1 and 30 seconds. While muscle tone is not completely lost in roosting birds during paradoxical sleep, their heads do show signs of drooping (240). Young chickens, for instance, sleep perching, with head bent forwards and wings drooping. More rarely, they sit with their legs folded under the body. Older birds tuck the head under the wings, whether sitting or perching (240). Periods of paradoxical sleep in the chicken are typically very brief, often less than 4 seconds, but they are increasingly frequent throughout the night. While in human beings the preponderance of REM sleep in the second half of the night is achieved by lengthening REM sleep periods, in the chicken, as in other birds, the periods remain short, but more episodes of REM sleep occur in the second half of the night (378).

Owls, which do not move their eyes when awake, do not show REMs when asleep, although they do show EEG signs of paradoxical sleep. These animals are also unusual in maintaining a tonic level of muscle activity in the neck which is as great during paradoxical sleep as during slow wave sleep. However, their increased arousal threshold during these periods (when they are harder to wake up) indicates that, despite the lack of eye movements or of loss in muscle tone, this is a true variety of paradoxical sleep, rather than representing periods of lighter sleep, or dozing (41).

In his book *Why We Sleep* (205) Jim Horne reports some recent work at the University of Arkansas indicating that some birds may have a sort of 'half-sleep' similar to dolphin and porpoise sleep. The glaucus winged gull (*Larus glaucescens*) for instance spends almost a fifth of its time asleep with one eye closed, and the other one open, with corresponding differences in hemispheric brain activation.

The similarities between avian sleep and mammalian sleep remain great, and are all the more remarkable because of the tenuous evolutionary link between birds and mammals. The implications of this will be discussed in the next chapter.

Reptiles

Reptiles are typically inactive for much of the time, but EEG studies are conflicting about whether this represents a true sleeping state. Crocodiles, for instance, have been reported not to sleep at all, in terms of not showing EEG signs of sleep (417). Other researchers have reported that the waking EEG of the crocodile shows large amplitude waves, which reduce during sleep, and are replaced by large spike-like waves (132). Two other studies have reported that crocodiles have periods of sleep marked by high voltage slow waves, associated with increased arousal threshold, consistent with all the signs of slow wave sleep (425, 298). These authors argued that previous workers may have neglected to make sure that the animals were at a preferred (high) temperature when they were allowed the opportunity to sleep.

During wakefulness, the reptilian EEG has been found, in more than one species, to be dominated by high voltage sharp waves and spikes. During behavioural sleep these high voltage waves diminished in frequency and amplitude, and arousal thresholds were demonstrably higher. There were no signs of slow wave sleep stages or paradoxical sleep (131, 216). This consensus of findings has been contradicted by observations of paradoxical sleep in two species of lizard, when there was almost complete muscle atonia, arousal thresholds were very high, and electrophysiological record-ings showed rapid eye movements and bursts of 5 to 10 Hz activity in the EEG (407).

Sleep in reptiles remains something of a mystery. There appear to be greater differences between species of reptile in sleep pattern than even between mammals and birds. One thing that is clear is that their neurophysiological state is highly temperature-dependent, and so far as crocodiles are concerned it seems that a high temperature is necessary for them to sleep soundly enough to show high voltage EEG slow wave sleep. Inconsistencies between the results of studies on the same species do not only involve crocodiles, and one might wonder whether the recordings that some studies report are of natural sleep at all. It is less than 20 years since it was asserted in a serious scientific journal that cattle never slept. Perhaps many of the reptiles are less stoical than they appear to be, and despite their inert, ponderous and sometimes fearsome appearance their natural timidity sometimes prevents normal rest and sleep in the laboratory. It remains possible that further careful and sensitive experimentation will uncover regularities in psychophysiological state in these creatures.

Animal hypnosis

More than two hundred years ago the Seminole Indians in the swamps of Florida discovered a peculiarity of alligator behaviour which is now demonstrated daily in parks such as Busch Gardens. It is not possible to tame one of these creatures, and every care has to be taken when handling it. Once caught in a noose it can be dragged up on to a table for a demonstration in front of an audience. When laid on its back, with its mouth held shut and its tail held still, the keeper slowly strokes its belly two or three times. Releasing the animal, more often than not, results in it remaining completely motionless until it is touched, when it springs again into writhing activity. (The alligator's jaw can exert enormous forces when closing, but the muscles controlling it's opening are not at all strong, and even a full-grown alligator's jaw can apparently be held shut, once it is closed, with one hand.)

This sort of 'freezing' behaviour is common to many animals, ranging from spiders to rabbits, although it is most commonly associated with birds and reptiles. It is induced primarily by physical restriction, although a sudden and violent stimulus may produce the same result. Drawing a chalk line in front of a chicken is reputed to 'hypnotize' it, but, of course, the chicken first has to be immobilized to ensure that it is looking at the line. Freezing or 'death-feigning' is not accompanied by muscle relaxation, and is sometimes referred to as a state of 'tonic immobility'. It is quite distinct from the catalepsy shown by narcoleptic patients, who fall down into REM sleep when over-stimulated, and there is no evidence that it is mediated through mechanisms normally controlling sleep.

Hibernation

One might assume that hibernating animals simply sleep through the winter. However, the inactivity is not all true sleep, and not all hibernators are inactive for the whole winter period. During hibernation body temperature is lowered, and metabolic rate reduced. In addition, some metabolic processes may be drastically altered.

Hibernation in some animals (such as the dormouse, weasel, ground squirrel and hamster) is a state of complete inactivity, coupled with lowered body temperature, for a matter of months. Another group of animals (such as squirrels and brown bears) become torpid, but periodically make foraging expeditions in fine weather, and are relatively easily roused from their winter sleep. The female polar bear gives birth to cubs and feeds them during the winter months. During these three months it does not eat or drink, and urea, instead of being concentrated in urine, is somehow either not produced or is recycled within the body (323).

Figure 10.3 The somnolent dormouse in *Alice in Wonderland* – probably the
            hazel mouse *Muscardinus avellanarius*, according to one authority.
Source: (278).

James Walker, Ralph Berger and others at the University of California at
Santa Cruz have made a number of studies of hibernation and torpor.
Electrophysiological measures of the sleep of ground squirrels showed that
during the summer they slept for about 16 hours per day, with 80 per cent
slow wave sleep and 20 per cent paradoxical (REM) sleep. The animals
entered hibernation from slow wave sleep. While hibernating at temperatures between 35 and 25 degrees C, they were asleep almost 90 per cent of
the time, of which 90 per cent was slow wave sleep, and a mere 10 per cent
paradoxical sleep, so that paradoxical sleep was actually reduced during
light hibernation, in real terms. When body temperature dropped below 25
degrees C the EEG amplitude was reduced to such an extent that slow wave
sleep could no longer be measured, and there were no signs of paradoxical
sleep either (421).

Desert-living round-tailed squirrels withdraw into a torpor when food is
scarce – a response called 'estivation'. The researchers at Santa Cruz were
able to induce this state in the laboratory by withdrawing food, and found
that as the animals entered this torpid state their body temperature dropped
every night by as much as 10 degrees C, returning to normal levels in the
two hours before daylight. Sleep time increased somewhat, but paradoxical
sleep, as during true hibernation, was reduced in both percentage and real
terms (419).

Berger argues that hibernation and the torpor of estivation are both energy-conserving processes, producing great reductions in the expenditure of energy during periods of privation, allowing the animal effectively to close up shop and wait for more favourable conditions. He further argues that normal sleep (and slow wave sleep in particular) has evolved as an adaptive mechanism of the same sort, whose primary function is to reduce energy expenditure.

CHAPTER 11

The Evolution and Functions of Sleep

It must be admitted straight away that the function of sleep remains a mystery, and its evolution remains a matter for conjecture. Although predictably affected by age and to some extent by drugs, diet and exercise, sleep still seems a largely autonomous process relatively impervious to the vicissitudes of life. The parallel to processes essential to metabolism, such as respiration and digestion, is obvious. The difference is that we understand the role these play in metabolism, as well as the mechanisms, or drives, regulating breathing, eating and drinking, while the functions of sleep remain opaque. In order to establish the physiological function of a process like this, it becomes necessary to understand its role in fulfilling physiological needs, which may not always be obvious, and which may be somewhat obscurely related to drive mechanisms.

It might appear that understanding the physiology regulating sleep drives should give a unique insight into its function. However, while physiologists have made great strides in understanding sleep mechanisms this has not greatly helped in the problem of what sleep is *for*. Only a larger understanding of the role of sleep in human functioning (including its psychology) can give us the answer to that question.

It is important here to distinguish needs from their related drive mechanisms. A good illustration of this distinction is provided by the control of breathing, which provides a supply of oxygen essential for life. The drive mechanism regulating the ventilation of the lungs is (somewhat unexpectedly) unaffected by oxygen levels in the blood, but is very sensitive indeed to its acidity – normally determined by carbon dioxide dissolved as carbonic acid. This system works very well when we are breathing the mixture of gases present in natural air. Breathing artificial mixtures of gases with no carbon dioxide can however result in catastrophic failures to breathe, even when adequate oxygen is available. Understanding the mechanism of this vital drive mechanism would give us little clue, in itself, of the nature of the need. A mere understanding of the drive system might lead one to argue that the system was designed to regulate the constancy of the internal environment (slavishly following the insight of the great physiologist, Claude Bernard) and maintain blood acidity at a constant level by invoking changes in gaseous exchange. Of course this would be a fatuous explanation, but so far as sleep is concerned we are at a level of ignorance much greater than nineteenth-century physiologists were in dealing with gross metabolism. The rather more subtle functions of sleep will probably be suggested even more obliquely by their drive mechanisms than those driving respiration.

The consequences of preventing sleep are well known. Generally speaking, people become increasingly sleepy as sleep is denied, and decrements in performance related to sleep loss can largely be explained in terms of involuntary lowering of arousal and 'microsleeps'. It remains unclear whether this is merely a consequence of the operation of the drive mechanism, or whether it reflects some real physiological need. Similarly, selective deprivation experiments, in which either REM sleep or slow wave (stages 3 and 4) sleep are prevented, have shown that when allowed ad lib sleep subjects show 'rebounds' of the sleep stage which had previously been denied (see Chapter 7). This may reflect a 'genuine' physiological need, or simply a peculiarity of the operation of the drive mechanism responding to very artificial conditions.

In the absence of any definitive answer to the question of why we sleep, this chapter will describe and assess the three major suggestions that have been made – first of all, that sleep serves an essential recuperative function, second, that it may serve no physiological purpose at all, and third (and not in any way as an alternative to the other two), that its function may best be established by a consideration of the way in which sleep has evolved in life on this planet.

Restorative theories

Theories relating sleep functions to processes of growth and bodily restoration have the advantage of making intuitive sense: we all feel the need to sleep, so it must be doing us good, and we all 'know' that sleep is essential for growth in children. Why shouldn't it have a similar role in adults?

Metabolic processes can broadly be divided into two categories, anabolic – in which complex substances are formed from simpler ones, energy is stored, and body tissues are built up, and catabolic – in which energy is made available by the conversion of complex substances into simpler waste products. Both processes occur simultaneously in the body, and over a lifetime they must of course balance out exactly. On the 24-hour time scale it makes sense to think of the expenditure of energy occuring during periods of activity, and the conservation of energy, and regrouping of resources to occur during sleep. Ian Oswald, of Edinburgh University's Department of Psychiatry, articulated a coherent theory incorporating these ideas twenty-five years ago (332).

Oswald's theory of REM sleep function was informed by his observations of the time course of recovery of normal sleep after drug overdoses and drug withdrawal, and other brain insults such as intensive ECT. He found that all these traumatic insults to the central nervous system were followed, in the patients who survived, by prolonged elevations in the quantity of REM sleep. The time scales involved were also very consistent with estimated times for the half-life of amino acids in the brain. (While brain nerve cells are not replaced if they die, there is a constant turnover of protein in brain tissue, so that in a six-week period about half the total protein in the brain is replaced.) He suggested that the increases in REM sleep time which occur after drug withdrawal or drug overdose are a manifestation of recovery processes going on in the brain, involving intensive neuronal protein synthesis. REM sleep quantity also seems to be well correlated with brain weight increase in the early years, across a range of species. High amounts of REM sleep in the very young could thus be explained in terms of a consequence of brain growth, and adult anabolic and recovery processes in the brain are similarly seen to require REM sleep.

Stage 4 sleep does not develop until about six months post-partum, but then and thereafter the quantity taken is well correlated with bodily growth in the juvenile. The nocturnal secretion of growth hormone (which stimulates somatic protein synthesis in the growing animal) is actually dependent on uninterrupted stage 4 sleep (375). In adulthood, a chronic lack of normal stage 4 sleep is found in sufferers from fibrositis, whose EEG during deep sleep is characterized by 'alpha-delta' patterns – a mixture of sleeping and waking EEG which typically results in the experience of fitful, 'unrestorative' sleep, leaving the patient feeling as tired next day as they did before going to bed. (See Chapter 12 (pp. 187–8) for more details of the syndrome of alpha-delta sleep.) Not only do these patients show aberrations in stage 4 sleep, but the disturbance of stage 4 sleep in healthy volunteers actually causes the symptoms of fibrositis to appear (305). All this evidence is consistent with a general anabolic function for sleep; REM sleep subserving brain growth, repair and memory functions, and slow wave (stage 4) sleep promoting bodily growth and repair.

People suffering from disorders affecting the secretion of thyroxine from the thyroid gland are of great interest with respect to this theory, as this hormone directly regulates metabolism and promotes anabolic processes. Oswald's group found that hyperthyroid patients (with overactive thyroid glands) showed an excess of stages 3 and 4 sleep, associated with increased plasma growth hormone levels. Thus the increased demands on tissue reserves which were made by the hyperthyroidism were compensated for by a matching increase in anabolic processes. Moreover, as the theory would predict, as treatment normalized their thyroid-gland activity the patients' levels of stages 3 and 4 sleep gradually reduced to normal levels (106). In the same way, patients with underactive thyroid glands (suffering from hypothyroidism) show little or no deep slow wave sleep, but it is restored as they respond to treatment (233).

Studies of patients suffering from anorexia nervosa have also provided direct evidence of the effects on sleep of prolonged starvation (85). These people were found to sleep little and fitfully. However, when putting on weight they slept more, and with fewer interruptions. Also, as the theory would predict, there was a change in the proportion of different sleep stages, so that there was a massive increase in the amount of deep slow wave sleep at the expense of light slow wave sleep. While these results support the anabolic theory for sleep function, some caution needs to be exercised in interpreting them, as sleep disorders frequently accompany psychiatric problems, and as patients get better they might naturally sleep more soundly, given an accumulated sleep debt. In fact normal people who go on starvation diets for short periods of time show increases in slow wave sleep – an apparent paradox until one considers that metabolic turnover has to increase during starvation to accommodate the demands on bodily food stores (382).

Studies of sleep in people during periods of illness, whether psychiatric or physical, may always be confounded by factors associated with the conditions involved, unrelated to sleep functions themselves. A series of studies of normal people, carried out by Colin Shapiro and others of Ian Oswald's Edinburgh group, in collaboration with two psychologists from the University of Tasmania, have provided some interesting confirmatory evidence of the close relation between sleep and metabolism. In these studies lean body mass was estimated by a novel technique developed at the Scottish Universities Research and Reactor Centre at East Kilbride, in which total body potassium can be estimated from the amount of a potassium isotope – potassium 40 – measured using a whole body counter. The amount of potassium in the body is a very good indication of lean body mass, and has been found to be highly correlated with metabolic rate. Comparing sleep patterns between individuals differing in body weight and composition in three separate studies, they have found that lean body mass consistently correlates positively with the amount of non-REM sleep (384).

The effects of exercise on sleep are not simple. The evidence, discussed in Chapter 9, appears to show that elevations in deep slow wave sleep can be caused by increases in energy expenditure, but that these need not be very great, and it appears that sleep mechanisms are more sensitive to increases in *rate* changes, rather than total amount of energy expended, and also that body-temperature changes crucially determine subsequent sleep quality. That is, increasing body temperature can produce elevations in deep slow wave sleep. The evidence here is therefore mixed, and somewhat difficult to interpret.

Direct measurement of cell division or protein synthesis in man is impractical, but there have been a number of studies on animals, reviewed by Kirstine Adam and Ian Oswald (5). In nocturnal animals the peak period of cell division (in almost every tissue studied) occurs at a time when the animal is asleep. In addition, during sleep, cells may divide in half the time that it takes during the waking period. Measurements of the rate of protein synthesis also show that it is at its greatest during the sleep period.

This account of sleep function, the Oswald theory, is an expression of what many non-specialists would subscribe to as being a commonsensical view of sleep being good for you, especially in growing children. While the theory is supported by a good deal of evidence, it is all, so to speak, correlational – there is no conclusive evidence linking sleep with restorative processes. The correlation of periods of growth in the young with high levels of REM sleep could of course be fortuitous, and need not indicate that REM sleep is essential to brain growth. The net increase in anabolism during sleep may not be a consequence of anything more than its inactivity reducing catabolic processes. This sceptical view of the weight of evidence for the restorative benefits of sleep has been expressed by theorists who believe it has no function at all, and it will be critically assessed in the next section – 'is sleep a waste of time?'.

Indeed the theory has already required some revision. Kirstine Adam for instance has pointed out that in some small mammals the time required for protein synthesis in the brain is too long to allow for the completion of significant amounts during their short REM periods, so that if REM sleep has any particular significance for brain protein synthesis in these animals it must be in influencing the quality of protein production rather than simply accelerating the rate (4). Nevertheless, the restorative view of sleep function remains a compelling explanation of most of the evidence, and despite years of accumulation of evidence nothing has emerged to discredit it.

Implications for memory

This theory implies that memory processes will be affected by the amount of REM sleep during the night, since it is indisputable that the consolidation of memories will involve protein changes of some sort in the brain. Twenty years ago I set out to test this hypothesis directly, depriving subjects of REM sleep and measuring the effects of the regime on the retention of material learned the day before (117). 10 pairs of yoked subjects were used, who had learned the same materials the evening before, and were both woken up whenever the experimental subject was roused from REM sleep. The retention of complex material (stories) was greatly reduced by REM deprivation, while the retention of lists of words was not. The retention of syntactically correct but meaningless sentences suffered an intermediate amount.

Others have confirmed that REM sleep deprivation has little effect on the retention of meaningless material (139). Following up on this, Andrew Tilley, working at the sleep laboratory in Hull, showed that REM sleep deprivation is also more disruptive of memory consolidation in human subjects than stage 4 sleep deprivation (408), so it is unlikely that the effects observed were non-specific consequences of a stressful regime. In this context a fascinating study of 3-month-old babies showed that babies who had apparently forgotten about a kickable overhead mobile and were reminded of its existence showed reminiscence (improved evidence of memory retention) in proportion to the amount of sleep intervening between the reminder and the test (124). Of course there is no direct evidence that REM sleep was implicated, but it is very tempting to speculate, given that babies' quiet sleep is largely REM, that the reactivation of old memories could be a function of REM sleep, as much as the consolidation of new ones.

Behavioural evidence from the Hull sleep laboratory (118) has further suggested that the advantage given to the retention of memories by REM sleep relies on an orderly sequence of REM sleep periods, in that the beneficial effect of REM sleep later in the night seemed to be dependent on the uninterrupted completion of a short perod of REM sleep early in the night. If true, could this be subserved by slow processes involving protein synthesis, initiated early in the night and continued periodically in REM sleep periods throughout the night? Comparing the brain to an automatic washing machine might be an oversimplification as a general model but is seems a useful metaphor to explain this sort of cyclical, programmed process.

Is sleep a waste of time?

During the early 1970s the commonsensical theories of restorative sleep were becoming enshrined as scientific fact long before they had been proven, when some dissenting voices started to question their whole basis. The most fully developed expression of this point of view has been presented by Ray Meddis (294, 295), arguing that sleep is a period of enforced inactivity, reducing metabolic demands and keeping the organism out of trouble during periods of the day when other essential needs have been satisfied. According to this view, sleep mechanisms are instincts which have evolved in the same way as those controlling the courtship and mating of birds and fish. Their sole function is the control of behaviour. This provocative theory graphically illustrated the weakness of the evidence supporting the restorative theories in that it could not be dismissed out of hand, and a thorough reconsideration of all the assumptions underlying our thinking about sleep function was required to meet its arguments. Even if this is all the theory has achieved, it will have done a great service.

Obviously, sleep mechanisms must have evolved, and any theory has to explain the variety of lifestyle across modern species, involving very great differences in total sleep time. If we take the 'waste of time' proposition seriously, it becomes difficult to explain why this particular instinct has become a universal, while other instincts are as diverse as the habitats of the creatures exhibiting them. In particular, it has to explain how this particular instinct remains as a determinant of stereotyped behaviour in mammals when the role of learning has become crucial in the expression of all other mammalian instincts. Nor can it explain why almost every known mammal shows the same patterning of sleep (although there is great variation in the total quantity taken). Despite enormous differences in lifestyle, all mammals seem to have to find time for a minimum amount of sleep. Thus the porpoise has even evolved a system of sleeping with the two sides of the brain alternately (315). If there were no other evidence for the absolute necessity of sleep, this would be eloquent enough on its own. This clearly suggests that sleep has acquired an essential role in physiology, whatever the evolutionary pressures which led to its appearance in primeval reptiles.

A more critical test of the essential nature of sleep is to consider the effects of sleep deprivation. Preventing the expression of some instincts (such as by crowding chickens in small cages) does not result in death, but may produce faster growth and egg-laying. Interfering with sleep, however, is a much more serious matter. Writing almost a hundred years ago, Marie de Manaceine reported from Saint Petersburg:

> Direct experiment has shown that animals entirely deprived of food for twenty days, and which have then lost more than half their weight, may yet escape death if fed with precaution – that is to say, in small amounts often repeated. On the other hand, I found by experimenting on ten puppies that the complete deprivation of sleep for four or five days (96 to 120 hours) causes irreparable lesions in the organism, and in spite of every care the subjects of these experiments could not be saved. Complete absence of sleep during this period is fatal to puppies in spite of the food taken during this time, and the younger the puppy the more quickly he succombed. (291)

With an experiment like this, it is crucially important to know how much physical ill-treatment the dogs were subjected to, to ensure wakefulness, and Manaceine wrote little to reassure one in this respect. Early American work on rats (345) involved keeping the animals awake by being revolved in cages. All died from bites inflicted on each other, and of course little can be said about the role of sleep from results like that! The puppy experiment was repeated by Nathanial Kleitman using 12 animals, which were deprived of sleep from 2 to 7 days. Unlike Manaceine, Kleitman gives full details of the methods he used to enforce wakefulness, stressing the importance he attached to avoiding any physical damage being inflicted on his dogs. A slight pull on the chain and a short walk would result in wakefulness persisting for some time. Control puppies (allowed ad lib sleep) were introduced to play with the experimental puppies, and this often banished somnolence entirely. Despite this relatively gentle regime two of the puppies died, and, like Manaceine's dogs, all showed a marked drop in red blood cells (246).

Allan Rechtschaffen and his colleagues at the University of Chicago have conducted a comprehensive set of experiments on sleep deprivation in the rat. They used pairs of rats, housed in cages whose floors were composed of discs suspended above water, divided in two by a partition. With one rat on each side of the division, the floor was rotated whenever the experimental animal went to sleep, or entered one of the sleep stages specifically being denied it. Both rats would then have to walk to avoid falling in the water. While the control rats had the same physical treatment as the experimental ones, they were permitted to sleep whenever the other rat was awake (358, 45).

The effects of total sleep deprivation (TSD) and of paradoxical sleep deprivation (PSD) were essentially similar (122, 257). Death was inevitable in the experimental animal, and the control animal suffered little if at all. TSD rats survived between 11 to 32 days and PSD rats survived 16 to 54 days. As the animals became sleep deprived, their appearance changed, with their fur becoming scrawny and dishevelled. They also typically developed sores on their tails in a regular pattern corresponding to the vertebral bones, as well as sores on their feet. In addition to eating more than usual (80 to 100 per cent above baseline in the last quarter of survival) they lost weight by about 20 per cent. This anomaly was not due to inefficient digestion (as judged from tests on faeces) and indirect calorimetry confirmed that the animals had increased their rate of energy expenditure, in a way that could not be simply explained by their levels of activity, to twice baseline levels by the final quarter of the survival period (44). Eight animals which were deprived of sleep, and developed all the symptoms of sleep loss described above, were allowed sleep ad lib before the final moribund stages. Three of them still died within a few days, but the other five recovered completely, with energy expenditure returning to normal after 24 hours. They also showed massive rebounds of paradoxical sleep.

Rechtschaffen and his colleagues dismiss the notion that, in the rat at least, sleep is merely for behavioural adaptation – the catastrophic consequences of deprivation must imply an important function for sleep (359). The only function that the pattern of symptoms developed by their animals suggests is that of thermo-regulation. Specifically, they suggest that loss of paradoxical sleep gives rise to excessive heat loss, and that loss of NREM sleep results in an increase of the preferred 'setpoint' of body temperature, increasing the need for greater energy expenditure to maintain that temperature. While their hypotheses are commendably restricted to the facts observed in their studies, they leave much unexplained. In the first place, it seems implausible that such a complex system as sleep should have evolved simply to maintain a particular level of body temperature – something which could be dealt with by a much simpler mechanism, one might have thought.

Although most human studies of sleep deprivation have only involved one or two nights of sleep deprivation, there are some in which sleep has been denied for as long as ten days – and without fatal consequences. Is the function of human sleep therefore different from the sleep of the rat? Rechtschaffen argues that the rate of development of sleep loss symptoms can be expected to be longer in human beings. Rats sleep 13.6 hours per day, humans 8.0 hours – thus symptom development should in the first place be 1.7 times slower in the human. Other factors can be argued to increase this differential. The small size of the rat gives it a much greater surface/mass ratio than the human, making it lose heat more quickly, and therefore perhaps six times more vulnerable to disruptions in thermo-regulation than humans. Relative survival times for starvation are 17 days for rats, 62 days for humans, again suggesting that humans might survive 3.7 times as long as rats, or 77 days of total sleep loss compared to the rat's 21 days. These arguments are all well supported, but in the end we have to admit that we do not know whether sleep deprivation on its own is lethal in humans, and we will probably never find out. The only indications come from 'natural experiments' (discussed in Chapter 2), when individuals suffer from 'fatal familial insomnia' (292). The indications from these cases are that the insomnia caused by the damage to the thalamus may well have had a part in causing death, but, again, it is difficult to attribute the precise cause of death when there was severe atrophy of brain structures as important as the ventral and mediodorsal thalamic nuclei. Systematic measures of energy expenditure and of food intake were not recorded from the patients, but they did show some symptoms consistent with an elevation in metabolic rate similar to that found in Allan Rechtschaffen's rats – pyrexia (high fever, or a resetting of the thermo-regulatory thermostat upwards), tachycardia and hypertension.

To know that sleep deprivation kills is not to know for certain that sleep is restorative in function – it is vital to understand the mechanisms involved as well. The contention that sleep serves no function has been useful in forcing a critical re-examination of our sometimes unwarranted preconceptions and assumptions about the role of sleep, but in the light of the evidence of the fatal effects of its deprivation, and its ubiquity throughout mammals, it seems safe to reject it. The Oswald theory has been particularly useful in the role that theory must have, of tying facts into bundles – almost everything we know about sleep fits in with the theory. This continual confirmation of the theory through correlational evidence is no proof of its correctness, however, and only a complete understanding of the physiology of sleep will ultimately indicate what it is actually *for*. The impulse to ascribe a functional role to sleep will obviously not be satisfied until we have a clearer understanding of the interactions of the slow neurophysiological swings which punctuate our circadian cycle. The attribution of functions to a process is never easy, boiling down to a matter of understanding and judgement, and scientific ground-rules are rather obscure on this point!

A weaker version of the 'waste of time' theory has been suggested by Jim Horne, a colleague of Ray Meddis at Loughborough University. In his book *Why We Sleep* he distinguishes *core sleep*, which is necessary, from *optional sleep* which is not (204). Evidence from sleep deprivation experiments – both partial and total, has shown that accumulated sleep 'debts' are made up to some extent on recovery nights, but never entirely. Thus the REM rebound, for instance, after REM sleep deprivation, accounts for approximately 50 per cent of the amount of REM sleep lost during the period of selective wakenings. Horne argues that evidence such as this indicates that only the first three hours of sleep during the night is truly necessary, core sleep, and the rest – optional sleep – has no physiological function, but in animals which sleep for longer than three hours it serves the function of reducing energy expenditure and keeping the animal immobile.

Horne rejects the evidence implicating sleep in restorative processes on the grounds that most of the experiments showing increased protein synthesis and cell growth during sleep have been conducted on small rodents. These animals, he argues, are rarely inactive when awake, so that the sleep period represents the only time when these processes *can* occur. Larger mammals, including human beings, are inactive and resting for much of the time, so that protein synthesis and cell division in these species may occur during the day. On the contrary, Horne suggests that the deep slow wave sleep stages may have a role in the recovery of brain tissues in mammals such as ourselves with high degrees of encephalization.

Is this distinction between core and optional sleep a useful one? I would argue not. Most of us eat more than we absolutely need to keep body and soul together, in both variety and quantity, but no biologist would consider it useful to say that because a proportion of feeding was optional that feeding was only partly functional. An understanding of the physiology of nutrition and its role in metabolism has given us a very good idea of the function of feeding. In the same way we may hope one day to have a definitive account of the functions of sleep.

Evolution and sleep

The orthodox view of the origins of sleep has been that slow wave sleep developed first, and paradoxical sleep (as REM sleep is called in animals) evolved in warm-blooded animals. Michel Jouvet for instance wrote in 1967, 'it is at least clear that in the course of evolution slow wave sleep preceded paradoxical sleep. The latter seems to be a more recent acquisition' (226). Elisabeth Hennevin and Pierre Leconte similarly asserted:

> Paradoxical sleep does not exist in fishes, reptiles or amphibians . . . It has been recorded in birds (the chicken, the pigeon), but its proportion is less than 0.3% of orthodox sleep . . . except among predatory birds . . . in fact paradoxical sleep does not appear with all its characteristics except in mammals. [My translation] (197)

This has been consistent with the idea that REM sleep is concerned with protein synthesis in the central nervous system (332) or with memory processes or the elaboration of fixed, instinctive responses (228) in that mammals have much better developed nervous systems than reptiles.

The nature of sleep in animals is obviously of some theoretical importance, and questions of the evolution of sleep and mechanisms of temperature regulation have become crucial issues in the debate about sleep function in man. Some of the evidence from modern reptiles indicates that their sleep may actually be more similar to human REM sleep than human SWS. This alternative analogy has the advantage of explaining both the anomaly of the appearance of REM sleep before SWS in the human foetus (when in embryology ontogeny normally follows phylogeny) and the loss of thermo-regulation in paradoxical sleep in mammals (196). (That is, during some periods of REM sleep they become reptilian-like in not making any compensations, by shivering or sweating, for changes in body temperature.)

However, there are problems with this analysis in that birds (which show unequivocal SWS) are conventionally viewed as having evolved along with dinosaurs and pterosaurs in parallel to the evolution of mammals from a common primeval reptile. Thus as Meddis says, 'the stem reptiles ancestral to birds, mammals, turtles and crocodiles must have been pre-adapted to develop this kind of sleep pattern (SWS) under certain conditions (such as homoeothermy)' (294). If we accept the persuasive evidence for some dinosaurs having been warm-blooded animals (102) then perhaps this problem could be rationalized by hypothesizing a common warm-blooded ancestor to mammals, dinosaurs and birds, which showed SWS, and diverged from the reptilian stem in pre-history (see Figure 11.1). In the absence of any possibility of actual evidence about the sleep patterns of animals now extinct one man's speculation is as good as another's!

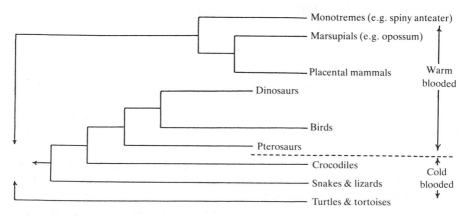

Figure 11.1 Evolutionary tree.   Source: (296).

Actual evidence about the nature of modern reptilian sleep is by no means unambiguous. Most laboratory studies of the EEG of the reptile (discussed in Chapter 10, p. 158) have shown few signs of slow waves in their periods of quiescence. This has been cited as evidence to suggest that REM sleep is 'reptilian' in origin, and that slow wave sleep is an evolutionarily recent, mammalian development. Evidence of EEG slow waves in 8-month-old crocodiles which were allowed to sunbathe suggests that thermo-regulatory behaviour (increasingly recognized as being a major determinant of the temperature of 'cold-blooded' animals) may be necessary for the production of slow wave sleep, and that this may be common to all reptiles, including the ancestral stem reptiles from which birds, mammals, dinosaurs and modern reptiles were evolved. This is a more parsimonious explanation than the ones involving either multiple stem ancestors or preadaptations. That is, all vertebrates share the same sleep mechanisms. Some of the difficulties involved in assessing the natural sleep of wild animals were discussed in Chapter 10. It seems that we must wait for more evidence on reptilian sleep before reaching any firm conclusions about its nature.

What determines how mammals sleep? Systematic comparisons between mammalian species with respect to sleep and other stable characteristics, such as size, metabolic rate, life span, and so on, ought to give an answer to this question, and provide clues as to its evolution and function. Harold Zepelin and Allan Rechtschaffen examined the correlations between sleep length, metabolic rate, lifespan, brain weight and other relevant variables for 53 species, finding a strong relationship between metabolic rate and total sleep taken (448). This evidence can be interpreted in terms of sleep being merely a mechanism for reducing energy consumption, as it can be argued that animals with high metabolic rates save much-needed energy reserves during sleep (419). As Ian Oswald has pointed out, it is also consistent with the view that sleep is a period of active recuperation, with high levels of metabolism demanding longer periods of sleep (333). Oswald further argued that since long sleepers amongst humans have higher body temperatures than short sleepers, longer sleep may be associated with higher metabolic rates even within a species. In this context the experiments by Jim Horne (discussed in Chapter 9, pp. 140–1) showing that bodily heating (by lying in a warm bath before bedtime) increases stage 4 sleep acquire a new significance, giving support to the Oswald position.

As we saw in Chapter 10, there can be great discrepancies between the findings from different laboratories concerning animals' sleep patterns, and calculations such as Zepelin and Rechtschaffen's, based on data from laboratory studies, must be treated with caution. In addition, while correlations provide a description of the extent to which different measures (such as sleep length and metabolic rate) vary together, any inferences made about whether one is caused by the other, or whether both are caused by some third factor, are inevitably speculative. Nevertheless, further analyses of this sort have been made, by Truett Allison and Domenic Cicchetti (10) and also by Ray Meddis (296).

Allison and Cicchetti included ratings, in their analysis, of the degree of 'safety' typically enjoyed by 39 species, and correlated these ratings, together with a number of other variables, with the amounts of REM and non-REM sleep that these animals reportedly took in the laboratory. The amount of REM sleep taken was found to correlate negatively with total danger (-0.69) and so did non-REM sleep (-0.40), indicating the importance of lifestyle and habitat in determining sleep patterns. Body size was negatively correlated with both non-REM sleep (-0.63) and REM sleep (-0.40). Thus body weight of an animal formed the best predictor of how much non-REM sleep it took, with larger animals sleeping less, and overall danger was the best predictor of the time spent in REM sleep every day, with the animals with most precarious lifestyles sleeping least in this state.

A particular problem with this analysis is posed by the inclusion of the large grazing animals, which spend much of their time feeding, and also habitually doze, rather than sleeping. Should dozing be counted as sleep or wakefulness? In addition, does it make sense to include these animals, which seem to sleep much less as well as qualitatively differently from most other mammals in a statistical procedure which assumes a certain homogeneity? Ray Meddis has argued that the grazers ought not to be included in this way. When they are removed from the correlations, the relationship between sleep length and body size (and metabolic rate) dwindles disappointingly, while the amount of REM sleep in the adult seems best predicted by the maturity of the animal at birth (its precocity). This analysis is somewhat controversial, and Zepelin, in a note following the chapter by Meddis on the evolution of sleep, strongly argued that it was most arbitrary for the ungulates to be removed from the analysis, leaving other grazers such as gorillas, rabbits, beavers and guinea pigs (447).

It would perhaps be overoptimistic to expect too much from correlations across species like this, when many of our estimates of sleep patterns are still somewhat unreliable. Precocity of an animal at birth, for instance, is commonly thought by biologists to be one way of resisting predation in animals which give birth in insecure habitats. Thus cats are born blind and immature, while some of their potential prey, such as guinea pigs, are born ready to run about. Precocity at birth may thus predict timidity in the adult, not only because these animals are largely preyed upon, but also because they are typically vulnerable from an early age. A subsequent inability to sleep soundly in a laboratory environment would be unsurprising. An artefact like this could well have inflated the negative correlation between precocity and REM sleep. Meddis is undoubtedly correct in being doubtful about correlations which are relatively small, even if statistically 'significant', but his reanalysis of the data without the ungulates (whatever the merits of the argument for doing so) does point up the difficulties inherent in this sort of exercise.

This chapter has set out to describe the sorts of theories that have been proposed, and to make some critical assessments of them. In an attempt to provide a balanced perspective of sleep functions Colin Shapiro has commented:

> Most systems of the body appear to be multi-functional, that is, having several 'operations' to perform and it seems reasonable to expect the same, a priori, of sleep. It would seem quite possible that sleep is subserving several processes simultaneously and when one is studying a single facet, the changes in sleep patterns one observes may be being dampened by the other (unaffected) inputs that normally comprise the 'summated' pattern seen in sleep records. (382)

The variety of alternative ideas (all plausible, and many compelling) advanced for the functions of sleep illustrate the degree of our ignorance, in spite of the wealth of data we have about sleep patterns and sleep mechanisms. To return to the basics, sleep appears to be ubiquitous and necessary. and is a complex function of the brain involving far-reaching changes in bodily physiology as well as brain physiology. It is difficult to believe that it does not have an important function, and the restorative theories provide a coherent account of what this might be.

Readers will have to decide for themselves whether sleep is good for them, or is a waste of time, although it might be advisable to keep an open mind on the subject – it is just possible that one day soon a new insight into sleep function will be achieved which will make us all wonder why it seemed such a mystery for so long. Until then, perhaps the safest thing would be to assume that it does do one some good, and get as much sleep as one can. (Afterwards, they might bring out a pill to abolish sleep, turn all bedrooms into offices and workshops, and condemn us to working Victorian mill hours – so make the most of it while you can!)

PART IV

CHAPTER 12

Adult Sleep Disorders

The nature and scale of sleep disorder

The nost common patterns of sleep disturbance are caused by psychological problems, although there are some, rarer, syndromes which have medical causes, or seem to be innately determined. The use of EEG/EOG recordings has been crucial in increasing understanding of these disorders of sleep, and has contributed to the development of a precise system of classification of sleep disorders, both on psychophysiological as well as medical critera. Especially in the United States, sleep disorders clinics have been set up which rely largely on EEG/EOG recordings, and their professional organization, the Association of Sleep Disorders Centres (26) has summarized the results of this recent research into an authoritative set of guidelines on the diagnosis of sleep disorders, some of which are extremely rare.

How many people sleep badly? Two sources of information are: the answers given by representative samples of the population to surveys, and the number of hypnotics – sleeping pills – prescribed by doctors (although, as we shall see, prescription rates are not as informative as they might seem). What is the matter with the sleep achieved by these people? Studies of people complaining of insomnia in the laboratory have the potential for identifying types of sleep disorder, but, again, as we shall see, do not necessarily explain why particular individuals complain about their quality of sleep. The effects of the drugs taken to alleviate sleep problems are also highly relevant to the development of disorders of sleep.

Insomnia and the sleeping pill habit

Sleep disturbance in adults is extremely common. A survey of over 1,000 households in Los Angeles in 1979 found that 38 per cent of their adult respondents complained of some sleep disorder (52). Dissatisfaction with sleep increased with age, especially among women. This confirmed the findings of a Scottish survey of a comparable size, conducted almost twenty years before (282). The American survey also enquired into the general and mental health correlates of sleep disorder, finding that over 50 per cent of the people complaining of insomnia had other recurring health problems. They were also significantly more likely to complain of tension, loneliness, depression and the need for help with emotional problems, but were not more likely than others to have made any use of mental health facilities. The general picture is thus of sleep disturbance being related to poor physical health, unhappiness and anxiety. A history of sleep disorder did not make it more likely for an individual to have received treatment for psychiatric illness (although it is of course commonplace for people suffering from emotional disorders to also have problems in sleeping).

How many people regularly take a sedative when going to bed? Statistics for the number of prescriptions for various preparations may be provided by pharmacists. Doctors, however, are not normally required to report what their patients complained of, or what they prescribed for them, and of course their profession jealously preserves a reputation for confidentiality. Consequently our assessment must rely on a certain amount of guesswork – first, as to the purpose for which the tablets were prescribed, and second, as to the proportion actually ingested, and by whom. At the time of the Scottish survey in Dundee and Glasgow (1961) the sedatives normally prescribed were barbiturates, and their respondents reported increasing dependence on them with age, especially among women, so that over 25 per cent of women aged 45 and over were in the habit of taking a sedative, while only about 15 per cent of 45-year-old men did so. A recent survey in France of over 1,000 respondents (353) showed that 10 per cent of the whole sample used hypnotics, 6 per cent on a chronic and frequent basis. Usage increased dramatically with age, with women showing the increase in hypnotic use between 45 and 54, and men showing their greatest increase over the age of 65.

Estimates of consumption levels in the United Kingdom (439) reflect a very marked change in prescribing habits over the past twenty years – of 14 million prescriptions for hypnotics in 1960, almost all were for barbiturates, while in 1973 the proportion of non-barbiturate hypnotics prescribed had increased to almost half the total, and by 1978 the barbiturate prescriptions were considerably fewer than half. A continuing survey of the prescribing habits of all 859 doctors who entered general practice in the United Kingdom in the year 1969/70 clearly shows that by 1976 barbiturates were prescribed essentially only to patients who had become dependent on them by these recently qualified general practitioners, and practically all new prescriptions for hypnotics were of the non-barbiturate variety (51).

Information about prescribing levels tells us when certain drugs cease to be prescribed (like the barbiturates) but does not necessarily indicate which other drugs took their place. This problem is particularly acute with the hypnotics since so many preparations can be prescribed to patients who complain of sleeplessness. Rare evidence of the medical response to patients presenting themselves with 'insomnia' is given by a survey of 5 general practitioners at the Aldermoor Health Centre, attached to the Southampton University Medical School (143). Of the 250 patients dealt with, only 4 were prescribed barbiturates, and the most popular drugs were nitrazepam (Mogadon), diazepam (Valium) and other benzodiazepines. However, almost half the prescriptions for the under-14s were for anti-histamines, and almost a third of those for the over 65s were for chlormethiazole, a powerful barbiturate-like sedative. (It is known that some milder drugs such as nitrazepam can cause confusion in the elderly, so these rather potent sedatives represent the lesser of two evils for these patients.) Chloral derivatives and anti-depressants were also given quite often, the former mainly to the under-14s, the latter to patients in middle age or older.

No single group of preparations can therefore be classed as 'hypnotic', as doctors obviously attempt to match prescriptions to patients' specific needs, and make use of a wide variety of drugs, some of which may also be prescribed for other reasons. This flexibility in usage means that data for the number and types of prescription must be interpreted with some caution. Over the years the benzodiazepines have become the most widely used psychotropic drugs, with the total number of prescriptions dispensed in Great Britain levelling off at about 30 million by the mid-1970s. About 13 million of these were accounted for by those marketed as hypnotics. However, an unknown number of the remaining 17 million 'anxiolytics' will have been prescribed as hypnotics – in the Southampton study diazepam was freely prescribed as a hypnotic – and of course the use that patients make of these drugs is also obscure.

The Department of Health has carried out an annual survey of 1 in 200 prescriptions in England and Wales, and 1 in 100 in Scotland. Their data show a general increase in the dispensation of anxiolytic benzodiazepines (marketed as anti-anxiety drugs, normally intended to be taken during the day) from the 1960s, which peaked in 1977. Over the following six years their prescription showed a pronounced drop, while the number of prescriptions for hypnotics continued to rise. This may reflect an increasing tendency to prescribe specifically 'hypnotic' benzodiazepine drugs for sleep problems, rather than diazepam (e.g. Valium) or another anxiolytic benzodiazepine. Some indication of more recent trends in prescribing over the 10-year period from 1980 to 1991 is given by the graph in Figure 12.1, referring particularly to prescriptions in England alone (also referred to in Chapter 9 on the effects of drugs). Prescriptions for 'hypnotic' benzodiazepines uncreased until 1987, but have consistently declined since, dropping by 2 million in 4 years. Prescriptions for 'anxiolytic' benzodiazepines have shown a much more dramatic reduction.

Official statistics on prescribing levels cannot provide more than a very rough guide to the prevalence of people taking hypnotic drugs. Dividing the number of prescriptions by the number in the adult population in the United Kingdom,

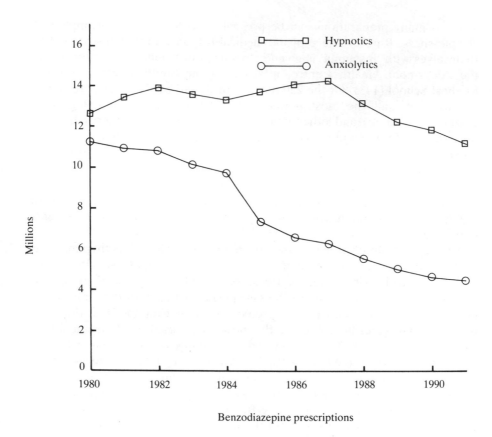

Figure 12.1 Prescribing levels for benzodiazepines in England, 1980–91.

Source: Data provided by the Department of Health, based on a sample of 1 in 200 prescriptions from 1980–1990, and normative data for 1991. Drugs classed as hypnotics are those indicated as such in *Goodman and Gilman's Pharmacological Basis of Therapeutics* (Seventh Edition), edited by Gilman, A., Goodman, L. S., Wall, T. W. and Murad, F. New York: Macmillan, 1985. This group comprises nitrazepam, flurazepam, triazolam, lorazepam and temazepam.

and assuming about 30 tablets in each prescription, would suggest that we all take a sedative on one night in ten. However relatively few individuals on repeat prescriptions in fact account for a disproportionate number of prescriptions, and most of us do without hypnotics. In addition, even when prescribed, dispensed and bought, the drugs may be left on the bathroom shelf, given to somebody to whom they weren't prescribed, or thrown away, rather than being taken as instructed. The only reliable way of finding out how many people take sleeping pills is to systematically ask them. A survey of psychotropic drug consumption in the general population carried out in 1977 in the United Kingdom (318) found that only 11 per cent of adults had taken 'sedatives' in a 2-week period, the same as that found 8 years previously (108) despite a large increase over the same period in the number of prescriptions. One explanation might be that the number of people taking repeat prescriptions had increased. Another possibility (and there is also some evidence for this) is that there has been a decline in the proportion of patients taking the drugs prescribed to them, and the development of a degree of scepticism towards medical authority between 1969 and 1977, so that patients became more likely to take drugs as they felt the need for them rather than as the doctor ordered.

Despite the lower than expected levels of consumption this survey confirmed previous British and American evidence (26, 52) that women are very much more likely than men to take hypnotics, and that this difference increases with age. The graph (Figure 12.2) based on evidence from West German respondents to a survey illustrate both these trends very well (394). This finding paradoxically contradicts laboratory evidence about the quality of sleep achieved, in general, by elderly men and women in the laboratory. There, men have almost twice as many wakenings and disturbances during the night as women, and, objectively, it would seem likely that a greater proportion of men would become dissatisfied with their sleep to the extent of demanding hypnotics. Are women generally more neurotic than men as they get older, or is this specifically a sleep problem? The survey evidence shows that the proportion of women taking anxiolytic or anti-anxiety drugs (such as Librium, or chlordiazepoxide) actually decreased with age. This demonstrates a lack of association between sleep disorder and general anxiety level, and contradicts the idea that the increase in sleep disorders with age amongst women is yet another symptom of a higher general level of neuroticism in women as they get older. No simple explanation can be offered for this sex difference.

The sleep of insomniacs

Psychophysiological studies of the sleep of insomniacs – that is, of people who complain to doctors of sleeping badly – have consistently shown that self-report of sleep quality does not predict quantity or quality of sleep as assessed in the laboratory at all reliably. Most people overestimate the time it takes to get to sleep (268). Insomniacs tend to have longer latencies to sleep onset, and do achieve less overall sleep than normal controls (308, 237). However, their complaints of lack of sleep or of failure to get to sleep may often seem out of proportion to the psychophysiological evidence, and some insomniacs will even report wakefulness when roused from stage 4 sleep (356).

Recent evidence, discussed in Chapter 2 (328), suggests that the normal

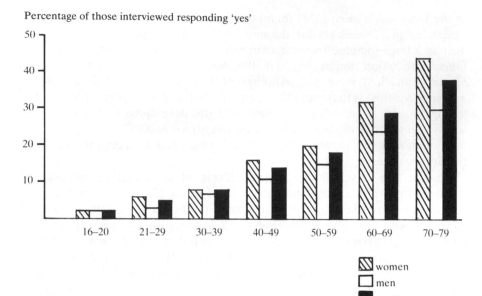

Percentage of those interviewed responding 'yes'

Figure 12.2 Age and consumption of sleep drugs. A survey conducted in West Germany asked respondents if they 'sometimes' took sleeping medication.
Source: (394).

transition from the experience of wakefulness to that of sleep is not all-or-none, but is a gradual one, during what the authors called a 'sleep onset period'. Sleep laboratory studies on both normals and insomniacs (193) have shown that the best estimate of an insomniac's definition of sleep onset is the beginning of the first 15 minutes of uninterrupted stage 2 sleep, rather than stage 2 sleep onset *per se*, which was found to be the best estimate of subjective sleep onset in normals. Insomniacs therefore do not only achieve less or worse sleep than normals, but their perception of it makes the problem worse. Some people demanding sedatives may not be deprived of sleep at all, but only of the experience of unconsciousness. Many 'normals' have less sleep than most 'insomniacs', without complaint. This fourfold typology can be illustrated in a single diagram (see Figure 12.3).

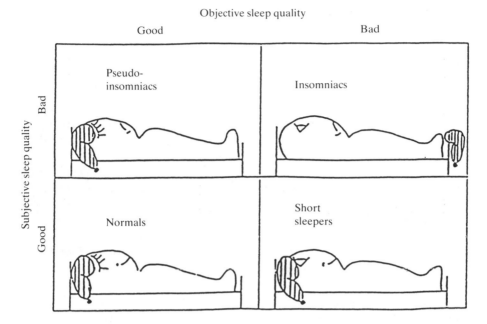

Figure 12.3 Types of sleepers. Satisfaction with sleep need not correlate well with objectively determined sleep quality.

Types of sleep disorder

This discussion will generally follow the taxonomy of sleep disorders arrrived at by the Association of Sleep Disorders Centres, based on psychophysiological evidence as well as on medical considerations. Of course some syndromes of sleep disorder are very common, while others may be very rare, even if very interesting from a theoretical point of view. (Readers who have a personal interest in the matter should bear this in mind: the most intractable sleep disorders tend to be extremely rare.)

Disorders of initiating sleep

In the Los Angeles survey referred to earlier (52) almost half of those who reported insomnia had difficulty in falling asleep. Worry and anxiety are commonly given as reasons for staying awake in bed. However, contrary to this usual view that it is worry or anxiety that causes difficulties in falling asleep, normal levels of anxiety and stress do not seem to have any simple effect on time taken to fall asleep in the laboratory. Insomniacs and good sleepers who were stressed by being required to do mental arithmetic problems after lights-out in the lab take no longer to get to sleep afterwards – the insomniacs taking slightly shorter than before, and the non-insomniacs taking longer (194). Another study compared the thoughts reported by non-insomniacs and insomniacs on falling asleep (144). Many of the patients had complained of being 'unable to fall asleep because [they] could not turn off [their] mind[s]'. Mental content reports of the period before sleep onset did not provide convincing evidence that worry or anxiety was causing the real delay in sleep onset shown by their insomniacs (44 versus 13 minutes in the controls). The authors of this study concluded that 'excessive rumination may be an epiphenomenon of sleeplessness', rather than its cause.

Subjects selected as being highly anxious have been found to sleep slightly less, more lightly, and with fewer wakenings than a control group, but generally had no problem in getting to sleep (367). The relationship between anxiety and this sleep disorder is obviously not simple. Robert Priest, a psychiatrist who has worked on sleep problems for much of his career, reports that in his clinical experience strong emotions of resentment or anger will more commonly prevent sleep than anxiety (352).

Very high levels of anxiety or worry must, however, be incompatible with sleep, and sleep always suffers during psychiatric crises, but the relationship between sleep and arousal is not simple, and can be paradoxical. For instance Ian Oswald has pointed out how bodily restraints and rhythmic stimulation can induce 'animal hypnosis' in a variety of species, and that this state of immobility is known to be accompanied by EEG signs of sleep. His own experiments on human volunteers confirmed that sleep could be induced in conditions that could only otherwise be described as highly arousing (331). 'Nervous yawning' is a very commonplace observation. Quite inappropriately, we have an overwhelming desire to yawn when in some crisis when in fact we have every reason to be extremely anxious. All this is consistent with the Pavlovian notion that impossible tasks or very disagreeable conditions can result in 'inhibitory experimental neuroses' – including withdrawal and sleep. A similar explanation, applied to infantile sleep behaviour by the neo-Freudian psychiatrist Harry Stack Sullivan, was that of the 'dynamism of somnolent detachment', by which the infant withdraws from anxiety-provoking situations (such as the absence of its mother) by falling asleep. Anxiety can thus actually cause sleep, although it may also frequently prevent it.

A recent interpretation of the aetiology of sleep-onset insomnia has been Elliot Weitzman's suggestion that it may be caused by a disturbance of biological rhythm. This syndrome, of regularly not going to bed until the early hours of the morning, and then being unwilling to get up until lunchtime, is quite common among students. These individuals are clearly getting plenty of sleep, but at the wrong time of day. The draconian cure proposed for such people with a chronic inability to fall asleep at a particular clock time ('chronotherapy') is to reset their circadian rhythms with a progressive phase delay of bedtime by 3 hours each week until the desired bed time is arrived at (430). It is unclear, however, how many patients have been sufficiently persistent (and have had sufficiently flexible lifestyles) to complete the course of treatment. Simply buying a loud alarm clock and getting up at an appropriate time every morning might achieve the same end – one's biological rhythms would settle down in a few days, just as after a transatlantic flight.

To sum up, difficulty in getting to sleep that is not due to pain or discomfort caused by some physical illness can sometimes be attributed to excessive levels of anxiety (in particular, apprehension about forthcoming and potentially stressful events) but is commonly caused either by feelings of resentment accompanied by rumination or by the lack of any pressure for sleep.

Disorders of maintaining sleep

Almost three-quarters of the Los Angeles survey's insomniacs reported difficulty in staying asleep, and just under half reported early wakening. These two symptoms both increased in frequency with age, especially the early wakenings. Arousals to light stage 1 sleep or wakefulness typically occur at the end of REM sleep periods in normals (259) but are not usually remembered because they are brief. Wakenings have to be longer than two minutes or so to be clearly recalled next day.

Lightened sleep, and relatively early wakenings are normal features of old age, and do not normally result in daytime sleepiness. Persistent maintenance insomnia in middle age or earlier is commonly associated with affective illness (depression and mania), drug abuse, alcoholism and respiratory illnesses. Affective disorders are associated with shortened REM latency (time between sleep onset and the first REM sleep period) and reduced stages 3 and 4. Monopolar depression (periodic depression with no manic episodes) is also associated with reduced sleep, repeated wakenings and early arousal (162, 256). Conventional wisdom in psychiatry has always attributed early wakenings to patients suffering from endogenous (severe, or psychotic) depression, and failure to get to sleep with exogenous (neurotic) depression. This 'classic' relationship has never been confirmed in the laboratory, despite the fact that these considerations have presumably been taken into account whenever these sorts of diagnoses have been made (82, 300).

Alpha-delta sleep

A minority of patients complaining of insomnia actually suffer from 'alpha-delta' sleep, in which the EEG patterns of wakefulness (the 10 Hz alpha rhythm) persist during slow wave sleep, and the 12 to 15 Hz spindling of stage 2 is superimposed on the low voltage mixed frequency EEG of stage REM sleep (192). These patients report not having slept at all, and feel that they derive little benefit from sleep, although they regularly sleep uninterruptedly for six hours or more. This syndrome is characteristic of patients suffering from fibrositis, as described in Chapter 11.

Sleep Apnoea Syndrome

The routine use of a measure of respiration in the night-time assessment of the sleep of patients complaining of maintenence insomnia led researchers at William Dement's laboratory to discover that the causation of insomnia in a few of them was entirely respiratory (176). Not only that, but this fact was unknown to them or their doctors, and, typically, they had a lengthy history of taking a variety of hypnotics which had only made their problems worse. These people suffer from sleep apnoea, in which respiration ceases during sleep until the build-up of carbon dioxide in blood causes them to wake up gasping for air.

In the past, the prevalence of sleep apnoea syndrome (SAS) in the United Kingdom has seemed extremely low compared to the United States, as judged by medical referrals (176). This apparent difference has been challenged, on the grounds that the problem may have been systematically underdiagnosed (17), rather than that Americans are more likely to be obese (288).

There is no clear demarcation between SAS, snoring, and normal. Careful studies of blood oxygen saturation and of related hypopnoeas (reductions, rather than complete cessations in airflow) and apnoeas during the night have shown that many normal subjects suffer from periodic, but short-lived breathing difficulties, without any serious disruption of sleep (47, 177). However, as these snorers get older, gain weight, take sedatives or drink, the symptoms may become more severe and ultimately result in significant desaturation of oxygen in blood, multiple wakenings, significant reduction in REM sleep, and the virtual elimination of deep slow wave sleep stages, 3 and 4. The prevalence of SAS in the population, based on surveys done in Israel, is now thought to be 1 to 2 per cent (320). Men are eight times more likely to be affected than women up to the age of the menopause, when the incidence amongst women increases. In the long term, SAS is associated with intellectual and memory impairment and a higher incidence of cardiovascular disease.

Parkes (341) distinguishes four categories of SAS:

1. *Central apnoea* Respiratory movements are absent and there is no oronasal airflow.
2. *Obstructive apnoea* The diaphragm and chest wall move with changes in intrathoracic pressure, but there is no airflow at the nose or mouth.
3. *Mixed apnoea*. Respiratory movements and airflow are absent early in the episode, followed by resumption of unsuccessful breathing. The opposite pattern does not occur.
4. *Sub-obstructive apnoea*. Reduced airflow with increased respiratory effort.

Parkes states that over 90 per cent of all cases of sleep apnoea are associated with airway obstruction, and that purely centrally mediated respiratory failure (with no mechanical obstruction to airflow implicated) is relatively rare.

As stated above, most of the cases with airway obstruction involve men over 40, many of them with a weight problem. More specifically, it seems that a thick short neck is highly associated with snoring and, more seriously, with apnoea during sleep (239).

Drug withdrawal

Alcoholics drying out and suffering from delirium tremens will have fitful sleep for 6 to 8 days with 50 to 100 per cent REM sleep accompanied by hallucinatory dreams (9). Disturbances of sleep continue for up to six months after the first 'good night's sleep', however, with delayed sleep onset and multiple wakenings through the night. Essentially similar symptoms result from withdrawal from the barbiturates (335). It has been argued that tolerance to CNS depressants (such as alcohol, barbiturates and the opiates) produces a syndrome of its own – Drug Dependency Insomnia – and any beneficial sleep-inducing properties of, for instance, barbiturate hypnotics are lost after a few weeks' use (235). It now seems that some of the benzodiazepines (minor tranquillizers) have a similarly disruptive effect on sleep on withdrawal. Drugs taken initially to deal with transient sleep problems (such as sleep-onset insomnia caused by some life crisis) can thus become the mainstay of a drug-dependent pattern of sleep – inducing a classic iatrogenic illness, where a course of medical treatment causes an illness in its own right.

Restless legs syndrome

Lastly, maintenance insomnia may be caused by periodic jerking movements in Ekbom's 'restless legs syndrome'. These are persistent and exaggerated forms of the twitches (myoclonal jerks) that most people occasionally experience on going to sleep, often associated with sensations of falling. Myoclonal jerks are as mysteriously involuntary as hiccups when we are awake, and little is known about the determinants of either. In this condition they occur every 20 to 30 seconds during slow wave sleep, disrupting sleep onset, and causing disturbance throughout the night. There is no known cure for this condition, and, as with sleep apnoea, heavy sedation is not beneficial.

Disorders of arousal

A group of disorders – somnambulism (sleepwalking), enuresis (bedwetting) and night terrors – have been classified together by Roger Broughton as being disorders associated with deep slow wave sleep (66).

Sleepwalking has already been discussed in Chapter 8. It fairly common: 15 per cent of all children have had at least one episode, and between 1 and 6 per cent suffer from frequent attacks (14). Laboratory studies show that typically, the sleeper sits up in bed, or gets up, in stage 3 or 4 sleep, following some particularly large slow waves in EEG (14). Generally the episode lasts less than 15 minutes, and after some apparently non-purposive, often repetitive activity the subject either goes back to sleep – often in their own bed – or wakes up. There is anecdotal evidence that this disorder runs in families as described in Chapter 8. There is evidence that enuresis and night terrors as well as somnambulism may be genetically associated (234).

Enuresis is of course invariable in babies. 'Primary' enuresis is defined as the persistence of bedwetting into childhood and 'secondary' enuresis as its reappearance after a period of successful bladder continence. Roger Broughton estimates that 10 to 15 per cent of 'nervous' children and 30 per cent of institutionalized children wet their beds. In addition 1 per cent of U.S. naval recruits are enuretic (despite screening for this amongst other disorders) as are 24 per cent of naval recruits discharged on psychiatric grounds (66). Studies of children have confirmed, as these figures would suggest, that enuresis is associated with emotional stress, and often reappears as late as adolescence. Enuresis typically occurs after a period of deep slow wave sleep. Recordings of pressure in the bladder have shown that bedwetting is preceded by an increasingly strong series of bladder contractions (which could also be stimulated by clicks, handclaps or other noises) quite unlike the pattern of bladder pressures recorded in normal controls. These excessive contractions did not always result in bedwetting, but invariably preceded those episodes that were recorded, which also always occurred during slow wave sleep arousals. This problem is almost certainly caused by overactivity in the autonomic nervous system, which controls all involuntary muscle (including the 'smooth muscle' of the guts and bladder, and heart muscle) (14).

Nightmares should be distinguished from night terrors, in that they consist of a frightening dream concerning some anxiety-laden topic, and normally occur during REM sleep. Waking up from an anxiety nightmare of this sort can be just as frightening as from a night terror, with the difference that reassurance is possible, as the fear is caused by the subject matter and plot of the dream. With night terrors it seems that the fear comes with no 'supporting' dream scenario. Typically, a child wakes its parents with an ear-splitting scream, and remains inconsolably terrified for 10 or 15 minutes before falling back again into a deep sleep. Next morning only the parents can remember the incident. Adults can also suffer from night terrors, although less commonly, and less spectacularly.

Another, related disorder of arousal, unrelated to autonomic system activity, is sleep paralysis, in which the flaccid paralysis of REM sleep intrudes into wakefulness. Attacks last up to 10 minutes, and can occur at sleep onset, or during the night's sleep at the end of an REM sleep period. Sleep paralysis can in itself be very frightening – especially if accompanied by hallucinations or preceded by a nightmare. The idea of pressure on the chest, or immobility, in the notions of 'incubus' and 'cauchmar' signifying being lain upon, and pressing down upon, must surely refer to sleep paralysis rather than the other two varieties of nightmare. It is of course very common indeed in patients suffering from narcolepsy (being one of the four defining symptioms associated in this syndrome (see below)) but is also relatively common in normal adolescence. In a sample of medical and nursing students 5 per cent reported sleep paralysis as having occurred at least once in the past year (166). People who regularly suffer from attacks may gain some 'lucidity', so that they recognize what is happening to them and wait for the resumption of control over their bodies in relative tranquillity (199).

The hypersomnias

Excessive daytime sleepiness may commonly be the result of a lack of adequate night-time sleep, caused for example by pain, jetlag or the effects of stimulant drugs at night. Sleep apnoea, although rare, is of course incompatible with normal sleep patterns, and most patients studied suffering from sleep apnoea in William Dements's laboratory also complained of sleepiness during the day (176).

Permanent daytime sleepiness may be a symptom of narcolepsy. This is a rare condition characterized by a tetrad of symptoms – sleep attacks and daytime somnolence, cataplexy, hypnagogic hallucinations and sleep paralysis. EEG/EOG studies of narcoleptic patients have been crucial in furthering understanding of this disorder. Night-time sleep is essentially normal, with the important difference that wakefulness is typically immediately followed by REM sleep, rather than a steady progression through the slow wave sleep stages (357). The tendency to do this is more marked in patients who also complain of cataplexy, and is common in daytime sleep attacks and night-time sleep onset.

Cataplexy is an extreme form of the helplessness that can be induced in anybody laughing hilariously, or being 'tickled to death'. Any extreme of emotion causes narcoleptics to fall down with flaccid paralysis of all muscles except the respiratory and oculomotor ones, just as in REM sleep. Hypnagogic hallucinations, the visual and auditory images that many people experience with the onset of sleep, are always reported by narcoleptics. Sleep paralysis, as noted above, is common in adolescence, but persists throughout life in patients suffering from narcolepsy, and is a wakening in which the flaccid paralysis of REM sleep is maintained.

Narcolepsy is a lifetime condition, largely genetically determined, which cannot be cured but which may be controlled with the help of stimulants during the day.

Cures and palliatives

Treatments for sleep apnoea syndrome

In the first place, patients suffering from SAS should not be sedated at night, either by hypnotics, anti-histamines or alcohol (320). Peripheral airway obstruction is the primary cause in the vast majority of cases. Obesity, defined as a body weight 20 per cent greater than that predicted from height from actuarial tables, is present in 60 to 70 per cent of the patients, and the worst symptoms are often completely eliminated through weight loss alone (179).

Obstructive sleep apnoea can be treated surgically, in an operation called uvulopalatopharyngoplasty, in which the back of the soft palate is removed, together with some other tissue in the throat. It has been reported to produce good reductions in sleep disturbance and in daytime somnolence in about 60 per cent of patients. For a major operation such as this, with all the risks of any surgery with total anaesthetic, it is important to be able to identify the patients who are most likely to benefit. It seems that the best results are obtained with those who do not have the worst symptoms at night (with apnoea/hypopnoea indices of under 30) and who are not obese (178).

A second, and less heroic treatment is a mechanical aid called nasal continuous positive airway pressure (nCPAP), where the patient wears a mask every night that is attached to a source of positive air pressure (400). Both inhalation and exhalation occur at high pressure, so neither receives any assistance from the pump. Rather, the effect of the high pressure is to inflate the pharynx, and maintain an airway. This treatment is reported to be highly effective, although compliance may be a problem.

The effects of hypnotic drugs

The dramatic change in prescribing habits in hypnotics in the late 1960s was not only a response to the epidemic of deaths through overdosing and the availability of relatively non-toxic alternatives, but also because of advances in understanding of the effects of barbiturates on sleep, and of their addictiveness, gained through EEG/EOG studies.

Ian Oswald and Robert Priest had shown that barbiturates reduce the amount of REM sleep when first taken, like many other drugs (335). As tolerance developed over a few days the level of REM sleep returned to normal, but on withdrawal the habitual user experienced vivid dreams and nightmares, with frequent night-time wakenings caused by a massive REM sleep rebound, with double the usual amount of REM sleep, lasting for five or six weeks. These symptoms may often have led patients to return to their doctors to ask for repeat prescriptions of the sedatives, ensuring a drug-dependent way of life in an otherwise healthy person. The change to prescribing minor tranquillizer, or benzodiazepine-based, hypnotics reduced the number of casualties from overdosing by the barbiturates, and initially it was assumed that these drugs were not habit-forming, as well as inducing a more 'natural' pattern of sleep.

The statistics for the number of prescriptions dispensed for hypnotic drugs do not support the view that the new hypnotics are any less habit-forming than the old ones: the same number, more or less, of prescriptions for hypnotics were dispensed in 1975 as in 1965 in the United Kingdom, without a great change in the number of people over the age of 40 (who are more liable to suffer from sleep problems). If the new drugs were indeed less habit-forming, the number of prescriptions should have gone down as the benzodiazepine-based hypnotics were introduced.

The immediate effects on sleep of the benzodiazepine-based hypnotics were discussed in Chapter 9. Their effects, especially in contrast with barbiturates, appear relatively harmless. There is evidence, however, that commonly used hypnotics may cause hangovers next day to the extent of measurably impairing performance on simple psychological tasks (222). Their half-life in blood (the time taken for peak concentrations to be reduced by half) may be as much as 100 hours for diazepam, or 30 hours for nitrazepam. A nightly dose will not have dissipated by morning, and repeatedly taking these drugs every day will gradually increase the amount of the drug in the body so that the regular user of sleeping pills will be permanently drugged. In addition, there is evidence that withdrawal from benzodiazepines causes anxiety and sleeplessness which may often be more acute than the level of sleeplessness the drug was originally taken to improve (346).

Some hypnotics, such as triazolam, have a very short half-life. Would their effects be any better? Kevin Morgan and Ian Oswald assessed the effects of two such drugs, one with a half-life of 15 hours (loprazolam) and another with a half-life of only 3 hours (triazolam). Their subjects were middle-aged and elderly people who suffered from poor sleep. Triazolam made the subjects feel more and more anxious during the day over a three-week period, while loprazolam made them feel calmer. On withdrawal from triazolam, they felt less anxious, but on their first drug-free day they still felt significantly more anxious than before having started taking the drug. The longer-acting effect of loprazolam resulted in increased anxiety on the third day after withdrawal (311). Low doses of these drugs do not impair performance on a vigilance task during the day. However, the Edinburgh group's elderly subjects reported incidents of absent-mindedness during the day, resulting in four accidents, three of which were associated with taking triazolam (310).

In another study from the Edinburgh laboratory elderly poor sleepers who took one of these two drugs over a similar period were found to have an immediate improvement in sleep quality, which was, however, not maintained when they were taking triazolam – by the third week they were sleeping almost as little as before they had started. On withdrawal sleep tended to be worse

than before, especially with triazolam (see Figure 12.4). The authors suspect
that the adverse effects of such drugs in increasing anxiety and sleeplessness
after withdrawal may be particularly great amongst elderly people (6).

Results like these described above have led many doctors to become
increasingly sceptical about the benefits of benzodiazepine hypnotics,
especially if taken for any length of time. The Committee on Safety of
Medicines in the United Kingdom, which regularly publishes advice to doctors,
has recently reported that dependence on benzodiazepines has become
increasingly worrying (80). Withdrawal symptoms may include anxiety,
depression, tremor, and even confusion and fits, as well as insomnia. These
symptoms can even occur following short periods of treatment, and it has been
suggested that up to half the patients who have taken these drugs for any length
of time will develop withdrawal symptoms if they stop. With regard to their
use as hypnotics, the Committee recommended that benzodiazepines 'should
be used to treat insomnia only when it is severe, disabling, or subjecting the
individual to extreme distress'. In addition, treatment should be intermittent
rather than continuous.

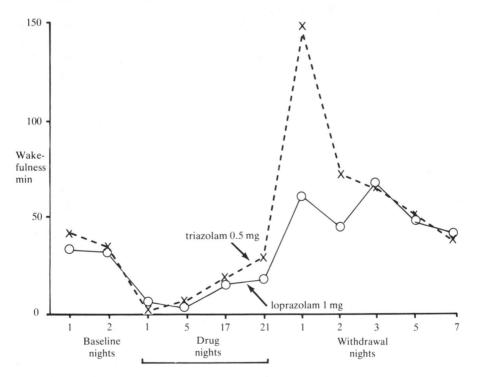

Note Immediate rebound after triazolam.

Figure 12.4 Minutes of wakefulness after first sleep onset before, during and after
intake of loprazolam 1 mg or triazolam 0.5 mg by the same nine subjects.
Source: (6).

It is hard to believe that we really need to take 15 million prescriptions to induce sleep every year, or that all of the patients who do so would have been severely distressed or disabled if they didn't. As many as 70 per cent of prescriptions for the minor tranquillizers (including the most popular hypnotics) are repeated prescriptions. The consequence is that a large number of people in this country have been taking benzodiazepines for months if not years, and any attempts to reduce the usage of these drugs will have to allow patients to reduce their dosages gradually, to avoid the most unpleasant withdrawal symptoms.

Sleep disorders clinics

It is well known that laboratory subjects' recollections of wakenings in the night are extremely inaccurate, and they are similarly rather imprecise about how long it took to get to sleep, or even of whether they were asleep (according to EEG/EOG criteria) or awake at any moment. Somebody consulting their doctor about a sleep problem may be in no position to provide such basic information about their own sleep as how long they slept, or how often they woke up. Patients can only offer their own impressions of their night's sleep, and describe how they feel. Even the most conscientious physician must rely on guesswork when attempting to make a diagnosis of primary insomnia on the basis of a patient's self-report.

In the United States a large number of sleep disorders clinics have been founded, offering routine night-time EEG/EOG assessment, giving objective information about the amount and quality of sleep achieved by any particular patient. There are only three or four of these in the United Kingdom. What benefits can they offer the patient?

A report from America on the effects of referral to such a clinic of 170 consecutive patients provides some indication (12). Almost a third of the patients were dealt with by interview, without spending any nights in the laboratory, but 117 of them were deemed to require polysomnographic assessment (including EEG/EOG recordings together with measures of respiration). Fifty-one of these were found to have sleep apnoea, which was obstructive in origin in 37. Patients with apnoea were significantly older than those without (52 compared to 42 years) and a good number of them were obese. Nine were treated surgically with tracheostomy, which was successful for eight of them. Eight patients were admitted and treated with a strict reducing diet, and three of the four who did achieve normal weights had fewer apnoeic attacks. The seriousness of this condition is demonstrated by the fact that two of these patients died in their sleep, one of them at the age of 47 with no other medically recognized disease. Twelve patients assessed in the clinic suffered from Ekbom's 'restless legs' syndrome.

In summing up the benefits of the clinic, the authors stress the importance of discouraging unnecessary referrals, and limiting EEG/EOG and respiratory recordings to those patients 'for whom a clinical indication is strong', and ascribe their success in achieving specific diagnoses in 90 per cent of the patients recorded to this selectivity. Several of the patients suffering from sleep apnoeas or narcolepsy were able to resume work, with treatment appropriate to their conditions. None of the patients actually given treatment actually died in the course of the study, while five of the untreated patients died. It is clear that a few selected patients can benefit enormously from this sort of assessment, and after a lifetime of taking inappropriate but highly potent drugs can at last be given some real relief from their symptoms.

Since it is only in the apnoeic syndrome that EEG/EOG and respiratory evidence is crucial in making a diagnosis, and few sleep disorders are life-threatening, this could be taken as an argument for not pursuing this sort of assessment, which is both costly and laborious. However, in view of the prevalence of the suffering caused by sleep disorders in general, and the widespread use of hypnotics, it could be argued that some relatively inexpensive system of recording EEG, EOG, EMG and respiration at home would improve both the accuracy of diagnosis and the suitability of prescribing in those patients who seem to be chronically in need of sedation.

Home recording devices do exist which use reusable magnetic tape to store the EEG/EOG and respiratory recordings. Since most of the cost of this sort of assessment arises from paying technicians to stay up all night in the sleep laboratory monitoring the equipment, and from the cost of non-reusable materials such as paper (a third of a mile of paper per night) such a system could be relatively inexpensive. A sleep assessment service based on home recordings could be provided by psychologists attached to group practices or health services. A postal survey of all the general practitioners in the Hull area in 1979 showed there was firm support for a proposed service like this amongst a sizeable majority of the doctors, and that a referral rate of three or four patients per year could be expected from each of them – more than enough demand to employ a psychologist and two or three nurses, in one city of about 250,000 people.

Enough is now known about the aetiology of sleep disorders to show that the palliatives offered in the past have been ineffective, and in some cases positively harmful. While there have certainly been great pharmacological improvements, in that modern sedatives are rarely lethal in overdose, they are almost as habit-forming as the drugs they replaced, and their long-term effects (over periods of years) have not been fully assessed.

CHAPTER 13

Children's Sleep Problems

Assessment of the nature of sleep problems in children poses problems different from those faced in assessing adult sleep disorders. As we have seen in Chapter 12, it is not always easy to judge what is wrong with an adult's sleep merely by listening to their own impressions of how they spend their nights. Many adults who sleep little or badly do not complain, while many others whose sleep appears normal in the laboratory do complain of poor sleep. So far as children are concerned, their opinions may not even be sought on whether they are sleeping well or badly – parents generally decide whether a sleep problem exists, rather than the individual child. A parent's expectations of how much a child ought to sleep, and when, will obviously determine whether they see the child as having a sleep problem. This will also often be treated within the family as a matter of managing the child, or of discipline, rather than being brought to the family doctor.

Essentially, therefore, a child's sleep problem is a parental problem. In the very young it may even be one that the child is not aware of. On the other hand children between about 4 and 12 years old may be well aware that that they are causing difficulties, but, again, 'their' sleep problem may be one that is only felt acutely by their parents. While the less common syndromes of sleep disorder suffered by adults, such as sleep apnoea, may also affect small children, these problems are mercifully rare. Difficulties in breathing are more common amongst premature babies, or those with a very low birth-weight, and these individuals are usually identified early in life by the medical profession. Breathing difficulties in very young babies are potentially life-threatening, and these patients ought to be treated in hospital. This chapter will not be concerned with the rarer, and more serious, disorders of sleep associated with medical conditions, but will confine itself to the far more common problems of sleep which confront many parents.

Infancy

During the first few weeks of life babies sleep as much during the day as during the night, waking up every 3 or 4 hours throughout the 24 hours. Some infants will settle down at night and not make any demands on their parents until morning from the age of 6 weeks, while others continue to wake up and cry at night for 3 months or longer. Laboratory evidence (discussed in Chapter 2) has shown that infants do not necessarily sleep through the night after they have stopped making demands for attention during the night. Rather, they periodically wake up, but remain quiet. Babies vary in temperament, some being content to lie awake in relative silence in a darkened room even if moderately wet and slightly hungry, while others will invariably summon their mothers at the tops of their voices.

Colic

A baby who screams for no apparent reason may seem to be a most unreasonable reproach to its mother, and it is all too easy to imagine that something seriously is amiss when a baby behaves like this. The colicky baby is inconsolably irritable for at least 3 hours a day. Marc Weissbluth (428) reports that colic is very common indeed, although the severity of the attacks, and their length, vary considerably. Typically, the attacks begin after the second week of life. Fifty per cent of infants will have settled down by their second month, and only 10 per cent will still be showing these symptoms after 4 months of age. Interestingly, premature babies will not show signs of colic until they have reached 2 weeks 'post-conception' age, rather than their age since birth, giving support to the view that these periodic paroxysms of screaming are an inevitable consequence of the developing nervous system in some babies. There is no evidence that colic is associated with any particular practices of child-rearing, and it is certainly not a consequence of neglect.

Little can be done to prevent or cure colic, and it is important to remain calm and patient, even when the baby screams and screams. Merely holding and cuddling often seems to have little effect. One tactic is to put a nappy on your shoulder, the baby face down facing over the shoulder, and walk up and down holding it firmly, singing softly. Eventually the crying will cease. Of the three that I have been involved in bringing up only one (fortunately) suffered from colic, and at her worst she could only be quietened by a ride in her carrycot in the car. (On one occasion this ride had to continue for 30 miles, although more commonly a trip around the block was enough.)

Most important, one must recognize when the child is beginning to pass through this difficult stage. It is then vital to establish a regular routine at bedtime, to facilitate the transition to normal, trouble-free nights. It has even been suggested (327) that it is the most solicitous mother who may do the most harm to the child's development of normal sleep patterns – that is, the parent may end up by maintaining the infant's disrupted sleep pattern, by continuing to get it up at the slightest sound after it has in fact recovered from its colicky phase, eventually making the child dependent on the mother's constant physical presence.

Toddlers

Origins of common sleep disorders in toddlers

There is a great reduction in the total amount of sleep taken by the child between 3 months and 3 years of age. Most of this reduction is during the day, with naps becoming shorter and fewer. Dr Spock (395) observes that towards the end of the first year most babies are down to two naps a day, and by the time they are 18 months old will have dropped one of these. Sleep during the night becomes uninterrupted. Many children at this stage will wake up rather earlier in the mornings than their parents would like to – for instance between 5 and 6 a.m. As with wakings during the night, there is no reason why a toddler should not be able to amuse itself in its cot until parents feel it is a reasonable time to get up, and if one is not too quick to run to children at the first sound it often transpires that they are perfectly happy to remain on their own, murmuring and muttering to themselves.

Parental tolerance of night wakenings in 1-year-old toddlers varies considerably. David Messer and Martin Richards report on the results of a postal survey, asking mothers how frequently their babies woke, and whether they thought there was a night-waking problem. Of those whose babies woke 5 times a week or more at night, 10 per cent regarded this as normal. Of those whose babies woke less frequently than this, 37 per cent felt that night waking was a real problem. Messer and Richards report that between a third and a fifth of infants will continue to wake at night during their pre-school years (302).

The definition of 'sleep problem' in this age range is thus most unclear – some parents tolerate multiple wakenings during the night as being perfectly normal, while others do not. It is still possible, however, to try and determine the incidence of disturbed sleep during infancy, and to correlate it with any psychosocial factors that may be relevant. A longitudinal study based on interviews with over 300 mothers in London (450) reported that 10 per cent of mothers reported 3 or more wakenings per night when the babies were 8 months old, and 22 per cent reported 1 wakening per night. Interviews were repeated when the children were 3 years old, and mothers were asked about other behavioural problems, as well as about sleep problems. Twenty-nine per cent of 3-year-olds were reported to have sleep problems, with 18 per cent having difficulty in getting to bed or to sleep, and 22 per cent waking up at night.

One-third of the children who had been reported as having a sleep problem at 8 months still had a sleep problem at the age of 3 – many more than would be expected by chance, and demonstrating good evidence of consistency in sleeping badly at both ages.

It was also found that 3-year-olds who slept badly were also more likely to have other behavioural problems – having tantrums or being more difficult to manage in general. A range of demographic and psychosocial measures did not show the circumstances of the poor sleepers to be worse than those who slept well, although the mothers of poor sleepers tended to be more depressed. Naturally, one might ask whether they were depressed because they were being kept awake every night by their infant. That is, given an association between depression in the mother and sleep disorder in the child, was the depression the cause or the consequence of the sleep problem? The authors investigated this by comparing the rate at which depression was developed amongst mothers who were not depressed at the 8-month interview, in those whose children had sleep problems at that age, and those whose children did not. There was no difference between these two groups in their likelihood of becoming depressed, indicating that it was perhaps depression in the mother which somehow caused at least a proportion of the children to develop sleep problems – a conclusion also supported by findings in two other studies (273, 362). It would be surprising indeed if only one factor (such as maternal depression) was responsible for all sleep problems in infancy and childhood, and it is highly likely that temperamental differences are responsible for a large number of the overactive, difficult and wakeful individuals.

Children may refuse to go to bed, or may persistently wake up and summon their parents at night, for no apparent good reason. Dr Richard Ferber (129) estimates that between 15 to 35 per cent of young children will behave like this. One reason he suggests is that anxiety and oversolicitous behaviour by parents dealing with a perhaps colicky baby may result in a toddler continuing to habitually demand attention during the night, long after any 'real' need for it is present. While a small baby may need to be rocked to sleep, a 2-year-old generally should not. It should be usual for a young child to have achieved enough independence to go to sleep and stay asleep all night on their own without any further attention.

Some objective evidence supporting this interpretation comes from a study comparing the night-time waking rates of children whose parents were routinely with them when they fell asleep (33 per cent of the sample of 122) with those whose parents were not. The 9-month-old infants who always had one parent with them when they fell asleep were twice as likely to wake during the night as those whose parents put them to bed awake (6.2 versus 3.1 awakenings a week) (2). While suggestive, this finding cannot be regarded as conclusive, as of course it may be that more difficult children (who were more likely to wake up later in the night) would be more likely to elicit more attention from parents, including sitting with them while they went to sleep.

Treatments of common sleep disorders in toddlers

A recent study conducted at the Child Development Unit at Cardiff University (50) assessed the usefulness of a child sleep disorders clinic, and examined the nature of sleep problems shown by the children referred to it. The 44 clients referred to the clinic ranged between 7 months and 4 years old, although most were under the age of 2. In general, they either suffered from frequent wakings during the night, or a combination of frequent wakings and difficulties in settling. Difficulty in settling on its own was not common. The treatment provided consisted of advice given by child-development advisers to the parents, with continuous monitoring of the child's progress with sleep diaries, kept by the parents.

A typical 8-month-old with settling and frequent waking problems was put on a regime of quiet play before bed, last bottle given in bed, soothing and relaxing techniques to settle and repetition of the relaxation arrangements when he woke at night with minimal stimulation, for example, no light, change, drinks or talking, although a quiet music cassette could be played. The child could only be picked up and soothed very quietly. By the end of three weeks there had been a great improvement, and there was only one difficult night in the fourth week. Before treatment began he had woken at least three times in every night for about half an hour, and had typically taken an hour and a half to get to sleep.

In this case the treatment was entirely successful. The techniques involved were similar to those which many parents might adopt spontaneously, and might sound merely 'common sense'. There may be other ways of dealing with a small child that are equally effective in reassuring him or her and allowing uninterrupted sleep. For instance, therapists at a similar sleep disorders clinic in London (363) advised parents to discuss the problem with the 2-year-olds and set agreed targets (such as sleeping in their own bed, and going to bed at an agreed time). They rewarded the children with surprises under the pillow if they went to bed at the right time, stories for settling quickly, and promises of surprise activities in the morning after an uninterrupted night. The advantage of following a treatment programme like either of these is probably as much to do with establishing a consistency of approach from night to night as anything else. When parents say, 'We've tried everything!', they probably mean it only too literally, changing their approach from night to night. While treatment programmes may differ in some of their approaches, there is no doubt whatsoever that it is essential to calm a toddler down before he or she can be expected to go to sleep, and to avoid turning a minor disagreement about bedtime into a battle. Calm firmness and consistency are essential. In addition, as the Cardiff group point out, it is important not to allow these sleep problems to continue after the age of 2: the older their clients with sleep problems, the longer it took to establish normal sleep patterns.

A different approach to sleep problems in infants is to provide *all* parents with guidance on the management of their infants' sleep, rather than simply those with problems. In an intervention study (3) the parents of 164 infants were visited at 4 months, given an information leaflet, and verbal instructions that they should normally put the babies to bed awake, and not have to stay with them until they went to sleep. Parents were asked to complete a daily sleep chart during the fifth month, and had another consultation with the pediatrician at the sixth month. The outcome of all this at 9 months was that the infants had only 2.5 wakings per week compared to 3.9 wakings in the control group (with no instructions). In addition, frequent night waking was twice as common in the control group as the intervention group (27 per cent versus 14 per cent). These findings provide further support for the notion that many sleep problems in infants are commonly attributable to parental overanxiety or oversolicitousness.

Disorders of arousal

These disturbances of deep slow wave sleep which result in bedwetting, night terrors, or sleepwalking are very much more prevalent amongst children than adults.

A longitudinal (follow-up) study of 212 normal, randomly selected children in Sweden (244) over a ten-year period has found that sleepwalking was a very common occasional occurrence, reported by 75 of the children in the sample. Thirty-five of these children were persistent sleepwalkers, in that they continued to walk in their sleep throughout the period of the study, although only 4 or 5 of them ever walked in their sleep more than once a month. The 7 children in the sample who reported night terrors all did so before the age of 7, and, interestingly, all of them later became sleepwalkers.

Regular bedwetting (several times a week either regularly or periodically during the year) was commoner in boys than girls every year between the ages of 4 and 16, although after the age of 9 there were no girls wetting their beds and only 2 or 3 boys.

Suggestions for treatment

Persistent sleepwalking can be dangerous – for instance children may roam outside the house or out of windows onto dangerous ledges. One solution is to tie the child to the bed by a piece of string attached to an anklet, so that they cannot get far without waking up. Episodes of sleepwalking tend to be associated with periods of worry or stress, in both adults and children. If there is an obvious source of worry, such as parental strife, then some reassurance may help relieve the child's mind.

While bedwetting can be the result of a disorder of arousal associated with deep slow wave sleep (66) it is now clear from studies at the Stanford Sleep Disorders Clinic (325) that many children may wet their beds in other sleep stages, or even when awake, and this less specific pattern may in fact be more common than the one specifically associated with stage 4 sleep. The Stanford therapists initially train their young clients to attempt to control their bladders when awake, after drinking quantities of fluid, both by withholding micturition for as long as possible, and by stopping in mid-stream, and starting again at will. After a few days of practice at controlling their bladders in this way most children stop wetting their beds. Those who do not may be provided with devices which detect wetness in the bed, setting off an alarm during the night. Finally, some children are prescribed imipramine, an anti-depressant drug one of whose side-effects is to improve bladder control. It's mode of action is still uncertain, but it can be very useful in proving to the worried child that dry nights are indeed possible, and a short course of treatment may solve the problem.

Night terrors are not uncommon, but rarely persistent. They may not bother the child as much as its parents, as children frequently forget the whole episode if they are promptly reassured and settled back to sleep. Like sleepwalking, night terrors tend to occur during periods of worry, and daytime reassurance about family problems may be enough to stop these terrifying screaming episodes in the first half of the night. As a last resort a family practioner may prescribe a benzodiazepine anti-anxiety drug for a short period, which would not only relieve any anxiety the child may be experiencing, but also lighten slow wave sleep.

Adolescence

Some teenage children rarely get up before noon at weekends, and frequently appear chronically sleepy. The obvious explanation is that for some reason connected with adolescence these young people need more sleep than they did when they were 11 or 12, when they got up earlier than their parents. Research from the Stanford Sleep Research Centre confirms that there are indeed changes in patterns of sleep during adolescence (75). Over a period of 7 years young people were invited to attend a summer camp at which observations were made of their sleep habits, and some of them were required to have their sleep monitored using EEG/EOG polygraphy. A total of 196 children between 7 and 9, 121 between 10 and 11, 124 between 12 and 13 and 168 between 18 and 22 took part.

Subjects were examined to determine their maturational stage, using a standardized system of classification based on breast development and pubic hair growth in girls and genital development and pubic hair growth in boys. These examinations allowed the children to be classified into 5 categories ('Tanner stages'). Those at Tanner stage 1 (pre-pubertal) were on average 10.5

years old, those at Tanner stage 5 (fully developed) on average 16.9 years old. They were given the opportunity of sleeping for 10 hours every night for three nights.

Measures of sleep patterns showed that the total amount of sleep taken remained constant across the five groups, but that the amount of deep slow wave sleep (stages 3 and 4) declined by 40 per cent between Tanner stage 1 and stage 5. Daytime alertness, assessed by the Multiple Sleep Latency Test, showed a decline in alertness between the pre-pubertal and mid-adolescent stages which remained low in late adolescents. (This test is based on the time taken to get to sleep during the day, given the opportunity.) This increase in daytime sleepiness (despite no reduction in the total amount of sleep taken) suggests that adolescence may indeed be associated with an increased need for sleep.

Comparing early adolescents sleeping as much as they liked with young college students who had slept between 7 and 9 hours (their preferred and habitual amounts of sleep) it was found that the college students were chronically sleepy during the day, some of them as sleepy as patients suffering from disorders of sleep, while the early adolescents were wide awake and alert. As parents exert less control over adolescents' bedtimes there is a tendency for bedtime to become later and later. A survey of adolescents' preferences found that nearly two-thirds of the sample endorsed the statement 'I enjoy staying up late' (351). The Stanford researchers speculate that many problems of adolescence, including communication problems with parents and the misuse of drugs, may have their origins in the normal adolescent's chronic sleepiness. They suggest that life for both parents and teenagers would greatly improve if only adolescents would sleep 1 hour longer every night.

Appendix
The Hull Sleep and Dreaming Questionnaire

The questionnaire was completed by 149 respondents, including 28 applicants to university, 19 students of nursing, 85 psychology students and 17 academic members of staff of the university. This sample was in no way representative of the country as a whole, but their answers could be taken to give some indication of relatively well-informed lay opinion of what seems obvious about sleep and dreaming.

The questionnaire is reproduced below (Table A), together with the number of respondents who agreed with the alternative answers. (In the version given to the respondents these alternatives alternated in order, so that 'True', or 'Always', sometimes appeared on the left, sometimes on the right. Here, for ease of comprehension, affirmative answers are all given on the right.)

Correlational analysis

Cluster analysis of correlation coefficients between responses to the questions suggests that the answers fall into two principle groups, or types. (That is, if a subject answered one question in a particular way, it tended to predict how they would respond to the others in its group, while not predicting how they might answer the questions in the other group.) These two clusters included 17 of the 23 questions.

Cluster analysis types

Type 1: questions 16, 23, 24, 14, 19, 20(-), 9(-)
Type 2: questions 15, 18, 21, 11, 17(-), 2(-), 12, 3(-), 10, 7

The first group, Type 1, included the questions about dreams foretelling the future, being caused by spirits, and so on, as well as (surprisingly) the proposition that dreaming is commonly accompanied by flaccid (relaxed) paralysis. That is, people who agreed with this statement tended to agree that dreams could be supernatural. Their belief in this proposition is therefore hardly likely to be based on the scientific evidence for it, which happens to be strong!

The second group, Group 2, of questions included those dealing with sleep being good for you, or necessary. People who subscribed to this view also endorsed the view that deprivation of dreaming sleep would drive you mad, and that cheese causes nightmares. Again, while some of their beliefs may have scientific support, others do not, and one cannot say that either of these clusters, or factors, represents a dimension of well-informed opinion.

Table A Beliefs about sleep questionnaire.

	(Never	Untrue Rarely	Maybe Sometimes	True Often	Always)
Sleep quality					
1. Lack of sleep gives you rings under the eyes		20	49	80	
2. Children need sleep to help them grow		22	34	93	
3. A strong alcoholic drink at bedtime improves sleep		51	44	54	
4. Adults need some sleep to stay healthy		4	12	133	
5. The prolonged use of sleeping pills is bad for you		3	18	128	
6. One hour's sleep before midnight is worth two afterwards		78	53	17	
7. A good night's sleep improves one's appearance		9	52	88	
8. Exercise improves the quality of sleep		4	49	96	
9. A warm nourishing drink at bedtime helps you to sleep		25	66	58	
10. A warm nourishing drink at bedtime reduces awakenings during the night		61	79	9	
11. There are some people who need no sleep at all		108	14	27	
Dreaming					
12. Dreams occur only in the few moments before you wake up		108	22	18	
13. Dreams are caused by spirits visiting the body during sleep	128	12	4	0	0
14. Dreaming is accompanied by flaccid (relaxed) paralysis		48	47	54	
15. Preventing people from dreaming will drive them mad		57	59	32	
16. Dreams can foretell the future	48	45	52	4	0
17. Most dreams are trivial and haphazard		45	58	46	
18. Cheese can cause nightmares		78	56	14	
19. Nightmares are caused by evil spirits visiting the body during sleep	138	8	2	1	0

Table A (*continued*)

	(Never	Untrue Rarely	Maybe Sometimes	True Often	Always)
20. Dreams are messages from the unconscious mind		6	72	71	
21. Interpreting dreams can throw light on mental processes		8	80	61	
22. Dreaming recurs three or four times every night		13	46	90	
23. The soul leaves the body and wanders during sleep	124	11	12	1	0

	No	Possibly	Certainly
24. In the holy scriptures of many religions there are accounts of messages from deities being received during dreams or of dreams foretelling the future (e.g. Pharoah's dream in the Old Testament, Mary's dream in the New Testament). Do you believe any of these accounts to be literally true?	53	76	19

Further Reading

Part I

Carlson, N. R., *Physiology of Behavior*, Massachusetts: Allyn and Bacon, 1991, ch. 9.

Precht, H. F. R. (1974), 'The behavioral states of the newborn infant (a review)', *Brain Research*, 76, 185–212.

Rechstchaffen, A and Kales, A. (eds), *A Manual of Standardized Terminology, Techniques and Scoring System for Sleep Stages of Human Adults*, Washington, DC: Public Information Service, US Government Printing Office, 1968.

Siegel, J. M. (1990), 'Mechanisms of sleep control', *Journal of Clinical Neurophysiology*, 7, 49–65.

Williams, R. L., Karacan, I. and Hursch, C. J., *Electroencephalography (EEG) of Human Sleep: Clinical applications*, New York: Wiley, 1974.

Part II

Arkin, A. M., Antrobus, J. S. and Ellman, S. J. (eds), *The Mind in Sleep*, 2nd edn, Hillsdale, New Jersey: Lawrence Erlbaum Associates, 1990.

Freud, S., *The Interpretation of Dreams. Standard edition of the complete psychological works of Sigmund Freud*, vol. 4, ed. and trans. J. Strachey, London: Hogarth Press, 1960.

Hobson, J. A., *The Dreaming Brain*, New York: Basic Books, 1988.

Rycroft, C., *The Innocence of Dreams*, Oxford: Oxford University Press, 1979.

Part III

Colquhoun, W. P. and Rutenfranz, J. (eds), *Studies in Shiftwork*, London: Taylor and Francis, 1980.

Horne, J., *Why We Sleep*, Oxford: Oxford University Press, 1988.

Mayes, A. (ed.), *Sleep Mechanisms and Functions*, London: Van Nostrand Reinhold (UK), 1983.

Monk, T. H. (ed.), *Sleep, Sleepiness and Performance*, London: Wiley, 1991.

Oswald, I. (1980), 'Sleep as a restorative process: human clues', *Progress in Brain Research*, 53, 279–88.

Part IV

Guilleminault, C. (ed.), *Sleep and its Disorders in Children*, New York: Raven Press, 1987.

Kryger, M. H., Roth, T. and Dement, W. C. (eds), *Principles and Practice of Sleep Medicine*, Philadelphia: Saunders, 1989.

Morgan, K., *Sleep and Ageing*, London: Croom Helm, 1987.

Parkes, J. D., *Sleep and its Disorders*, London: Saunders, 1985.

References

(1) Achermann, P. and Borbely, A. A. (1990), 'Simulation of human sleep: ultradian dynamics of electroencephalographic slow-wave activity', *Journal of Biological Rhythms*, *5*, 141–57.

(2) Adair, R., Bauchner, H., Philipp, B., Levenson, S. and Zuckerman, B. (1991), 'Night waking during infancy: role of parental presence at bedtime', *Pediatrics*, *87*, 500–4.

(3) Adair, R., Zuckerman, B., Bauchner, H., Philipp, B., and Levenson, S. (1992), 'Reducing night waking in infancy: a primary care intervention', *Pediatrics*, *89*, 585–8.

(4) Adam, K. (1980), 'Sleep as a restorative process and theory to explain why', *Progress in Brain Research*, *53*, 289–305.

(5) Adam, K. and Oswald, I. (1983), 'Protein synthesis, bodily renewal and the sleep-wake cycle', *Clinical Science*, *65*, 561–7.

(6) Adam, K., Oswald, I. and Shapiro, C. (1984), 'Effects of loprazolam and of triazolam on sleep and overnight urinary cortisol', *Psychopharmacology*, *82*, 389–94.

(7) Agnew, H. W., Webb, W. B. and Williams, R. L. (1964), 'The effects of stage four sleep deprivation', *Electroencephalography and Clinical Neurophysiology*, *7*, 68–71.

(8) Agnew, H. W., Webb, W. B. and Williams, R. L. (1966), 'The first night effect: an EEG study of sleep', *Psychophysiology*, *2*, 263–6.

(9) Allen, R. P., Wagman, A., Faillace, L. A. and MacIntosh, M. (1971), 'EEG sleep recovery following prolonged alcohol intoxication in alcoholics', *Journal of Nervous and Mental Disease*, *152*, 424–33.

(10) Allison, T. and Cicchetti, D. V. (1976), 'Sleep in mammals: ecological and constitutional correlates, *Science*, *194*, 732–4.

(11) Allison, T. and Goff, W. R. (1968), 'Sleep in a primitive mammal, the spiny anteater', *Psychophysiology*, *5*, 200.

(12) Ancoli-Isreal, S., Kripke, D. F., Menn, S. J. and Messin, S. (1981), 'Benefits of a sleep disorders clinic in a veterans administration medical center', *The Western Journal of Medicine*, *135*, 14–18.

(13) Anders, T., Emde, R. and Parmelee, A. (eds), *A Manual of Standardized Terminology, Techniques and Criteria for Scoring of States of Sleep and Wakefulness in Newborn Infants*, Los Angeles, CA: UCLA Brain Information Service, NINDS Neurological Information Network, 1971.

(14) Anders, T. F. and Weinstein, P. (1972), 'Sleep and disorders in infants and children – a review', *Pediatrics*, *50*, 312–24.

(15) Angus, R. R., Heslegrave, R. J. and Myles, W. S. (1985), 'Effects of prolonged sleep deprivation, with and without chronic physical exercise, on mood and performance', *Psychophysiology*, *22*, 276–82.

(16) Antrobus, J. S., Dement, W. and Fisher, C. (1964), 'Patterns of dreaming and dream recall: an EEG study', *Journal of Abnormal and Social Psychology*, *69*, 341–4.

(17) Apps, M. C. P., Moore Gillon, J. C. and Stradling, J. R. (1983), 'Underdiagnosis of obstructive sleep apnoea in Britain', *The Lancet*, *1*, 1054.

(18) Arkin, A. M. (1966), 'Sleep-talking: a review', *Journal of Nervous and Mental Disease*, *143*, 101–22.

(19) Arkin, A. M., 'Sleeptalking'. In A. M. Arkin, J. S. Antrobus and S. J. Ellman (eds), *The Mind in Sleep: Psychology and psychophysiology*, Hillsdale, New Jersey: Lawrence Erlbaum Associates, 1978, ch. 15.

(20) Arkin, A. M., Toth, M. F., Baker, J. and Hastey, J. M. (1970), 'The frequency of sleep talking in the laboratory among chronic sleep talkers and good dream recallers. The degree of concordance between the content of sleep talking and mentation recalled in wakefulness', *Journal of Nervous and Mental Disease*, *151*, 369–74, 375–93.

(21) Arnold, G. W., 'Rest and sleep'. In A. F. Fraser (ed.), *Ethology of Farm Animals*, Amsterdam: Elsevier, 1985.

(22) Aschoff, J. (1965), 'Circadian rhythms in man', *Science*, *148*, 1427–32.

(23) Aserinsky, E. and Kleitman, N. (1953), 'Regularly occuring periods of eye motility, and concomitant phenomena, during sleep', *Science*, *118*, 273–4.

(24) Aserinsky, E. and Kleitman, N. (1955), 'A motility cycle in sleeping infants as manifested by ocular and gross bodily motility', *Journal of Applied Physiology*, *8*, 11–18.

(25) Aserinsky, E., Lynch, J. A., Mack, M. E., Tzankoff, S. P. and Hurn, E. (1985), 'Comparison of eye motion in wakefulness and REM sleep', *Psychophysiology*, *22*, 1–10.

(26) Association of Sleep Disorders Centres (1979), 'Diagnostic classification of sleep and arousal disorders', *Sleep*, *2*, 1–137.

(27) Aston-Jones, G. (1985), 'Behavioural functions of locus coeruleus derived from cellular attrubutes', *Physiological Psychology*, *13*, 118–26.

(28) Aston-Jones, G. and Bloom, F. E. (1981), 'Norepinephrine-containing locus coeruleus neurons in behaving rats exhibit pronounced responses to non-noxious environmental stimuli', *Journal of Neuroscience*, *1*, 887–900.

(29) Aston-Jones, G., Ennis, M., Pieribone, V. A., Nickell, W. T. and Shipley, M. T. (1986), 'The brain nucleus locus coeruleus: restricted afferent control of a broad efferent network', *Science*, *234*, 734–7.

(30) Baekeland, F. and Laski, R. (1966), 'Exercise and sleep patterns in college athletes', *Perceptual and Motor Skills*, *23*, 1203–7.

(31) Bakin, H. (1970), 'Sleep walking in twins', *The Lancet*, *2*, 446–7.

(32) Barber, B. (1966), 'Factors underlying individual differences in dream reporting', *Psychophysiology*, *6*, 247–8.

(33) Becker, R. de, *Dreams, or the Machinations of the Night*, trans. Michael Heron, London: Allen and Unwin, 1968.

(34) Belvedere, E. and Foulkes, D. (1971), 'Telepathy and dreams: a failure to replicate' (abstract), *Perceptual and Motor Skills*, *33*, 783–9.

(35) Belyavin, A. and Nicholson, A. N. (1987), 'Rapid eye movement sleep in man: modulation by benzodiazepines', *Neuropharmacology*, *26*, 485–91.

(36) Benca, R. M., Kushida, C. A., Everson, C. A., Kalski, R., Bergmann, B. M. and Rechtschaffen, A. (1989), 'Sleep deprivation in the rat: VII. Immune function', *Sleep*, *12*, 47–52.

(37) Berger, R. J. (1963), 'Experimental modification of dream content by meaningful verbal stimuli', *British Journal of Psychiatry*, *109*, 722–40.

(38) Berger, R. J. (1984), 'Slow wave sleep, shallow torpor and hibernation: homologous states of diminished metabolism and body temperature', *Biological Psychology*, *19*, 305–26.

(39) Berger, R. J. and Oswald, I. (1962), 'Effects of sleep deprivation on behaviour, subsequent sleep, and dreaming', *Journal of Mental Science*, *108*, 457–65.

(40) Berger, R. J. and Oswald, I. (1962), 'Eye movements during active and passive dreams', *Science*, *137*, 601–3.

(41) Berger, R. J. and Walker, J. M. (1972), 'Sleep in the burrowing owl (*Speotyto cunicularia hypugaea*)', *Behavioural Biology*, *7*, 183–94.

(42) Berger, R. J., Olley, P. and Oswald, I. (1962), 'The EEG, eye movements and dreams of the blind', *Quarterly Journal of Experimental Psychology*, *14*, 183–6.

(43) Bergmann, B. M. and Rechtschaffen, A. (1989), 'Sleep deprivation in the rat: III. Total sleep deprivation', *Sleep*, *12*, 13–21.

(44) Bergmann, B. M., Everson, C. A., Kushida, C. A., Fang, V. S., Leitch, C. A., Schoeller, D. A., Refetoff, S. and Rechtschaffen, A. (1989), 'Sleep deprivation in the rat: V. Energy use and medication', *Sleep*, *12*, 31–41.

(45) Bergmann, B. M., Everson, C. A., Kushida, C. A., Gilliland, M. A., Obermeyer, W. and Rechtschaffen, A. (1989), 'Sleep deprivation in the rat: II. Methodology', *Sleep*, *12*, 5–12.

(46) Bert, J., Kripke, D. F. and Rhodes, J. M. (1970), 'Electroencephalogram of the mature chimpanzee: 24 hour recordings', *Electroencephalography and Clinical Neurophysiology*, *28*, 368–73.

(47) Berry, D. T. R., Webb, W. B. and Block, A. J. (1984), 'Sleep apnea

syndrome: a critical review of the apnea index as a diagnostic criterion', *Chest*, *84*, 529–31.

(48) Besterman, T. (1933), 'Report of an inquiry into pre-cognitive dreams', *Proceedings of the Society for Psychical Research*, *41*, 186–204.

(49) Betts, T. A. and Alford, C. (1985), 'Beta-blockers and sleep: a controlled trial', *European Journal of Clinical Pharmacology*, *28*, 65–8.

(50) Bidder, R. T., Gray, O. P., Howells, P. M. and Eaton, M. P. (1986), 'Sleep problems in pre-school children: community clinics', *Child: Care, health and development*, *12*, 325–37.

(51) Birmingham Research Unit of the Royal College of General Practitioners (1978), 'Practice activity analysis, 4. Psychotropic drugs', *Journal of the Royal College of General Practitioners*, *28*, 122–4.

(52) Bixler, E. O., Kales, A., Soldatos, C. R., Kales, J. D. and Healey, S. (1979), 'Prevalence of sleep disorders in the Los Angeles metropolitan area', *American Journal of Psychiatry*, *136*, 1257–62.

(53) Bjerner, B. (1949), 'Alpha depression and lowered pulse rate during delayed actions in a serial reaction test: a study in sleep deprivation', *Acta Physiologica Scandinavica*, *19*, Supplement 65, 1–93.

(54) Blake, H. and Gerard, R. W. (1937), 'Brain potentials during sleep', *American Journal of Physiology*, *119*, 692–703.

(55) Bokert, E. (1968), 'The effects of thirst and related auditory stimulation on dream reports', *Dissertation Abstracts*, *28*, 122–31.

(56) Bonnet, M., 'Performance during sleep'. In W. B. Webb (ed.), *Biological Rhythms, Sleep and Performance*, Chichester: John Wiley, 1982, ch. 8.

(57) Borbely, A., *Secrets of Sleep*, trans. Deborah Schneider, London: Longman, 1986.

(58) Borbely, A. A. and Neuhaus, H. U. (1979), 'Sleep-deprivation: effects on sleep and the EEG in the rat', *Journal of Comparative Physiology*, *133*, 71–87.

(59) Borbely, A. A. and Tobler, I. (1989), 'Endogenous sleep-promoting substances and sleep regulation', *Physiological Reviews*, *69*, 605–70.

(60) Bosinelli, M., Cicogna, P. and Molinari, S. (1974), 'The tonic-phasic model and the testing of self-participation in different stages of sleep', *Italian Journal of Psychology*, *1*, 35–65.

(61) Bradley, C. and Meddis, R. (1974), 'Arousal threshold in dreaming sleep', *Physiological Psychology*, *2*, 109–14.

(62) Brazier, M. A. B., *A History of the Electrical Activity of the Brain*, New York: Macmillan, 1961.

(63) Breger, L. (1967), 'Function of dreams', *Journal of Abnormal Psychology*, *72*, 1–28.

(64) Breger, L., Hunter, I. and Lane, R. W., *The Effect of Stress on Dreams*, New York: International Universities Press, 1971.

(65) Brezinova, V. and Oswald, I. (1972), 'Sleep after a bedtime beverage', *British Medical Journal*, *2*, 431–3.

(66) Broughton, R. J. (1968), 'Sleep disorders: disorders of arousal?', *Science*, *159*, 1070–8.

(67) Bunnell, D. E., Bevier, W. and Horvath, S. M. (1983), 'Effects of exhaustive exercise on the sleep of men and women', *Psychophysiology*, *20*, 50–8.

(68) Buysse, D. J., 'Drugs affecting sleep, sleepiness and performance'. In T. H. Monk (ed.), *Sleep, Sleepiness and Performance*, Wiley: London, 1991.

(69) Caekebeke, J. F. V., Van Dijk, J. G. and Van Sweden, B. (1990), 'Habituation to K-complexes or event-related potentials during sleep', *Electroencephaligraphy and Clinical Neurophysiology*, Supplement 41, 168–72.

(70) Callaway, C. W., Lydic, R., Baghdoyan, H. A. and Hobson, J. A. (1987), 'Pontogeniculooccipatal waves: spontaneous visual system activity during rapid eye movement sleep', *Cellular and Molecular Neurobiology*, *2*, 105–49.

(71) Carey, W. B. (1974), 'Night-waking and temperament in infancy', *Journal of Pediatrics*, *84*, 756–8.

(72) Carlson, N. R., *Physiology of Behavior*, 4th edn, Boston: Allyn and Bacon, 1991.

(73) Carskadon, M. A. and Dement, W. C. (1975), 'Sleep studies on a 90-minute day', *Electroencephalography and Clinical Neurophysiology*, *39*, 145–55.

(74) Carskadon, M. A. and Dement, W. C. (1981), 'Cumulative effects of sleep restriction on daytime sleepiness', *Psychophysiology*, *18*, 107–13.

(75) Carskadon, M. A. and Dement, W. C., 'Sleepiness in the normal adolescent'. In C. Guilleminault (ed.), *Sleep and Its Disorders in Children*, New York: Raven Press, 1987.

(76) Cartwright, Rosalind, *Night Life*, New Jersey: Prentice Hall, 1977.

(77) Caton, R. (1875), 'The electric currents of the brain', *British Medical Journal*, *2*, 278–82.

(78) Chenen, A. M. L., van Hulzen, Z. J. M. and van Luijtelaar, E. L. J. M. (1983), 'Paradoxical sleep in the dark period of the rat: a dissociation between electrophysiological and behavioural characteristics', *Behavioural and Neural Biology*, *37*, 350–6.

(79) Cohen, D. B. and Wolfe, G. (1973), 'Dream recall and repression: evidence for an alternative hypothesis', *Journal of Consulting and Clinical Psychology*, *41*, 349–55.

(80) Committee on Safety of Medicines (1988), 'Benzodiazepines, dependence and withdrawal symptoms', *Current Problems*, no. 21, 1988.

(81) Corcoran, D. W. J. (1962), 'Noise and loss of sleep', *Quarterly Journal of Experimental Psychology*, *14*, 178–82.

(82) Costello, C. G. and Selby, M. M. (1965), 'The relationship between sleep patterns and reactive and endogenous depression', *British Journal of Psychiatry*, *111*, 497–501.

(83) Crick, F. and Mitchison, G. (1983), 'The function of REM sleep', *Nature*, *304*, 111–14.

(84) Crick, F. and Mitchison, G. (1986), 'REM sleep and neural nets', *Journal of Mind and Behavior*, 7, 229–49.

(85) Crisp, A. H. and Stonehill, E., *Sleep, Nutrition and Mood*, London: Wiley, 1977.

(86) Czeisler, C. A., Allan, J. S., Strogatz, S. H., Ronda, J. M., Sanchez, R., Rios, C. D., Freitag, W. O., Richardson, G. S. and Kronauer, R. E. (1986), 'Bright light resets the human circadian pacemaker independent of the timing of the sleep-wake cycle', *Science*, *233*, 667–71.

(87) Czeisler, C. A., Johnson, M. P., Duffy, J. F., Brown, E. N., Ronda, J. M. and Kronauer, R. E. (1990), 'Exposure to bright light and darkness to treat physiologic maladaptation to night work', *New England Journal of Medicine*, *322*, 1253–9.

(88) Czeisler, C. A., Kronauer, R. E., Allan, J. S., Duffy, J. F., Jewett, M. E., Brown, E. N. and Ronda, J. M. (1989), 'Bright light induction of strong (type O) resetting of the human circadian pacemaker', *Science*, *244*, 1328–33.

(89) Daan, S., Beersma, D. G. M. and Brobely, A. A. (1984), 'The timing of human sleep: recovery process gated by a circadian pacemaker', *American Journal of Physiology*, *246*, R.161–78.

(90) Darwin, E., *Zoonomia, or, The Laws of Organic Life*, 2nd, corrected edn, London: J. Johnson, 1796.

(91) Davis, H., Davis, P. A., Loomis, A. L., Harvey, E. N. and Hobart, G. (1937), 'Human brain potentials during the onset of sleep', *Journal of Neurophysiology*, *1*, 24–38.

(92) De Andres, I., Gutierrez-Rivas, E., Nava, E. and Reinoso-Suarez, F. (1976), 'Independence of sleep–wakefulness cycle in an implanted head "encephale isole"', *Neuroscience Letters*, *2*, 13–18.

(93) Deary, I. J. and Tait, R. (1987), 'Effects of sleep disruption on cognitive performance and mood in medical house officers', *British Medical Journal*, *295*, 1513–16.

(94) Delorme, F., Froment, J. L. and Jouvet, M. (1966), 'Supression du sommeil par la *p*-chlormethamphetamine et la *p*-chlorophenylalanine', *Comptes rendus société biologique* (Paris), *160*, 2347–51.

(95) Delorme, F., Vimont, P. and Jouvet, D. (1964), 'Etude statistique du cycle veille-sommeils chez le chat', *Comptes rendus société biologique* (Paris), *58*, 2128–30.

(96) Dement, W. C. (1960), 'The effect of dream deprivation', *Science*, *131*, 1705–7.

(97) Dement, W. C., 'Studies on the function of rapid eye movement (paradoxical) sleep in human subjects'. In Jouvet, M. (ed.), *Aspects anatomo-fonctionnels de la physiologie du sommeil*, Paris: Editions du Centre Nationale de la Recherche Scientifique, 1965, pp. 571–608.

(98) Dement, W., *Some Must Watch While Some Must Sleep*, Stanford: Stanford University Press, 1972; repr. San Francisco: Freeman, 1974.

(99) Dement, W. C., 'Sleep deprivation and the organization of the behavioral states'. In C. D. Clemente, D. P. Purpura and F. E. Mayer (eds), *Sleep and the Maturing Nervous System*, New York: Academic Press, 1972, pp. 319–55.

(100) Dement, W. and Kleitman, N. (1957), 'The relation of eye movements during sleep to dream activity: an objective method for the study of dreaming', *Journal of Experimental Psychology*, *53*, 339–46.

(101) Dement, W. and Wolpert, E. A. (1958), 'The relation of eye movements, body motility, and external stimuli to dream content', *Journal of Experimental Psychology*, *55*, 543–53.

(102) Desmond, A. J., *The Hot-Blooded Dinosaurs*, London: Futura, 1977.

(103) Dickson, P. R. (1984), 'Effect of a fleecy woolen underlay on sleep', *Medical Journal of Australia*, *140*, 87–9.

(104) Doering, C. H., Kraemer, H. C., Brodie, K. H. and Hamburg, D. A. (1975), 'A cycle of plasma testosterone in the human male', *Journal of Clinical Endocrinology Metabolism*, *40*, 492.

(105) Dunleavy, D. L. F. and Oswald, I. (1973), 'Phenelzine, mood response and sleep', *Archives of General Psychiatry*, *28*, 353–6.

(106) Dunleavy, D. L. F., Oswald, I., Brown, P. and Strong, J. A. (1974), 'Hyperthyroidism, sleep and growth hormone', *Electroencephalography and Clinical Neurophysiology*, *36*, 259–63.

(107) Dunne, J. W., *An Experiment with Time*, New York: Macmillan, 1927.

(108) Dunnell, K. and Cartwright, A., *Medicine Takers, Prescribers, and Hoarders*, London: Routledge and Kegan Paul, 1972.

(109) Easton, P. A., West, P., Meatherall, R. C., Brewster, J. F., Lertzman, M. and Kryger, M. H. (1987), 'The effect of excessive ethanol ingestion on sleep in severe chronic obstructive pulmonary disease', *Sleep*, *10*, 224–33.

(110) Eguchi, K. and Sato, T. (1980), 'Characterization of the neurons in the region of solitary tract nucleus during sleep', *Physiology and Behavior*, *23*, 99–102.

(111) Eguchi, K. and Sato, T. (1980), 'Convergence of sleep-wakefulness subsystems onto single neurons in the region of cats' solitary tract nucleus', *Arch. Ital. Biol.*, *118*, 331–45.

(112) Ellingson, R. J. (1964), 'Studies of the electrical activity of the developing human brain', *Progress in Brain Research*, *9*, 26–53.

(113) Ellis, H. D. and Young, A. W. (1990), 'Accounting for delusional misidentifications', *British Journal of Psychiatry*, *157*, 239–48.

(114) Emerson, R. W., *Lectures and Biographical Sketches*, Boston: Houghton Mifflin, 1884.

(115) Emmons, W. H. and Simon, C. W. (1956), 'The non-recall of material presented during sleep', *American Journal of Psychology*, *69*, 76–81.

(116) Empson, J. A. C. (1977), 'Periodicity in body temperature in man', *Experientia*, *33*, 342–3.

(117) Empson, J. A. C. and Clarke, P. R. F. (1970), 'Rapid eye movements and remembering', *Nature*, *227*, 287–8.

(118) Empson, J. A. C., Hearne, K. M. T. and Tilley, A. J., 'REM sleep and reminiscence'. In W. P. Koella (ed.), *Sleep 1980: Circadian rhythms, dreams, noise and sleep*, Basle: S. Karger, 1981.

(119) Empson, W. (1964), 'The Ancient Mariner', *Critical Quarterly*, 6:4; republished in W. Empson, *Argufying: Essays on literature and culture*, ed. with an introduction by J. Haffenden, Iowa City: University of Iowa Press, 1987.

(120) Ephron, H. S. and Carrington, P. (1966), 'Rapid eye movement sleep and cortical homeostasis', *Psychological Review*, *73*, 500–26.

(121) Evans, F. J., Gustafson, L. A., O'Connell, D. N., Orne, P. T. and Shor, R. E. (1970), 'Verbally induced behavioral responses during sleep', *Journal of Nervous and Mental Diseases*, *150*, 171–87.

(122) Everson, C. A., Bergmann, B. M. and Rechtschaffen, A. (1989), 'Sleep deprivation in the rat: III. Total sleep deprivation', *Sleep*, *12*, 13–21.

(123) Everson, C. A., Gilliland, M. A., Kushida, C. E., Pilcher, J. J., Fang, V. S., Refetoff, S., Bergmann, B. M. and Rechtschaffen, A. (1989), 'Sleep deprivation in the rat: IX. Recovery', *Sleep*, *12*, 60–7.

(124) Fagen, J. W. and Rovee-Collier, C. (1983), 'Memory retrieval: a time-locked process in infants', *Science*, *222*, 1349–51.

(125) Faraday, Ann, *Dream Power*, London: Hodder and Stoughton, 1972.

(126) Faraday, Ann, *The Dream Game*, London: Maurice Temple Smith, 1975.

(127) Feinberg, I., Fein, G., Walker, J. M. *et al.* (1979), 'Flurazepam effects on sleep EEG', *Archives of General Psychiatry*, *36*, 95–102.

(128) Feinberg, I., Koresko, R. L. and Heller, N. (1967), 'EEG sleep patterns as a function of normal and pathological aging in man', *Journal of Psychiatric Research*, *5*, 107.

(129) Ferber, R., 'The sleepless child'. In C. Guilleminault (ed.), *Sleep and Its Disorders in Children*, New York: Raven Press, 1987.

(130) Firth, H. (1973), 'Habituation during sleep', *Psychophysiology*, *10*, 43–51.

(131) Flanigan, W. F. Jnr (1973), 'Sleep and wakefulness in chelonian reptiles: 1. The red-footed tortoise', *Sleep Research*, *2*, 82.

(132) Flanigan, W. F. Jnr, Wilcox, R. H. and Rechtschaffen, A. (1973), 'The EEG and behavioral continuum of the crocodilian, *Caiman sclerops*', *Electroencephalography and Clinical Neurophysiology*, *34*, 521–38.

(133) Folkard, S. and Monk, T. H., 'Individual differences in the circadian response to a weekly rotating shift system'. In A. Reinberg, N. Vieux and P. Andlauer (eds), *Night and Shift Work: Biological and social aspects*, Oxford: Pergamon Press, 1981, pp. 365–74.

(134) Foulkes, D., *Dreaming: A cognitive-psychological analysis*, Hillsdale, New Jersey: Lawrence Erlbaum Associates, 1985.

(135) Foulkes, D. and Pope, R. (1973), 'Primary visual experience and secondary cognitive elaboration in state REM: a modest confirmation and extension', *Perceptual and Motor Skills*, *37*, 107–18.

(136) Foulkes, D. and Rechtschaffen, A. (1964), 'Presleep determinants of dream content: effects of two films', *Perceptual and Motor Skills*, *19*, 983–1005.

(137) Foulkes, D. and Vogel, G. (1966), 'Mental activity at sleep onset', *Journal of Abnormal Psychology*, *70*, 231–43.

(138) Foulkes, D., Pivik, T., Steadman, H. S., Spear, P. S. and Symonds, J. D. (1967), 'Dreams of the male child: an EEG study', *Journal of the American Psychoanalytical Association*, *18*, 747–82.

(139) Fowler, M. J., Sullivan, M. J. and Ekstrand, B. R. (1973), 'Sleep and memory', *Science*, *179*, 302–4.

(140) Frazer, J. G., *Folk-lore in the Old Testament*, vol. 2, London: Macmillan, 1918.

(141) Frazier, K. (ed.), *Science Confronts the Paranormal*, New York: Prometheus Books, 1986.

(142) Friedmann, J., Globus, G., Huntley, A., Mullaney, D., Naitoh, P. and Johnson, L. (1977), 'Performance and mood during and after gradual sleep reduction', *Psychophysiology*, *14*, 245–50.

(143) Freeman, G. K. (1978), 'Analysis of primary care prescribing – a "constructive" coding system for drugs', *Journal of the Royal College of General Practitioners*, *28*, 547–51.

(144) Freedman, R. R. and Sattler, H. L. (1982), 'Physiological and psychological factors in sleep-onset insomnia', *Journal of Abnormal Psychology*, *91*, 380–9.

(145) Freemon, F. R., McNew, J. J. and Ross Adey, W. (1971), 'Chimpanzee sleep stages', *Electroencephalography and Clinical Neurophysiology*, *31*, 485–9.

(146) Freud, S., *Project for a Scientific Psychology* (1895), in *Complete Psychological Works, Standard Edition*, vol. 1, trans. and ed. J. Strachey, London: Hogarth Press, 1966.

(147) Freud, S., *The Interpretation of Dreams*, trans. A. A. Brill, London: George Allen and Unwin Ltd, 1913; rev. edn, 1932.

(148) Freud, S., *Introductory Lectures on Psycho-Analysis*, standard edition, *15–16*, pp. 128–9.

(149) Friedman, R. C., Bigger, J. T. and Kornfeld, D. S. (1971), 'The intern and sleep loss', *New England Journal of Medicine*, *285*, 201–3.

(150) Friedman, S. and Fisher, C. (1967), 'On the presence of a rhythmic, diurnal, oral instinctual drive cycle in man: a preliminary report', *Journal of the American Psycho-analytic Association*, *15*, 317–43.

(151) Fuller, C. A., Lydic, R., Sulzman, F. M., Albers, H. E., Pepper, B. and Moore-Ede, M. C. (1981), 'Circadian rhythm of body temperature persists after suprachiasmatic lesions in the squirrel monkey', *American Journal of Physiology*, *241*, R385–91.

(152) Gahagan, L. (1936), 'Sex differences in recall of stereotyped dreams, sleep-talking and sleep-walking', *Journal of Genetic Psychology*, *48*, 227–36.

(153) Gaillard, J.-M. and Blois, R. (1989), 'Differential effects of flunitrazepam on human sleep in combination with flumazenil', *Sleep*, *12*, 120–32.

(154) Gaillard, J.-M., Nicholson, A. N. and Pascoe, P. A., 'Neurotransmitter systems'. In M. H. Kryger, T. Roth and W. C. Dement (eds), *Principles and Practice of Sleep Medicine*, Philadelphia: W. B. Saunders, 1989, ch. 19.

(155) Galton, F., *Inquiries Into the Human Faculty and its Development*, London: Macmillan, 1883.

(156) Gander, P. H., Kronauer, R. E. and Graeber, R. C. (1985), 'Phase shifting two coupled circadian pacemakers: implications for jet lag', *American Journal of Physiology*, *249*, R704–19.

(157) Garber, Marjorie B., *Dream in Shakespeare*, New York: Yale University Press, 1974.

(158) Garfield, P. L. *Creative Dreaming*, New York: Simon and Schuster, 1974.

(159) Gauthier, P. and Gottesmann, C. (1983), 'Influence of total sleep deprivation on event-related potentials in man', *Psychophysiology*, *20*, 351–5.

(160) Giannocorou, M. (1984), M.Sc. dissertation, University of Hull.

(161) Gilliland, M. A., Bergmann, B. M. and Rechtschaffen, A. (1989), 'Sleep deprivation in the rat: VIII. High EEG amplitude sleep deprivation', *Sleep*, *12*, 53–9.

(162) Gillin, J. C., Duncan, W., Pettigrew, K. D., Frankel, B. L. and Snyder, F. (1979), 'Successful separation of depressed, normal and insomniac subjects by EEG sleep data'. *Archives of General Psychiatry*, *36*, 85–90.

(163) Globus, G. G., Gardner, R. and Williams, T. A. (1969), 'Relation of sleep onset to rapid eye movement sleep', *Archives of General Psychiatry*, *21*, 151–4.

(164) Glover, T. R. *The Conflict of Religions and the Early Roman Empire*, London: Methuen, 1909.

(165) Goldsmith, O. *A History of The Earth and Animated Nature*, vol. 1, Liverpool: Nuttal and Dixon, 1811.

(166) Goode, G. B. (1962), 'Sleep paralysis', *A.M.A. Archives of Neurology*, *6*, 228–34.

(167) Goodenough, D. R., 'Dream recall: history and current status'. In A. M. Arkin, J. S. Antrobus and S. J. Ellman (eds), *The Mind in Sleep*, New Jersey: Lawrence Erlbaum Associates, 1978.

(168) Goodenough, D. R., Shapiro, A., Holden, M and Steinschriber, L. (1959), '"Dreamers" and "non-dreamers"', *Journal of Abnormal and Social Psychology*, *59*, 295–302.

(169) Goodenough, D. R., Witkin, H. A., Koulack, D. and Cohen, H. (1975), 'The effects of stress films on dream affect and on respiration and eye-movement activity during REM sleep', *Psychophysiology*, *12*, 313–320.

220 *References*

(170) Gorer, G. 'Psychoanalysis in the world'. In Charles Rycroft (ed.), *Psychoanalysis Observed*, London: Constable, 1966.
(171) Gresham, S. C., Webb, W. B. and Williams, R. L. (1963), 'Alcohol and caffeine: effect on inferred visual dreaming', *Science*, *134*, 1226–7.
(172) Griffin, M. L. and Foulkes, D. (1977), 'Deliberate pre-sleep control of dream content: an experimental study', *Perceptual and Motor Skills*, *45*, 660–2.
(173) Griffin, S. J. and Trinder, J. (1978), 'Physical fitness, exercise and human sleep', *Psychophysiology*, *15*, 447–50.
(174) Griffith, R. M., Miyagi, O. and Tago, A. (1958), 'The universality of typical dreams: Japanese vs. Americans', *American Anthropologist*, *60*, 1173–9.
(175) Gross, J., Byrne, J. and Fisher, C. (1965), 'Eye movements during emergent stage 1 EEG in subjects with lifelong blindness', *Journal of Nervous and Mental Disease*, *141*, 365–70.
(176) Guilleminault, C., Eldridge, F. L. and Dement, W. C. (1973), 'Insomnia with sleep apnea: a new syndrome', *Science*, *181*, 856–8.
(177) Guilleminault, C. and Dement, W. C., 'Sleep apnea syndrome and related sleep disorders'. In R. L. Williams and I. Kornean (eds), *Sleep Disorders: Diagnosis and treatment*, New York: Wiley, 1978, pp. 9–28.
(178) Guilleminault, C., Hayes, B., Smith, L. and Simmons, F. B. (1983), 'Palatopharyngoplasty and obstructive sleep apnea syndrome', *Bull. Europ. Physiopath. Resp.*, *19*, 595–9.
(179) Guilleminault, C., Tilkian, A. and Dement, W. C. (1976), 'The sleep apnea syndromes', *Annual Review of Medicine*, *27*, 465–84.
(180) Haider, I. and Oswald, I. (1971), 'Effects of amylobarbitone and nitrazepam on the electrodermogram and other features of sleep', *British Journal of Psychiatry*, *118*, 519–22.
(181) Halberg, F. (1969), 'Chronobiology', *Annual Review of Physiology*, *31*, 675–725.
(182) Halberg, F., Halberg, E., Barnum, C. P. and Bittner, J. J. (1959), 'Physiologic periodicity in human beings and mice, the lighting regimen and daily routine'. In R. B. Withrow (ed.), *Photoperiodism and Related Phenomena in Plants and Animals*, Washington DC: AAAS.
(183) Hall, C. S. (1951), 'What people dream about', *Scientific American*, *184*, 60–3.
(184) Hamilton, P., Wilkinson, R. T. and Edwards, R. S., 'A study of four days partial sleep deprivation'. In W. P. Colquhoun (ed.), *Aspects of Human Efficiency: Diurnal rhythm and loss of sleep*, London: English Universities Press, 1972.
(185) Hansel, C. E. M., *ESP and Parapsychology: A re-evaluation*, New York: Prometheus Books, 1980.
(186) Hartmann, E. (1968), 'The effect of four drugs on sleep in man', *Psychopharmacologia*, *12*, 346–53.
(187) Hartmann, E., 'Long-term administration of psychotropic drugs: effects

on human sleep'. In R. L. Williams and I. Karacan (eds), *Pharmacology of Human Sleep*, New York: Wiley, 1976, pp. 211–23.

(188) Hartmann, E., *The Sleeping Pill*, New Haven: Yale University Press, 1978.

(189) Haslam, D. R., 'The military performance of soldiers in continuous operations: exercises "early call" I and II'. In L. C. Johnson, D. I. Tepas, W. P. Colquhoun and M. J. Colligan (eds), *Biological Rhythms, Sleep and Shift Work*, New York: Spectrum Publications, 1981, pp. 435–58.

(190) Haslam, D. R. (1982), 'Sleep loss, recovery sleep, and military performance', *Ergonomics*, 25, 163-78.

(191) Hauri, P. (1966), 'Effects of evening activity on early night sleep', *Psychophysiology*, 4, 267–77.

(192) Hauri, P. and Hawkins, D. R. (1973), 'Alpha-delta sleep', *Electroencephalography and Clinical Neurophysiology*, 34, 233–7.

(193) Hauri, P. and Olmstead, E. (1983), 'What is the moment of sleep onset for insomniacs?', *Sleep*, 6, 10–15.

(194) Haynes, S. N., Adams, A. and Franzen, M. (1981), 'The effects of presleep stress on sleep-onset insomnia', *Journal of Abnormal Psychology*, 90, 601–6.

(195) Hebb, D. O. (1968), 'Concerning imagery', *Psychological Review*, 75, 466–74.

(196) Heller, H. C. and Glotzbach, S. F. (1977), 'Thermoregulation during sleep and hibernation: environmental physiology II', *International Review of Physiology*, 15, 147–88.

(197) Hennevin, E. and Leconte, P. (1971), 'La fonction du sommeil paradoxal', *Année psychologique*, 72, 489–505.

(198) Herman, J. H., Ellman, S. J. and Roffwarg, H. P., 'The problem of NREM dream recall re-examined'. In A. M. Arkin, J. S. Antrobus and S. J. Ellman (eds), *The Mind of Sleep*, New York: Wiley, 1978.

(199) Hishikawa, T., 'Sleep paralysis'. In C. Guilleminault, W. C. Dement and P. Passuant (eds), *Narcolepsy*, New York: Spectrum, 1976.

(200) Hobson, J. A. and McCarley, R. W. (1977), 'The brain as a dream state generator: an activation-synthesis hypothesis of the dream process', *American Journal of Psychiatry*, 134, 1335–48.

(201) Hockey, G. R. J. (1970), 'Effect of loud noise on attentional selectivity', *Quarterly Journal of Experimental Psychology*, 22, 28–36.

(202) Hockey, G. R. J. (1970), 'Changes in attention allocation in a multi-component task under loss of sleep', *British Journal of Psychology*, 61, 473–80.

(203) Holt, R. R., 'On the nature and generality of mental imagery'. In P. Sheehan (ed.), *The Function and Nature of Imagery*, New York: Academic Press, 1972.

(204) Horne, J. A. (1981), 'The effects of exercise upon sleep: a critical review', *Biological Psychology*, 12, 241–90.

(205) Horne, J., *Why We Sleep: The functions of sleep in humans and other mammals*, Oxford: Oxford University Press, 1988.

(206) Horne, J. A. and Moore, V. J. (1985), 'Sleep EEG effects of exercise with and without additional body cooling', *Electroencephalography and Clinical Neurophysiology*, *60*, 33–8.

(207) Horne, J. A. and Pettitt, A. N. (1985), 'High incentive effects on vigilance performance during 72 hours of total sleep deprivation', *Acta Psychologica*, *58*, 123–39.

(208) Horne, J. A. and Porter, J. M. (1976), 'Time of day effects with standardized exercise upon subsequent sleep', *Electroencephalography and Clinical Neurophysiology*, *40*, 178–84.

(209) Horne, J. A. and Reid, A. J. (1985), 'Night-time sleep EEG changes following body heating in a warm bath', *Electroencephalography and Clinical Neurophysiology*, *60*, 154–7.

(210) Horne, J. A. and Wilkinson, R. T. (1985), 'Chronic sleep reduction: daytime vigilance performance and EEG measures of sleepiness, with particular reference to "practice" effects', *Psychophysiology*, *22*, 69–77.

(211) Horton, R. H., *Stories of the Early Church*, vols. 1–4, London: Edward Arnold, 1963.

(212) Hull, C. L. (1962), 'Psychology of the scientist: IV. Passages from the "idea books" of Clark L. Hull', *Perceptual and Motor Skills*, *15*, 807–22.

(213) Humble, R., *Marco Polo*, London: Weidenfeld and Nicolson, 1975.

(214) Hume, K. I. (1986), Paper presented at the December 1986 meeting of the Psychophysiology Society (UK), Charing Cross Hospital, London.

(215) Hume, K. I. and Mills, J. N. (1977), 'Rhythms of REM and slow-wave sleep in subjects living on abnormal time schedules', *Waking and Sleeping*, *1*, 291–6.

(216) Huntley, A. C. and Cohen, H. B. (1980), 'Further comments on "sleep" in the desert iguana, *Dipsosaurus dorsalis*', *Sleep Research*, *9*, 111.

(217) Immelman, V. K. and Gebbing, H. (1962), 'Schlaf bei Giraffen', *Z. Tierpsychol.*, *19*, 84–92.

(218) Inouye, S.-I. T. and Kawamura, H. (1979), 'Persistence of circadian rhythmicity in a mammalian hypothalamic "island" containing the supra-chiasmatic nucleus', *Proc. natl. Acad. Sci. USA*, *76*, 5962–6.

(219) Jacobs, L., Feldman, M., and Bender, M. B. (1972), 'Are the eye movements of dreaming sleep related to the visual images of the dreams?', *Psychophysiology*, *9*, 393–401.

(220) James, W., *The Will to Believe, and Other Essays*, London: Longmans, 1896.

(221) Johns, M. W. and Masterton, J. P. (1974). 'Effects of flurazepam on sleep in the laboratory', *Pharmacology*, *11*, 358–64.

(222) Johnson, L. C. and Chernik, D. A. (1982), 'Sedative-hypnotics and human performance', *Psychopharmacology*, *76*, 101–13.

(223) Johnson, L. C. and Lubin, A. (1967), 'The orienting reflex during waking and sleeping', *Electroencephalography and Clinical Neurophysiology*, *22*, 11–21.

(224) Johnson, L. C., Naitoh, P., Moses, J. M. and Lubin, A. (1974), 'Interaction of REM deprivation and stage 4 deprivation with total sleep loss: experiment 2', *Psychophysiology*, *11*, 147–59.

(225) Jones, H. S. and Oswald, I. (1968), 'Two cases of health insomnia', *Electroencephalography and Clinical Neurophysiology*, *24*, 378–80.

(226) Jouvet, M. (1967), 'Neurophysiology of the states of sleep', *Psychological Review*, *47*, 117–34.

(227) Jouvet, M. (1972), 'The role of monoamines and acetylcholine-containing neurons in the regulation of the sleep-walking cycle', *Rev. Physiol.*, *64*, 166–307.

(228) Jouvet, M., 'Does a genetic programming of the brain occur during paradoxical sleep?' In P. Buser and A. Buser-Rogeul (eds), *Cerebral Correlates of Conscious Behaviour*, Amsterdam: Elsevier/North Holland, 1978.

(229) Jouvet, M. and Renault, J. (1966), 'Insomnie persistante après lesions des noyaux du raphe chez le chat', *C.R. Soc. Biol.* (Paris), *160*, 1461–5.

(230) Jouvet, M., Denoyer, M., Hitahama, K. and Sallanon, M., 'Slow wave sleep and indolamines: a hypothalamic target'. In A. Wauquier (ed.), *Slow Wave Sleep: Physiological, pathophysiological and functional aspects*, New York: Raven Press, 1989, pp. 91–108.

(231) Kahn, E., Dement, W. C., Fisher, C. and Barmcak, J. E. (1962), 'Incidence of colour in immediately recalled dreams', *Science*, *137*, 1055–6.

(232) Kahn, E. and Fisher, C., 'The sleep characteristics of the normal aged male', *Journal of Nervous and Mental Disorders*, *148*, 477–82.

(233) Kales, A., Hewser, G., Jacobson, A., Kales, J. D., Hanley, J., Zweizig, J. R. and Paulson, M. J. (1967), 'All night sleep studies in hypothyroid patients before and after treatment', *Psychosomatics*, *14*, 33–7.

(234) Kales, A., Jacobson, A., Paulson, M. J., Kales, J. and Walter, R. D. (1966), 'Somnambulism: psychophysiological correlates', *Archives of General Psychiatry*, *14*, 586–94.

(235) Kales, A., Malmstrom, E. J., Scharf, M. B. and Rudin, R. T., 'Psychophysiological and biochemical changes following use and withdrawal of hypnotics'. In A. Kales, (ed.), *Sleep Physiology and Pathology*, Philadelphia: Lippincott, 1969.

(236) Kales, A., Tan, T. L., Kollar, E. J., Naitoh, P., Preston, T. A. and Malmstrom, E. J. (1970), 'Sleep patterns following 205 hours of sleep deprivation', *Psychosomatic Medicine*, *32*, 189–200.

(237) Karacan, I., Salis, P. J. and Hursch, C. J. (1971), 'New approaches to the evaluation and treatment of insomnia', *Psychosomatics*, *12*, 81–8.

(238) Katayama, Y., DeWitt, D. S., Becker, D. P. and Hayes, R. L. (1986), 'Behavioral evidence for cholinoceptive pontine inhibitory area: descending

control of spinal motor output and sensory input', *Brain Research*, *296*, 241–62.

(239) Katz, I., Stradling, J., Slutsky, A. S., Zamel, N. and Hoffstein, V. (1990), 'Do patients with obstructive sleep apnea have thick necks?', *American Review of Respiratory Disease*, *141*, 1228–31.

(240) Key, B. J. and Marley, E. (1962), 'The effect of the sympathomimetic amines behaviour and electrocortical activity of the chicken', *Electroencephalography and Clinical Neurophysiology*, *14*, 90–105.

(241) Keys, A., *The Biology of Human Starvation*, Minneapolis: University of Minnesota Press, 1986.

(242) King-Hele, D., *Erasmus Darwin and the Romantic Poets*, London: Macmillan, 1950.

(243) Kjellberg, A. (1977), 'Sleep deprivation and some aspects of performance: I. Problems of arousal changes. II. Lapses and other attentional effects. III. Motivation, comment and conclusions', *Waking and Sleeping*, *1*, 139–43; 145–8; 149–53.

(244) Klackenberg, G., 'Incidence of parasomnias in children in a general population'. In C. Guilleminault (ed.), *Sleep and Its Disorders in Children*, New York: Raven Press, 1987.

(245) Klein, R. and Armitage, R. (1979), 'Rhythms in human performance: 1.5 hour oscillations in cognitive style', *Science*, *204*, 1326–7.

(246) Kleitman, N. (1927), 'Studies on the physiology of sleep: V. Some experiments on puppies', *American Journal of Physiology*, *84*, 386–95.

(247) Kleitman, N., 'The basic rest-activity cycle in relation to sleep and wakefulness'. In A. Kales (ed.), *Sleep: Physiology and Pathology*, Philadelphia: Lippincott, 1969.

(248) Kluvitse, C. D. (1984), M.Sc. dissertation, University of Hull.

(249) Knauth, P., Landau, K., Droge, C., Schwitteck, M., Widynski, M. and Rutenfranz, J. (1980), 'Duration of sleep depending on the type of shiftwork', *International Archives of Occupational and Environmental Health*, *46*, 167–77.

(250) Koestler, A., *The Act of Creation*, London: Hutchinson, 1964; London: Pan Books, 1966, pp. 213–14.

(251) Kohlschutter, E. (1892), 'Messungen der Festigheit des Schlafes', *Zeitschrift für Rechtscmedizin*, *17*, 209–53, quoted in M. Bonnet, 'Performance during sleep'. In W. B. Webb (ed.), *Biological Rhythms, Sleep and Performance*, Chichester: Wiley, 1982, ch. 8.

(252) Kohsaka, M., Fukuda, N., Honma, K., Honma, S. and Morita, N. (1992), 'Seasonality in human sleep', *Experientia*, *48*, 231–3.

(253) Koukkou, M. and Lehmann, D. (1968), 'EEG and memory storage in sleep experiments with humans', *Electroencephalography and Clinical Neurophysiology*, *25*, 455–62.

(254) Kristal, M. B. and Noonan, M. (1979), 'Note on sleep in captive giraffes (*Giraffa camelopardalis reticulata*)', *South African Journal of Zoology*, *14*, 108.

(255) Kronauer, R. E., Czeisler, C. A., Pilato, S. F., Moore-Ede, M. C. and Weitzman, E. D. (1982), 'Mathematical model of the human circadian system with two interacting oscillators', *American Journal of Physiology*, *242*, R3–17.

(256) Kupfer, D. J. (1976), 'REM latency: a psychobiologic marker for primary depressive disease', *Biological Psychiatry*, *11*, 159–74.

(257) Kushida, C. A., Bergmann, B. M. and Rechtschaffen, A. (1989), 'Sleep deprivation in the rat: IV. Paradoxical sleep deprivation', *Sleep*, *12*, 22–30.

(258) Kushida, C. A. Everson, C. A., Suthipintharm, P.; Sloan, J., Soltani, K., Bartnicke, B., Bergmann, B. M. and Rechtschaffen, A. (1989), 'Sleep deprivation in the rat: VI. Skin changes', *Sleep*, *12*, 42–6.

(259) Langford, G. W., Meddis, R. and Pearson, A. J. D. (1972), 'Spontaneous arousals from sleep in human subjects', *Psychonomic Science*, *28*, 228–30.

(260) Langford, G. W., Meddis, R. and Pearson, A. J. D. (1974), 'Awakening latency from sleep for meaningful and non-meaningful stimuli', *Psychophysiology*, *11*, 1–5.

(261) Lefebure, Molly, *Samuel Taylor Coleridge: A bondage of opium*, London: Gollancz, 1974.

(262) Lehmann, D. and Koukkou, M. (1974), 'Computer analysis of EEG wakefulness-sleep patterns during learning of novel and familiar sentences', *Electroencephalography and Clinical Neurophysiology*, *37*, 73–84.

(263) Lehman, M. N., Silver, R., Gladstone, W. R., Kahn, R. M., Gibson, M. and Bittman, E. L. (1987), 'Circadian rhythmicity restored by neural transplant: immunocytochemical characterization with the host brain', *Journal of Neuroscience*, *7*, 1626–38.

(264) Levi, Primo, *If This is a Man*, trans. Stuart Woolf, London: The Orion Press, 1960.

(265) Levi, Primo, *The Truce*, trans. Stuart Woolf, London: The Bodley Head, 1965.

(266) Lewis, Bernard, *The Assassins: A radical sect in Islam*, New York: Octagon Books, 1980.

(267) Lewis, H. B., Goodenough, D. R., Shapiro, A. and Sleser, I. (1966), 'Individual differences in dream recall', *Journal of Abnormal Psychology*, *71*, 52–9.

(268) Lewis, S. A. (1969), 'Subjective estimates of sleep: an EEG evaluation', *British Journal of Psychology*, *60*, 203–8.

(269) Lindsley, D. B., Schreiner, L. H., Knowles, W. B. and Magoun, H. W. (1950), 'Behavioral and EEG changes following chronic brain stem lesions in the cat', *Electroencephalography and Clinical Neurophysiology*, *2*, 483–98.

(270) Lisper, H.-O. and Kjellberg, A. (1972), 'Effects of 24 hours sleep deprivation on rate of decrement in a 10 minute auditory reaction time task', *Journal of Experimental Psychology*, *96*, 287–90.

(271) Lister, S. J. (1981), 'A theoretical formulation of the effects of sleep loss', Ph.D. thesis, University of Hull.

(272) Loomis, A. L., Harvey, E. N. and Hobart, G. A., 'Cerebral states during sleep as studied by human brain potentials', *Journal of Experimental Psychology*, *21*, 127–44.

(273) Lozoff, B., Wolf, A. W. and Davis, N. S. (1985), 'Sleep problems seen in pediatric practice', *Pediatrics*, *75*, 477–83.

(274) Lubin, A., Moses, J. M., Johnson, L. C. and Naitoh, P. (1974), 'The recuperative effects of REM sleep and stage 4 sleep on human performance after complete sleep loss: experiment 1', *Psychophysiology*, *11*, 133–46.

(275) Lugaresi, E., Medori, R., Montagna, P., Baruzzi, A., Cortelli, P., Lugaresi, A., Tinuper, P., Zucconi, M. and Gambetti, P. (1986), 'Fatal familial insomnia and dysautonomia with selective degeneration of thalamic nuclei', *New England Journal Of Medicine*, *315*, 997–1003.

(276) Lukas, J. S. and Kryter, K. D., 'Awakening effects of simulated sonic booms and subsonic aircraft noise'. In B. L. Welch and A. S. Welch (eds), *Psychological Effects of Noise*, New York: Plenum Press, 1970.

(277) Lydic, R., Scroene, W. C., Czeisler, C. A., and Moore-Ede, M. C. (1980), 'Suprachiasmatic region of the human hypothalamus: homolog to the primate circadian pacemaker?', *Sleep*, *2*, 355–61.

(278) Lyman, C. P., 'Why bother to hibernate?' In C. P. Lyman, J. S. Willis, A. Malan and L. C. H. Wang (eds), *Hibernation and Torpor in Mammals and Birds*, New York: Academic Press, 1982.

(279) McCarley, R. W. and Hobson, J. A. (1977), 'The neurobiological origins of psychoanalytic dream theory', *American Journal of Psychiatry*, *134*, 1211–21.

(280) McCarley, R. W. and Massaquoi, S. (1986), 'A limit cycle mathematical model of the REM sleep oscillator system', *American Journal of Physiology*, *251*, R1011–R1029.

(281) Macdonald, D. G., Schicht, W. W. and Frazier, R. E. (1975), 'Studies of information processing in sleep', *Psychophysiology*, *12*, 624–9.

(282) McGhie, A. and Russell, S. M. (1962), 'The subjective assessment of normal sleep patterns', *Journal of Mental Science*, *8*, 642–54.

(283) McGinty, D. J. and Harper, R. M. (1976), 'Dorsal raphe neurons: depression of firing during sleep in cats', *Brain Research*, *101*, 569–74.

(284) McGregor, D., *The Dream World of Dion McGregor*, New York: Geis, 1964.

(285) McKellar, P., *Imagination and Thinking*, London: Cohen and West, 1957.

(286) McKellar, P., 'Imagery from the standpoint of introspection'. In P. Sheehan (ed.), *The Function and Nature of Imagery*, New York: Academic Press, 1972.

(287) MacNeice, L., *The Strings are False*, London: Faber, 1965; London: Faber, 1982, p. 198.

(288) McNicholas, W. T., Tarlo, S. M. and Phillipson, E. A. (1982) 'Is sleep apnoea more common in North America?', *The Lancet*, *1*, 458.

(289) Magnes, J., Moruzzi, G. and Pompeiano, O. (1961), 'Synchronization

of the EEG produced by low-frequency electrical stimulation of the region of the solitary tract', *Archives Italiennes de Biologie*, *99*, 33–67.

(290) Mahowald, M. W. and Schenck, C. H., 'REM sleep behavior disorder'. In M. H. Kruger, T. Roth and W. C. Dement (eds), *Principles and Practice of Sleep Medicine*, Philadelphia: Saunders, 1989, pp. 389–401.

(291) Manaceine, M. de, *Sleep: Its physiology, pathology, hygiene and psychology*, London: Walter Scott, 1897.

(292) Manetto, V., Medori, R., Cortelli, P., Montagna, P., Tinuper, P., Baruzzi, A., Rancurel, G., Hauw, J.-J., Vanderhaeghen, J.-J., Mailleux, P., Bugiani, O., Tagliavini, F., Bouras, C., Ruzzuto, N., Lugaresi, E. and Gambetti, P. (1992), 'Fatal familial insomnia: clinical and pathologic study of five new cases', *Neurology*, *42*, 312–19.

(293) Manseau, C. and Broughton, R. J. (1984), 'Bilaterally synchronous ultradian EEG rhythms in awake adult humans', *Psychophysiology*, *21*, 265–73.

(294) Meddis, R. (1975), 'On the function of sleep', *Animal Behaviour*, *23*, 676–91.

(295) Meddis, R., *The Sleep Instinct*, London: Routledge and Kegan Paul, 1977.

(296) Meddis, R., 'The evolution of sleep'. In A. Mayes (ed.), *Sleep Mechanisms and Functions*, Wokingham: Van Nostrand, 1983.

(297) Meddis, R., Pearson, A. J. D. and Langford, G. (1973), 'An extreme case of healthy insomnia', *Electroencephalography and Clinical Neurophysiology*, *35*, 391–4.

(298) Meglasson, M. D. and Huggins, S. E. (1979), 'Sleep in a crocodilian, *Caiman sclerops*', *Comparative Biochemistry and Physiology*, *63A*, 561–7.

(299) Meier-Ewart, K., Matsubayashi, K. and Benter, L. (1985), 'Propranolol: longterm treatment in narcolepsy-cataplexi', *Sleep*, *8*, 95–104.

(300) Mendels, J. and Hawkins, D. R. (1967), 'Sleep and depression', *Archives of General Psychiatry*, *16*, 344–54.

(301) Merrick, A. W. and Sharp, D. W. (1971), 'Electroencephalography of resting behavior in cattle, with observations on the question of sleep', *American Journal of Veterinary Research*, *32*, 1893–7.

(302) Messer, D. and Richards, M., 'The development of sleeping difficulties'. In I. St James-Roberts, G. Harris and D. Messer, *Infant Crying, Feeding and Sleeping*, Hemel Hempstead: Harvester Wheatsheaf, 1993.

(303) Michelson, E. (1897), 'Intersuchungen über die Tiefe des Schlafes', *Psychologic Arbeiten*, *2*, 84–117.

(304) Middleton, W. C. (1942), 'The frequency with which a group of unselected college students experience colour dreaming and colour hearing', *Journal of General Psychology*, *27*, 221–9.

(305) Moldofsky, H. *et al.* (1975), 'Musculoskeletal symptoms and non-REM sleep disturbance in patients with "fibrositis syndrome" and healthy subjects', *Psychosomatic Medicine*, *37*, 341–53.

(306) Molinari, S. and Foulkes, D. (1969), 'Tonic and phasic events during sleep: psychological correlates and implications', *Perceptual and Motor Skills*, *29*, 343–68.

(307) Monod J. and Guidasci, S. (1976), 'Sleep and brain malformation in the neonatal period', *Neuropaediatrie*, *7*, 229–49.

(308) Monroe, L. J. (1967), 'Psychological and physiological differences between good and bad sleepers', *Journal of Abnormal Psychology*, *72*, 255–64.

(309) Moore, R. Y. and Eichler, V. B. (1972), 'Loss of a circadian adrenal corticosterone rhythm following suprachiasmatic lesions in the rat', *Brain Research*, *42*, 201–6.

(310) Morgan, K., Adam, K. and Oswald, I. (1984), 'Effects of loprazolam and of triazolam on psychological function', *Psychopharmacology*, *82*, 386–8.

(311) Morgan, K. and Oswald, I. (1982), 'Anxiety caused by a short-life hypnotic', *British Medical Journal*, *284*, 942.

(312) Moruzzi, G. and Magoun, H. W. (1949), 'Brain stem reticular formation and activation in the EEG', *Electroencephalography and Clinical Neurophysiology*, *1*, 455–73.

(313) Moscovitz, E. and Berger, R. J. (1969), 'Rapid eye movements and dream imagery: are they related?', *Nature*, *224*, 613–14.

(314) Mukhametov, L. M. and Polyakova, I. G. (1981), 'EEG investigation of the sleep in porpoises (*Phocoena phocoena*)', *Zhurnal Visshei Nerundi Deyatelnosti Pavlova*, *31*, 333–9.

(315) Mukhametov, L. M., Supin, A. Y. and Polyakova, I. G. (1977), 'Interhemispheric asymmetry of the electroencephalographic sleep patterns in dolphins', *Brain Research*, *134*, 581–4.

(316) Mullaney, D. J., Johnson, L. C., Naitoh, P., Friedmann, J. K. and Globus, G. G. (1977), 'Sleep during and after gradual sleep reduction', *Psychophysiology*, *14*, 237–44.

(317) Mullaney, D. J., Kripke, D. F., Fleck, P. A. and Johnson, L. C. (1983), 'Sleep loss and nap effects on sustained continuous performance', *Psychophysiology*, *20*, 643–51.

(318) Murray, J., Dunn, G., Williams, P. and Tarnopol, A. (1981), 'Factors affecting the consumption of psychotropic drugs', *Psychological Medicine*, *11*, 551–60.

(319) Naitoh, P., Johnson, L. C. and Lubin, A. (1971), 'Modification of surface negative slow potential (CNV) in the human brain after total sleep loss', *Electroencephalography and Clinical Neurophysiology*, *30*, 17–22.

(320) Nasser, S. and Rees, P. J. (1992), 'Sleep apnoea: causes, consequences and treatment', *British Journal of Clinical Practice*, *46*, 39–43.

(321) Nathan, P. W., *The Nervous System*, Harmondsworth: Pengiun, 1969.

(322) Needham, J., *Science and Civilisation in China*, vol. 2, Cambridge: Cambridge University Press, p. 364.

(323) Nelson, R. A., Wahner, H. W., Jones, J. D., Ellefson, R. D. and Zollman, P. E. (1973), 'Metabolism of bears before, during and after winter sleep', *American Journal of Physiology*, *224*, 491–6.

(324) Ngubane, H., *Body and Mind in Zulu Medicine*, London: Academic Press, 1976.

(325) Nino-Murcia, G. and Keenan, S., 'Enuresis and sleep'. In C. Guilleminault (ed.), *Sleep and Its Disorders in Children*, New York: Raven Press, 1987.

(326) Norton, R. (1970), 'The effects of acute sleep deprivation on selective attention', *British Journal of Psychology*, *61*, 157–61.

(327) Ogden, T. H. (1985), 'The mother, the infant and the matrix: interpretations of aspects of the work of Donald Winnicott', *Contemp. Psychoanal.*, *21*, 346–71.

(328) Ogilvie, R. D., Wilkinson, R. T. and Allison, S. (1989), 'The detection of sleep onset: behavioral, physiological, and subjective convergence', *Sleep*, *12*, 458–74.

(329) Omwake, K. and Loranz, M. (1933), 'Study of ability to wake at a specified time', *Journal of Applied Psychology*, *17*, 468–74.

(330) Oswald, I. (1959), 'Sudden bodily jerks on falling asleep', *Brain*, *82*, 92–103.

(331) Oswald, I. (1959), 'Experimental studies of rhythm, anxiety and cerebral vigilance', *Journal of Mental Science*, *105*, 269–94.

(332) Oswald, I. (1969), 'Human brain protein, drugs and dreams', *Nature*, *223*, 893–7.

(333) Oswald, I. (1980), 'Sleep as a restorative process: human clues', *Progress in Brain Research*, *53*, 279–88.

(334) Oswald, I. and Adam, K. (1980), 'The man who had not slept for 10 years', *British Medical Journal*, *281*, 1684–5.

(335) Oswald, I. and Priest, R. G. (1965), 'Five weeks to escape the sleeping pill habit', *British Medical Journal*, *2*, 1093–9.

(336) Oswald, I., Merrington, J. and Lewis, S. (1970), 'Cyclical "on demand" oral intake by adults', *Nature*, *225*, 959–60.

(337) Oswald, I., Taylor, A. M. and Treisman, M. (1960), 'Discriminative responses to stimulation during human sleep', *Brain*, *83*, 440–53.

(338) Padgam, C. A. (1975), 'Colours experienced in dreams', *British Journal of Psychology*, *66*, 25–8.

(339) Papakostopoulos, D. and Fenelon, B. (1975), 'Spatial distribution of the Contingent Negative Variation (CNV) and the relationship between the CNV and reaction time'. *Psychophysiology*, *12*, 74–8.

(340) Parker, A., *States of Mind: ESP and altered states of consciousness*, New York: Taplinger, 1980.

(341) Parkes, J. D., *Sleep and its Disorders*, London: Saunders, 1985.

(342) Parkes, J. D. and Lock, C. B. (1989), 'Genetic factors in sleep disorders', *Journal of Neurology, Neurosurgery and Psychiatry*, special supplement, 101–8.

(343) Parmelee, A., Wenner, W. H., Akiyama, Y., Stern, E. and Flescher, J., 'Electroencephalography and brain maturation'. In A. Minkowski (ed.), *Symposium on Regional Development of the Brain in Early Life*, Philadelphia: Davis, 1967.

(344) Pasnau, R. O., Naitoh, R., Stier, S. and Kollar, E. J. (1968), 'The psychological effects of 205 hours of sleep deprivation', *Archives of General Psychiatry*, *18*, 496–505.

(345) Patrick, G. T. W. and Gilbert, J. A. (1896), 'On the effects of loss of sleep', *Psychological Review*, *3*, 469–83.

(346) Petursson, H. and Lader, M. H. (1981), 'Withdrawal from long-term benzodiazepine treatment', *British Medical Journal*, *283*, 643–5.

(347) Pieron, H., *Le Problème physiologique du sommeil*, Paris: Masson, 1913.

(348) Pivik, R. T., Bylsma, F. W. and Cooper, P. (1986), 'Sleep-wakefulness rhythms in the rabbit', *Behavioural and Neural Biology*, *45*, 275–86.

(349) Portnoff, G., Baekelannd, F., Goodenough, G. R., Karacan, I. and Shapiro, A. (1968), 'Retention of verbal materials perceived immediately prior to onset of NREM sleep', *Perceptual and Motor Skills*, *22*, 751–8.

(350) Prechtl, H. F. R. (1974), 'The behavioural states of the newborn infant (a review)', *Brain Research*, *76*, 185–212.

(351) Price, V. A., Coates, T. J., Thoresen, C. E. and Grinstead, O. A. (1978), 'Prevalence and correlates of poor sleep among adolescents', *American Journal of Disorders of Childhood*, *143*, 583–6.

(352) Priest, R., 'Sleep and its disorders'. In R. N. Gaine and B. L. Hudson (eds), *Current Themes in Psychiatry*, London, 1983.

(353) Quera-Salva, M. A., Orluc, A., Goldenberg, F. and Guilleminault, C. (1991), 'Insomnia and use of hypnotics: study of a French population', *Sleep*, *14*, 386–91.

(354) Ralph, M. R., Foster, R. G., Davis, F. C. and Menaker, M. (1990), 'Transplanted suprachiasmatic nucleus determines circadian period', *Science*, *247*, 975–8.

(355) Rechtschaffen, A. (1978), 'The singlemindedness and isolation of dreams', *Sleep*, *1*, 97–109.

(356) Rechtschaffen, A. and Monroe, L., 'Laboratory studies of insomnia'. In A. Kales (ed.), *Sleep: Physiology and pathology*, Philadelphia: Lippincott, 1969.

(357) Rechtschaffen, A., Wolpert, E. A., Dement, W. C., Mitchell, S. A. and Fisher, C. (1963), 'Nocturnal sleep of narcoleptics', *Electroencephalography and Clinical Neurophysiology*, *15*, 599–609.

(358) Rechtschaffen, A., Bergmann, B. M., Everson, C. A. and Gilliland, M. A. (1989), 'Sleep deprivation in the rat: X. Integration and discussion of the findings', *Sleep*, *12*, 68–87.

(359) Rechtschaffen, A., Bergmann, B. M., Everson, C. A., Kushida, C. A. and Gilliland, M. A. (1989), 'Sleep deprivation in the rat: I. Conceptual issues', *Sleep*, *12*, 1–4.

(360) Rechtschaffen, A. and Kales, A. (eds), *A Manual of Standardized Terminology, Techniques and Scoring System for Sleep Stages of Human Adults*, Washington, DC: Public Information Service, US Government Printing Office, 1968.

(361) Reinberg, A., Andlauer, P., DePrins, J., Malberg, W., Vieux, N. and Baurdeleau, P. (1984), 'Desynchronization of the oral-temperature circadian-rhythm and intolerance to shift work', *Nature*, *308*, 272–4.

(362) Richman, N. (1981), 'A community survey of characteristics of 1 to 2-year-olds with sleep disruptions', *J. Am. Acad. Child Psychiatry*, *20*, 281–91.

(363) Richman, N., Douglas, J., Hunt, H., Lansdown, R. and Levere, R. (1985), 'Behavioural methods in the treatment of sleep disorders – a pilot study', *Journal of Child Psychology and Psychiatry*, *26*, 581–91.

(364) Robertson, J., *The Ladybird New Testament*, London: Ladybird Books, 1981.

(365) Roffwarg, H. P., Dement, W. C., Muzio, J. N. and Fisher, C. (1962), 'Dream imagery: relationship to rapid eye movements of sleep', *Archives of General Psychiatry*, *7*, 235–58.

(366) Roger, H., *Les Troubles du sommeil – hypersomnies, insomnies, parasomnies*, Paris: Masson et Cie, 1932.

(367) Rosa, R. R., Bonnet, M. H. and Kramer, M. (1983), 'The relationship of sleep and anxiety in anxious subjects', *Biological Psychology*, *16*, 119–26.

(368) Ruckebusch, Y. (1972), 'The relevance of drowsiness in the circadian cycle of farm animals', *Animal Behaviour*, *20*, 637–43.

(369) Ruckebusch, Y. (1972), 'Development of sleep and wakefulness in the foetal lamb', *Electroencephalography and Clinical Neurophysiology*, *32*, 119–28.

(370) Ruckebusch, Y., Barbey, P. and Guillemot, P. (1970), 'Les états de sommeil chez le cheval (*Equus caballus*)', *Comptes Rendus Séances Société Biologique*, *164*, 658–64.

(371) Rundell, O. H., Lester, B. K., Griffiths, W. J. and Williams, H. L. (1972), 'Alcohol and sleep in young adults', *Psychopharmacologia*, *26*, 201–18.

(372) Rycroft, C., *The Innocence of Dreams*, Oxford: Oxford University Press, 1979.

(373) St Ambrose's prayer: a modern and more wrought translation of the prayer was given to me by my colleague John Bernasconi:
Suppress our foe's infernal arts,
Lest sensual dreams defile our hearts,
With vain deluding thoughts that creep
On heedless minds disarmed with sleep.

(374) Sanders, N. K., *The Epic of Gilgamesh*. An English version with an introduction, Harmondsworth: Pengiun, 1960.

(375) Sassin, J. F., Parker, D. C., Johnson, L. C., Rossman, L. G., Mace, J. W. and Gotlin, R. W. (1969), 'Effects of slow wave sleep deprivation on

human growth hormone release in sleep: preliminary study', *Life Science*, *8*, 1299–307.
(376) Saul, L. J. and Curtis, G. C. (1967), 'Dream form and strength of impulse in dreams of falling and other dreams of descent', *International Journal of Psychoanalysis*, *48*, 281–7.
(377) Schacter, D. L. (1976), 'The hypnagogic state: a critical review of the literature', *Psychological Bulletin*, *83*, 452–81.
(378) Schlehuber, C. J., Flaming, D. G., Lange, G. D. and Spooner, C. E. (1974), 'Paradoxical sleep in the chick (*Gallus domesticus*)', *Behavioral Biology*, *11*, 537–46.
(379) Schneider, Elisabeth, *Coleridge, Opium and Kubla Khan*, New York: Octagon Press, 1975.
(380) Seligman, M. E. P. and Yellen, A. (1987), 'What is a dream?', *Behavioural Research and Therapy*, *25*, 1–24.
(381) Shanon, B. (1979), 'Semantic processing during sleep', *Bulletin of the Psychonomic Society*, *14*, 382–4.
(382) Shapiro, C. M. (1982), 'Energy expenditure and restorative sleep', *Biological Psychology*, *15*, 229–39.
(383) Shapiro, C. M., Catteral, J. R., Oswald, I. and Flenley, D. C. (1981), 'Where are the British sleep apnea patients?', *The Lancet*, *2*, 534–5.
(384) Shapiro, C. M., Catteral, J., Warren, P., Oswald, I., Trinder, J., Paxton, S. and East, B. W. (1986), 'Lean body mass and non-rapid eye movement sleep', *British Medical Bulletin*, *294*, 22.
(385) Shulman, S., *Nightmare*, London: David and Charles, 1979.
(386) Siegel, J. M. and McGinty, D. J. (1977), 'Pontine reticular formation neurons: relationship to discharge of motor activity', *Science*, *196*, 678–80.
(387) Siegel, J. M. (1985), 'A behavioral approach to the analysis of reticular formation unit activity'. In T. E. Robinson (ed.), *Behavioral Approaches to Brain Research*, New York: Oxford University Press, 1983.
(388) Siegel, J. M. (1990), 'Mechanisms of sleep control', *Journal of Clinical Neurophysiology*, *7*, 49–65.
(389) Snyder, F. (1970), 'The phenomenology of dreaming'. In H. Madow and L. H. Snow (eds), *The Psychodynamic Implications of the Physiological Studies on Dreams*, Springfield, Illinois: Charles C. Thomas, 1970.
(390) Sokolov, E. N., *Perception and the Conditional Reflex*, New York: Pergamon Press, 1963.
(391) Sokolov, E. N. and Paramonova, N. P. (1961), 'Progressive changes in the orienting reflex in man during the development of sleep inhibition', *Pavlov Journal of Higher Nervous Activity*, *11*, 217–26.
(392) Soldatos, C. R., Kales, J. D., Scharf, M. B., Bixler, E. O. and Kales, A. (1980), 'Cigarette smoking associated with sleep difficulty', *Science*, *207*, 551–3.
(393) Sontag, S., *Trip to Hanoi*, London: Panther, 1969.

(394) Spiegel, R. and Azcona, A. (1985), 'Sleep and its disorders'. In M. S. J. Pathy (ed.), *Principles and Practice of Geriatric Medicine*, London: Wiley.

(395) Spock, B., *Baby and Child Care*, London: W. H. Allen, 1979.

(396) Stephan, F. K. and Zucker, I. (1972), 'Circadian rhythms in drinking behavior and locomotor activity of rats are eliminated by hypothalamic lesion', *Proceedings of the National Academy of Sciences, U.S.A.*, 69, 1583–6.

(397) Steiger, A., Holsboer, F. and Benkert, O. (1987), *Psychopharmacology*, 92, 110–14.

(398) Steriade, M., Pare, D., Bouhassira, D., Deschenes, M. and Oakson, G. (1989), 'Phasic activation of lateral geniculate and perigeniculate thalamic neurons during sleep with ponto-geniculo-occipital waves', *Journal of Neuroscience*, 9, 2215–29.

(399) Stone, B. M. (1980), 'Sleep and low doses of alcohol', *Electroencephalography and Clinical Neurophysiology*, 48, 706–9.

(400) Sullivan, C. E., Issa, F. G., Berthon-Jones, M. and Eves, L. (1981), 'Reversal of obstructive sleep apnoea by continuous positive airway pressure applied through the nares', *The Lancet*, 1, 862–5.

(401) Szymusiak, R. and McGinty, D. (1986), 'Sleep-related neuronal discharge in the basal forebrain of cats', *Brain Research*, 370, 82–92.

(402) Szymusiak, R. and McGinty, D. (1989), 'Sleep-walking discharge of basal forebrain projection neurons in cats', *Brain Research Bulletin*, 22, 423–30.

(403) Taub, J. M. and Berger, R. J. (1969), 'Extended sleep and performance: the Rip Van Winkle effect', *Psychonomic Science*, 16, 204–5.

(404) Taub, J. M. and Berger, R. J. (1973), 'Performance and mood following variations in the length and timing of sleep', *Psychophysiology*, 10, 559–70.

(405) Taub, J. M. and Berger, R. (1976), 'Effects of acute sleep pattern alteration depend on sleep duration'. *Physiological Psychology*, 4, 412–20.

(406) Taub, J. M., Globus, G. G., Phoebus, E. and Drury, R. (1971), 'Extended sleep and performance', *Nature*, 233, 142–3.

(407) Tauber, E. S., Rofas-Ramire, J. and Hernandez-Peon, R., (1968), 'Electrophysiological and behavioural correlates of wakefulness and sleep in the lizard *Ctenosaura Pectinata*', *Electroencephalography and Clinical Neurophysiology*, 24, 424–33.

(408) Tilley, A. J. and Empson, J. A. C. (1978), 'REM sleep and memory consolidation', *Biological Psychology*, 6, 293–300.

(409) Tilley, A. J. and Wilkinson, R. T. (1982), 'Sleep and performance of shiftworkers'. *Human Factors*, 24, 629–41.

(410) Tinbergen, N., *The Study of Instinct*, London: Oxford University Press, 1951.

(411) Toutain, P.-L. and Ruckebusch, Y. (1972), 'Secretions nasolabiales au cours du sommeil paradoxal chez les bovins', *Comptes rendus acad. sc.* (Paris), 274, 2519–22.

(412) Trulson, M. E. and Jacobs, B. L. (1979), 'Raphe unit activity in freely moving cats: correlation with level of behavioral arousal', *Brain Research*, 163, 135–50.

(413) Turnbull, R., *The Forest People*, London: Jonathan Cape, 1961.

(414) Twain, M., *The Adventures of Tom Sawyer*, London: Dent, 1943, pp. 64–5; originally published 1876.

(415) Ullman, M., Krippner, S. and Vaughan, A., *Dream Telepathy*, New York: Macmillan, 1973.

(416) Ursin, R. (1968), 'Sleep stages in the cat', *Brain Research*, *11*, 347–56.

(417) Van Twyver, H. (1973), 'Polygraphic studies of the American alligator', *Sleep Research*, *2*, 87.

(418) Vogel, G. W., Thurmond, A., Gibbons, P., Sloan, K., Boyd, M. and Walker, M. (1975), 'REM sleep reduction effects on depression syndromes', *Archives of General Psychiatry*, *32*, 765–77.

(419) Walker, J. M. and Berger, R. J. (1980), 'Sleep as an adaption for energy conservation functionally related to hibernation and shallow torpor', *Progress in Brain Research*, *53*, 255–78.

(420) Walker, J. M., Floyd, T. C., Fein, G., *et al.* (1978), 'Effects of exercise on sleep', *Journal of Applied Physiology*, *44*, 945–51.

(421) Walker, J. M., Glotzbach, S. F., Berger, R. J. and Heller, H. C. (1977), 'Sleep and hibernation in ground squirrels (*Citellus* spp.): electrophysiological observations', *American Journal of Physiology*, *233*, R213–R221.

(422) Walter, W. G., *The Living Brain*, London: Duckworth, 1953.

(423) Walters, W. J. and Lader, M. H. (1970), 'Hangover effects of hypnotics in man', *Nature*, *229*, 637–8.

(424) Ward, D. (ed. and trans.), *The German Legends of the Brothers Grimm*, Philadelphia: ISHI; London: Millington Books, 1981.

(425) Warner, B. F. and Huggins, S. E. (1978), 'An encephalographic study of sleep in young caimans in a colony', *Comparative Biochemistry and Physiology*, *59A*, 139–44.

(426) Webb, W. B. and Agnew, H. W. (1964), 'Sleep cycling within twenty-four hour periods', *Journal of Experimental Psychology*, *74*, 158–64.

(427) Webb, W. B. and Agnew, H. W., Jr. (1975), 'The effects on subsequent sleep of an acute restriction of sleep length', *Psychophysiology*, *12*, 367–70.

(428) Weissbluth, M. (1982), 'Sleep duration and infant temperament', *J. Pediatr.*, *99*, 817–19.

(429) Weissbluth, M., 'Sleep and the Colicky Infant'. In C. Guilleminault (ed.), *Sleep and Its Disorders in Children*, New York: Raven Press, 1987.

(430) Weitzman, E. D. (1981), 'Sleep and its disorders', *Annual Review of Neuroscience*, *4*, 381–417.

(431) Weitzman, E. D. and Pollak, C. P. (1982), 'Effects of flurazepam on sleep and growth hormone release during sleep in healthy subjects', *Sleep*, *5*, 343–9.

(432) West, J. L., 'A general theory of hallucinations and dreams'. In J. L. West (ed.), *Hallucinations*, New York: Grune and Stratton.

(433) Wilkinson, R. T. (1959), 'Rest pauses in a task affected by lack of sleep', *Ergonomics*, *2*, 373–80.

(434) Wilkinson, R. T. (1961), 'Interaction of lack of sleep with knowledge of results, repeated testing and individual differences', *Journal of Experimental Psychology*, *62*, 263–71.

(435) Wilkinson, R. T. (1962), 'Muscle tension during mental work under sleep deprivation', *Journal of Experimental Psychology*, *64*, 565–71.

(436) Wilkinson, R. T. (1970), 'Methods for research on sleep deprivation and sleep function', *International Psychiatry Clinics*, *7*, 369–81.

(437) Wilkinson, R. T., Tyler, P. D. and Varey, C. A. (1975), 'Duty hours of young hospital doctors: effects on the quality of work', *Journal of Occupational Psychology*, *48*, 219–29.

(438) Williams, H. L., Lubin, A. and Goodnow, J. J. (1959), 'Impaired performance with acute sleep loss', *Psychological Monographs*, *73*, (14, whole no. 484).

(439) Williams, P. (1983), 'Psychotropic drug prescribing'. *The Practioner*, *227*, 77–81.

(440) Williams, R. L., Agnew, H. W. and Webb, W. B. (1964), 'Sleep patterns in young adults: an EEG study', *Electroencephalography and Clinical Neurophysiology*, *17*, 376–81.

(441) Williams, R. L., Karacan, I. and Hursch, C. J., *Electroencephalography (EEG) of Human Sleep: Clinical applications*, New York: Wiley, 1974.

(442) Wolff, P. H. (1959), 'Observations on newborn infants'. *Psychosomatic Medicine*, *21*, 110–18.

(443) Wood, A. J. J. (1984), 'Pharmacologic differences between beta blockers', *American Heart Journal*, *108*, 1070–7.

(444) Woodworth, R. S. (1938) cited in P. McKellar, *Imagination and Thinking*, London: Cohen and West, 1957.

(445) Wynn, V. T. (1972), 'Measurements of small variations in absolute pitch', *Journal of Physiology* (London), *220*, 627.

(446) Yules, R. B., Freedman, D. K. and Chandler, K. A. (1966), 'The effect of ethyl alcohol on man's electroencephalographic sleep cycle', *Electroencephalography and Clinical Neurophysiology*, *20*, 109–11.

(447) Zepelin, H. Note by Harold Zepelin. In A. Mayes (ed.) *Sleep Mechanisms and Functions*, London: Van Nostrand, 1983, p. 93.

(448) Zepelin, H. and Rechtschaffen, A. (1974), 'Mammalian sleep, longevity, and energy metabolism'. *Brain, Behaviour and Evolution*, *10*, 425–70.

(449) Zir, L. M., Smith, R. A. and Parker, D. C. (1971), 'Human growth hormone release in sleep: effect of daytime exercise on subsequent sleep', *Journal of Clinical Endocrinology*, *32*, 662–5.

(450) Zuckerman, B., Stevenson, J. and Bailey, V. (1987), 'Sleep problems in early childhood: continuities, predictive factors, and behavioural correlates', *Pediatrics*, *80*, 664–71.

(451) Zung, W. W. K. and Wilson, W. P. (1971), 'Time estimation during sleep'. *Biological Psychiatry*, *3*, 159–64.

Index